Blessed and Beautiful

LLOYD JOHN OGILVIE INSTITUTE
OF PREACHING SERIES

SERIES EDITORS:

Mark Labberton

Clayton J. Schmit

The vision of the Lloyd John Ogilvie Institute of Preaching is to proclaim Jesus Christ and to catalyze a movement of empowered, wise preachers who seek justice, love mercy, and walk humbly with God, leading others to join in God's mission in the world. The books in this series are selected to contribute to the development of such wise and humble preachers. The authors represent both scholars of preaching as well as pastors and preachers whose experiences and insights can contribute to passionate and excellent preaching.

OTHER VOLUMES IN THIS SERIES:

The Eloquence of Grace: Joseph Sittler and the Preaching Life edited by James M. Childs Jr. and Richard Lischer

The Preacher as Liturgical Artist: Metaphor, Idenitity, and the Vicarious Humanity of Christ by Trygve David Johnson

Ordinary Preacher, Extraordinary Gospel: A Daily Guide for Wise, Empowered Preachers by Chris Neufeld-Erdman

FORTHCOMING VOLUMES IN THIS SERIES:

Bringing Home the Message: How Community Can Multiply the Power of the Preached Word by Robert K. Perkins

Decolonizing Preaching: The Pulpit as Postcolonial Space by Sarah A. N. Travis

Blessed and Beautiful

Multiethnic Churches
and the Preaching that Sustains Them

Lisa Washington Lamb

CASCADE *Books* • Eugene, Oregon

BLESSED AND BEAUTIFUL
Multiethnic Churches and the Preaching That Sustains Them

Lloyd John Ogilvie Institute of Preaching Series 4

Cascade Books
An Imprint of Wipf and Stock Publishers
199 W. 8th Ave., Suite 3
Eugene, OR 97401

www.wipfandstock.com

ISBN 13: 978-1-62032-812-5

Cataloging-in-Publication data:

Blessed and beautiful : multiethnic churches and the preaching that sustains them / Lisa Washington Lamb.

Lloyd John Ogilvie Institute of Preaching Series 4

x + 212 p. ; 23 cm. Includes bibliographical references.

ISBN 13: 978-1-62032-812-5

1. Ethnicity—Religious aspects—Christianity. 2. Preaching. 3. Memory—Religious aspects—Christianity. I. Title. II. Series.

BX1970 L24 2014

Manufactured in the U.S.A.

Contents

Intro: The Joy of Cat-Herding

When it comes to the Super Bowl, I admit I'm in it for the ads. A few years ago, Electronic Data Systems (EDS) put out a Super Bowl commercial in which cowboys testified to the extraordinary challenges of herding cats. As one remarked, "Anybody can herd cattle—but holding together ten thousand half-wild shorthairs—now that's another thing altogether." This enormously popular commercial vividly portrayed a phrase already popular in the management world. Leaders lamented that uniting their people around a common vision was a lot like herding cats. Check it out: http://www.youtube.com/watch?v=Pk7yqlTMvp8.

But you may already know this firsthand. If you're a pastor or preparing to be one, welcome to the wild world of cat-herding. Shepherding sheep, in biblical times, was far from easy: heavy rods and long staffs were tools of the trade for a reason. But today's communities and congregations are increasingly complex, and herding docile sheep doesn't begin to capture the chaos of the task. But I'm guessing that you like it that way, since you picked up this book. You're energized by the vision of a dynamic, diverse, reconciled, and reconciling body of believers, somehow coalescing around the joyful call to follow and worship our good and beautiful God. Yes, you'll get some scratches. In the ad, one cat-boy points to another and says, "*His* face is just ripped to shreds." But then another affirms, "I'm living the dream. I wouldn't do nothin' else. It ain't an easy job but when you bring a herd into town and you ain't lost one of them, ain't a feeling like it in the world." These words capture the heart of a pastor, a herder of God's motley flock who labors tirelessly toward their reconciliation with God and each other, a work made possible solely through the work of Jesus Christ. What

I love about this ad is that it takes something impossible and makes it seem possible. Not easy—but possible, and deeply satisfying. Cat-boys share in a rich community as they carry out their task.

One of the coolest things we get to do as leaders of faith communities is preach. Our time in the pulpit, or behind the beat-up music stand, is a highly leveraged moment, crammed with opportunities to shape culture, form hearts, and proclaim truth. More and more of us are finding ourselves carrying out this task in a context of ethnic and socioeconomic diversity. For many pastors, that new reality barely registers an impact on the content and form of their sermons. Their commitment is to the timeless, transcultural truths of the gospel—why muddy the waters with talk of ethnic distinctions? These folks are like sheepherders whose fluffy flocks have evolved into wonderfully multicolored cats, but they steadfastly refuse to acknowledge the change. I will argue here that there are real losses to this approach. Other pastors actively celebrate diversity in their sermons and work hard to name the distinctive treasures, heartaches, and even sins of the cultures in their midst, calling their members to risky repentance and deep unity. These pastors are pursuing a vision that has captured their hearts and imaginations. That approach has costs as well: their faces tend to sport more scratches.

MEMORIES OF HOME

This book seeks to give you fuel for the journey. If we let the metaphor encourage us, it's interesting to note that, though ornery at times and not particularly amenable to herding, cats have a remarkable ability to find their way home. Take the tomcat, Ninja. Ninja journeyed with his family from Utah to Washington state in 1996. He promptly disappeared, only to show up a year later at his old home in Utah, a whopping 850 miles away.[1] Evidently cats have magnetized cells in their brains that act like tiny compasses that help them to know which way is north. We humans don't seem to have those. But as the body of Christ, we do have something like them. We have the words of Scripture, and when the Word is preached it functions to build into our brains our homing instinct, magnetically drawing us together and calling us toward our shared and ultimate true home.

This book is about the neglected yet magnetic power of memory for forming congregations that dwell in the midst of ethnic and cultural

1. http://www.pbs.org/wnet/nature/episodes/extraordinary-cats/homing-instinct/2170/

diversity. We'll define the terms *ethnicity* and *culture* more along the way, but for now let me put forward the idea that one of the primary characteristics of an ethnic group is its *shared memory*. John Higham puts it this way:

> [A] means of generalizing about American ethnic groups, and distinguishing among them, lies at hand, surprisingly neglected. It lies in the recognition that all such groups arise from, or must create, a community of memory . . . memory is what binds an ethnic group together, assigning its tasks and maintaining its identity. Memory recalls and fixates a particular origin, from which it projects a continuity of subsequent experience.[2]

If we are paying attention to Higham, we preachers will take a deep breath and reach for a PowerBar. No wonder it is hard, building cohesion and *esprit de corps* in church between members of different ethnic backgrounds. We don't just look different and prefer different dance moves. Powerful forces of memory pull us towards those who share the strong binding agent of shared ancestry, and we tend to let those forces sort us into churches as well.[3] For much of U.S. history, the church has evaded the problem, passively allowing that sifting to run its course, so that segregation persists in church long after many schools and other secular institutions have found ways to integrate. We still hear the persistent argument from sheer pragmatism that it is not a battle worth fighting, due to the inherent instability in heterogeneous group formation.[4] Some churches that are composed of diverse individuals have tackled the problem with a certain, "check your ethnic identity and history at the door" approach, in which generalized gospel claims trump ethnic particularities. This is certainly efficient and on one level easier, but whether it is truly effective or faithful to the New Testament vision of the church is doubtful.

Here, I'll argue for an approach that proclaims the transcultural good news in ways that enable various listeners to transcend powerful cultural identities and come together as church, and yet at the same time hear, honor, and tenderly name a range of other memories at play in any diverse

2. Higham, "The Amplitude of Ethnic History," 62.

3. Gregory Stanczak writes, "Religion remains one of the most enduring institutions in which racial and ethnic sorting continues in most communities today both within and outside the United States." He explains this on the basis of the demographics of a given area and the fact that, "[R]eligiosity cannot be dissected from one's culture and social experience" (Stanczak, "Strategic Ethnicity," 859).

4. Gary McIntosh and Alan McMahan make this argument in *Being the Church in a Multi-Ethnic Community*, 119–31.

gathering of people. This sort of preaching pays attention to the contextual, cross-cultural, and countercultural elements of gospel as well as the trans-cultural elements.[5] Its work is funded by a rich understanding of the theological dimensions of memory itself, and communal memory in particular. It understands the power of Jesus Christ to heal and transform memories through much more creative means than simply erasing them. The preachers who endeavor to do that kind of work well are my true heroes. They are the cat-herders, out on the frontier of the church, living the dream with scratched, scarred faces and a glint in their eyes. Are you in?

---

5. This fourfold typology is eloquently articulated in the *Nairobi Statement on Worship and Culture: Contemporary Challenges and Opportunities* (1996), which can be found online at http://www.worship.ca/docs/lwf_ns.html.

1

Race, Ethnicity, and Culture

As we prepare to address the challenges and opportunities of building ethnically diverse congregations, we need to take a closer look at salient aspects of the terms race, ethnicity, and culture, both as modern scholars have conceived those terms and as postmodern scholars continue to construct their meaning. A central challenge in discussions of multiethnic churches is how (and whether) they are capable of fostering healthy ethnic identity in their members. Ethnic-specific churches have historically been strong settings for transmitting and preserving values and traditions, especially for marginalized minority communities. Are multiethnic churches able to do the same, or is strong identity formation a necessary loss of affiliation with them? A survey of terms will sharpen our response to that question. We will be particularly interested in the insights that come from viewing ethnic groups and cultures through the lens of memory, understanding them as *communities of memory*. John Higham writes, "[A] means of generalizing about American ethnic groups, and distinguishing among them, lies at hand, surprisingly neglected. It lies in the recognition that all such groups arise from, or must create, a community of memory . . . memory is what binds an ethnic group together, assigning its tasks and maintaining its identity. Memory recalls and fixates a particular origin, from which it projects a continuity of subsequent experience."[1] Can a multiethnic congregation

1. Higham, "Amplitude of Ethnic History," 62.

house those memories that shape identity? To what extent should we expect it to, and toward what ends?

Memory's capacities and vicissitudes will focus our discussions of ethnic identity, reconciliation, and intergroup relations, both sociologically and theologically. Some currently popular postmodern conceptions of ethnicity and culture, while highlighting neglected aspects, are at risk of losing the dimension of the shared past, due to their emphasis on individual choice and on present and future-oriented aspects of identity construction. Cultures must reckon with the past—and they always do, whether through denial, distortion, nostalgia, or courageous truth-telling. William James Booth, arguing for the importance of a sense of continuity with the past, observes,

> The groups of identity politics, then, are actors with histories and projects, groups that sometimes speak of past injustices inflicted by earlier generations of other groups, and as such they must in some sense be continuous actors. Indeed, this would seem fundamental to speaking . . . about a group as something other than a mere passing aggregate, a transient aggregate of shared interests or views. Enduringness, and with it accountability, matter and are at the core of our claims about political or group membership. The absence of reflection on these issues from current identity debates is a loss of a vital element in our understanding of the moral/political life of a community.[2]

Shared memories, often undisclosed to outsiders, function powerfully to unite ethnic and other groups within themselves, to distinguish them from other groups, and to keep alive both vibrant ethnic heritage and bitter hostilities. All societies, and the ethnic groups that may reside within them, find ways to narrate wounds suffered and wounds inflicted, triumphant moments, and honorable deeds done. Some do so in ways that allow them to celebrate, mourn, and transcend their past, and that enable them to forge meaningful connections with other cultures. Other groups' narrations leave them mired in the past and stranded in isolation. The church is uniquely equipped to stand at the nexus of multiple, and at times contested, narrations of history in ways that honor the past(s) and call its various members toward a reconciled future. The proclamation of Scripture can propel the church to remember well together, in ways that

---

2. Booth, *Communities of Memory*, 4.

highlight particular hermeneutical vantage points, while crafting language that creates new interpretive and relational spaces congregants may inhabit together.[3]

Here we will seek to place emerging secular understandings of social identity in conversation with theological perspectives on culture. Discourse surrounding them has seen seismic shifts in how theorists approach them. Central to these discussions is the changing notion of *identity* itself, whether individual or collective. Modern, Western notions of identity have tended to stress social groups of various kinds as bounded objects, with a high degree of internal homogeneity. This is less and less true in postmodern discourse. Richard Handler notes, "In current scholarly analyses of collective identities, there is a tension between the notion that identity is essential, fundamental, unitary, and unchanging, and the notion that identities are constructed and reconstructed through historical action."[4]

RACE AND RACIAL THEORY

Historic Use of the Term

All three terms are elusive and complex, but the term *race* has had by far the most troublesome and tainted history. Its use in the past four hundred years has been rooted in categorizations of groups of people according to geographical origin and phenotype. In part due to the perceived need to legitimate colonialist subjugation of others, a hierarchy of value and privilege inevitably accompanied that typology, particularly in the areas of beauty and intelligence. Biological determinism and essentialism informed the racial taxonomic schemes of such eighteenth-century European scientists as Swedish botanist Carolus Linnaeus and German anatomist Friederich Blumenbach.[5] Scientists now so widely acknowledge that this type of racial theory is based on flawed assumptions, that it is questionable whether *race* is even a useful term today. It has inevitably led to what Douglas Sharp

3. Mark Lau Branson develops the concept of our shared words constructing a "house of language," tracing its lineage through Heidegger and Nietzsche, in Branson, "Ecclesiology," 2.

4. Handler, "Is 'Identity' a Useful Concept?," 29.

5. Linnaeus' taxonomy divided humans into four races: white Europeans, black Africans, yellow Asians, and red Americans. The closer a race resided to the Caucasus Mountains, the more superior their race was considered to be. Blumenbach added a fifth race, the Malays. See Cokley, "Critical Issues," 224.

calls the, "universe-maintenance scheme legitimating the racialized social order."[6] Sweeping theories of genetically determined racial differences are simply no longer in play in the scientific or sociological community today.

Throughout the history of the United States, racial classification discourse has shifted, in part depending on the political aims of those in power. Race has been magnified and used as a tool of oppression, and it has been artificially erased at other times, in attempts to unite the nation. Political institutions, made up primarily of members of the dominant culture, blurred ethnic difference in the creation of *whiteness*, at various times classifying Arab, Polish, Italian, Armenian, and numerous other immigrants as white, and at times not. The same courts and civil institutions denied rights and freedoms to Native and African Americans on the basis of such policies as blood quantum requirements for tribal membership, and the "one drop rule" for establishing Black identity (and often for denying basic civil rights).

The vision of national unity led North American institutions to meet the challenge of rising immigration numbers with the melting pot image and its accompanying assimilation strategies. The years following the Civil Rights movement saw a rise in the rhetoric of sameness. The ideal of *color-blindness* came to dominate. Clarence J. Pendleton, the chair of the 1985 U.S. Commission on Civil Rights, reported to the nation, "We are working on a color-blind society that has opportunities for all and guarantees success for none."[7] The cost of the rhetoric of melting pots and color-blindness, and aspects of the assertions made by those who argue that we have achieved a "post-racial" society, has been the loss of identity, pride, and recognized spaces in which marginalized voices find a hearing. The melting pot metaphor, and the ideology behind it, may overlook or deny numerous factors of history that still cause access to opportunity to be influenced by pigmentation. The current challenge is to develop an understanding of race that does not obscure or negate difference, yet does not root that difference in biology in a way that leads to a determinist or essentialist understanding.

This tension in terminology is a microcosm of the dilemma of the postmodern era, with its skepticism of all totalizing schemas, or "incredulity toward meta-narratives," as Jean-Francois Lyotard now famously phrased it.[8] For the twentieth century, even more than most, difference

---

6. Sharp, *No Partiality*, 125.

7. Cited in Omi and Winant, *Racial Formation in the United States*, 1.

8. Lyotard, *The Postmodern Condition*, xxiv.

proved to be a source and locus of violence and exclusion, particularly in Europe. Enlightenment thinkers in the liberal tradition of Kant, Locke, and Descartes had urged the modern world to step outside the particularities of history and cultural context, appealing to universal principles based on the foundation of reason alone. Postmodernists have objected strenuously to the assumption of neutrality inherent in that quest for certainty. They have brought to the surface the hermeneutical processes that have always been at play in descriptions of truth, and the ways those processes are influenced by our social, economic, and geographical location. Kevin Vanhoozer notes, "Postmodernity is the condition of being so exposed to plurality and otherness that one becomes conscious of the contingency of one's own language, culture, and way of life."[9] Postmodernism has contributed significantly to an awareness of *situatedness*, and has added needed complexity to the discussion of difference, particularly in the area of race.

Contemporary Use of the Term

Race theorists have historically been far too quick to connect observable differences between populations with generalizations about moral character and intelligence, and thus have legitimated and perpetuated racist beliefs and practices. While the jury is still out on the extent to which there is a genetic basis for some differences between those of differing geographical ancestry, scientists agree that racial classifications tend to be imprecise and arbitrary, and deny gradations. Thus, the current reevaluation of racial terminology is surely a movement forward. Yet it may be premature to simply eliminate the word from our vocabulary, as some scholars do today. Shawn Kelley summarizes the tension in the word's ongoing use:

> Race remains a particularly vexing category. It seems to have no intellectual grounding or legitimacy, yet it has negatively impacted the lives of millions of people for hundreds of years. It is now accepted by very few serious intellectuals, yet for most of the modern era it was accepted by virtually all serious intellectuals in virtually all academic and religious disciplines. We have thus reached a bewildering paradox: if we accept the reality of race then we may be on the slippery slope towards legitimizing racism, yet if we deny its reality we become powerless to confront it. If we wish to get anywhere in our discussion we need to find a way to recognize the historical centrality of race without falsely elevating race as a

9. Vanhoozer, "Pilgrim's Digress," 77.

biological category. We need to take race seriously without giving
in to racial thinking. We need, in short, to look at race as a social
and intellectual construct.[10]

Kelley insightfully articulates the dilemma of how to continue to speak
of racial difference, given the shifts that have occurred in understanding,
and the rhetorical and attitudinal changes that still need to take place. What
language will best reflect and shape new understanding and actions? The
scientific community currently lacks consensus regarding the ongoing
usefulness of the term. Many prefer to speak of *populations*, wanting to
maintain some term with which to describe genetic differences that occur
on the basis of bio-geographical ancestry, such as the disproportionate occurrence of certain diseases in specific populations. Given the problematic
associations with the term, an alternate term may be the best way forward
for many discussions. Today the classifications remain in arenas such as
census data, as one means toward better distribution of resources and votes.

In the realm of ethnic and racial identity theory, Kevin Cokley makes
an interesting recommendation. He asserts that, "When researchers are interested in how individuals see themselves relative to their cultural beliefs,
values, and behaviors, ethnic identity is the more appropriate construct to
study. However, when researchers are more interested in how individuals
construct their identities in response to an oppressive and highly racialized
society, racial identity is the more appropriate construct to study."[11] Even
that distinction, though, is frequently blurred, since identities that may be
consciously based in values and beliefs are frequently constructed in highly
racialized contexts. Still, Cokley has rightly pointed to another appropriate
ongoing use for the highly problematic term, *race*. For the purposes of this
book, the term will rarely be used, due to its charged history and the current lack of scholarly consensus as to its appropriate use.

ETHNICITY

Ethnicity is a term that carries less baggage than race, yet its meaning is
similarly elusive. Its vernacular use today often overlaps with race and
with culture. It tends to be a more pliable concept with a greater degree
of individual choice involved. Traditionally, an ethnic group is defined as

10. Kelley, *Racializing Jesus*, 23–24.
11. Cokley, "Measurement of Ethnic and Racial Identity," 225.

one that shares a (real or presumed) common lineage, with its accompanying language, history, values, patterns of behavior, and certain stylistic expressions such as music, dress, and dance. Today, ethnicity is understood less as a biologically determined or determinative phenomenon and more in terms of common environment and history, with that history's ensuing shared values and beliefs, or what one might call a *worldview*. Ethnic theorists vary in their emphases, with instrumentalists focusing on the common political causes of ethnic groups, and constructivists emphasizing ethnic identity construction and its permeability in different contexts.[12] Here we will consider two recent theories of ethnicity: the *identity politics* or multiculturalist movement, and the *postethnic* or cosmopolitan perspective. Then we will look at some of the recent attempts to measure levels of ethnic identification.

Multiculturalism and Identity Politics Movements

In a strong backlash from the assimilation-driven politics of earlier decades, the multiculturalist movement grew rapidly in the United States in the 1980s, bringing to academia and politics a great concern for the formation and preservation of ethnic identity, and paralleling similar movements in areas of gender and sexual preference. The concurrent rise of postmodern thought fueled this movement. Anselm Min's concise summary of postmodernity speaks to the concerns of the multiculturalists. He argues, "Postmodernity is a philosophy of difference. It universalizes difference and accentuates it so as to denounce naïve assumptions of unity, universality, and totality."[13] Heated debates continue in academia between essentialists, who seek to preserve classic Western texts as core to college curricula, and deconstructionists, who seek to expand the canon to include marginalized voices. Legislation toward equal treatment of various minority groups has also pressed the agenda of the public recognition of the legitimacy of minority groups. Multiculturalists have contributed to society's awareness of the profound loss that occurs when voices from the margin are not heard, and when equal rights are not granted to all.

However, some limitations of the movement have become apparent. It has tended to highlight *difference* as the ultimate means of constructing identity. It has labored hard to preserve and protect that difference, without

12. Conde-Frazier et al. make this point in *Many Colored Kingdom*, 19.

13. Min, *Solidarity of Others*, 66.

a corresponding ethic with which to unite societies. Charles Taylor cites
the "tight common purpose" that balanced individual freedom in Rous-
seau's vision of society, arguing that this common vision can be a casualty
of multiculturalism.[14] Arthur Schlesinger Jr. raised this objection more
stridently, arguing, "The cult of ethnicity exaggerates differences, intensi-
fies resentments and antagonisms, and drives ever deeper wedges between
races and nationalities."[15] Numerous scholars have argued that Schlesinger's
vision obscures differences in the name of an American unity that is better
described as *uniformity*.[16] Yet he is right to note the lack of a compelling
basis for unity in much of the multiculturalist literature, which is rooted in
modernist conceptions of individual rights.[17] Vanhoozer's critique of the
excesses of postmodernity applies to many strands of the multiculturalist movement. He writes, "Human situatedness . . . has become the focus
of postmodern investigations. The result: every issue is ultimately about
identity politics, about where, what, and who one is. Postmoderns are so
preoccupied with the situated self that they cannot get beyond it."[18] As we
consider how preaching may participate in this conversation, at this point
we will simply ask: when are preachers called to speak words that transcend
difference, uniting listeners around a larger vision? When are preachers
called to name and even highlight difference?

Kenneth Appiah raises a different concern. He notes the tendency of
the multicultural movement to create a politics of identity that requires political acknowledgement of ethnic and other differences that some would
prefer to view as personal dimensions of their identity. He concludes, "[A]
politics of identity can be counted on to transform the identities on whose
behalf it ostensibly labors. Between the politics of recognition and the
politics of compulsion, there is no bright line."[19] The perception of compulsion and the ensuing highly charged environment surrounding the debate
explains in part the waning appeal of the multiculturalist agenda in recent
years.

14. Taylor, "Politics of Recognition," 50.

15. Schlesinger Jr., *Disuniting of America*, 102.

16. Conde-Frazier et al., *Many Colored Kingdom*, 15.

17. Higham writes, "Multiculturalism . . . lacks a vision of what is wants the country
to become. For young people in search of some common purpose beyond the confines
of their own endowment, multiculturalism offers no nourishing center or beckoning
horizon" ("Multiculturalism and Universalism," 230).

18. Vanhoozer, "Pilgrim's Digress," 76.

19. Appiah, "Identity, Authenticity, Survival," 163.

Affiliative, Individual, Choice-Based Models

Historian David Hollinger has proposed an alternative to multiculturalism, which he calls a *post-ethnic* perspective, or a rooted cosmopolitanism. Noting that cosmopolitanism among intellectuals has tended toward breadth at the expense of awareness of history, he advocates, " . . . the critical renewal of cosmopolitanism in the context of today's greater sensitivity to roots."[20] He argues that ethnic identity is acquired through *affiliation*, whether prescribed or chosen. The affiliation model seeks to correct the sometimes rigidly ascribed fixed distinctions that can arise in multiculturalism. As he states it, "Multiculturalism breeds an enthusiasm for specific, traditional cultures that can sometimes mask a provinciality from which individuals are eager to escape through new, out-group affiliations."[21] While the last thing a multiculturalist would want to be called is conservative, Appiah's and Hollinger's critiques point to its drive to conserve the distinctive characteristics of marginalized groups, sometimes at the cost of pliability.

Hollinger's work parallels the rise of social theorists who emphasize what sociologist Gerardo Marti calls, "the malleability of ethnic identity."[22] These theorists hold to an instrumental or situational understanding of ethnicity. Among them is Jonathan Okamura, who writes, "The individual actor has the option, on the one hand, of emphasizing or obfuscating his ethnic identity, or on the other, of assuming other social identities that he holds."[23] Some aspects of this theory can lead to a highly individualistic, choice-based understanding of identity, one that thrives in the consumer culture of North America today. Weakened family and social structures mean that rituals and traditions are being displaced by mass media and marketing. This has elevated the element of individual, independent choice in identity construction. Working with a similarly pliable definition of ethnicity, Manuel Castells has demonstrated two other models on which identity may be based in a postmodern environment. One he labels *resistance identity*, which is rooted in a challenge to perceived powers, and the other he calls *project identity*, which is forward-looking and goal-oriented.[24]

20. Hollinger, *Postethnic America*, 5.
21. Ibid, 107.
22. Marti, *A Mosaic of Believers*, 170.
23. Okamura, "Situational Ethnicity," cited in Marti, *Mosaic*, 170.
24. Castells, *Power of Identity*, 8.

At this point it will be instructive to consider briefly the goals of one ethnically diverse church. Mosaic Church of Los Angeles exemplifies the pursuit of a common, project-based identity that transcends ethnicity. While intentionally diverse, the church leadership consciously obscures ethnic difference and seeks to create a new culture for all its members, based in common commitment to transcendent values. They are intentionally monocultural in their congregational life.[25] They have provided a haven for young third and fourth generation immigrants, who are seeking a change from the ethnic-specific churches of their parents and grandparents, and for white people who are drawn to diversity. However, many African Americans perceive Mosaic as white-dominated.[26] In explaining this reality, Marti, a former pastor of Mosaic, asserts, "The more highly committed people are to a single ethnic expression, the less likely they are to come to and stay at Mosaic."[27]

The portrait Marti paints is of a church that has embraced a highly pliable conception of ethnicity, along with an embrace of the culture of globalization and its marketing methods, in the service of conveying a (type of) Christian message. Much is to be commended in the unity of purpose among Mosaic's members, and in the strong corporate identity that is founded upon baptism into Christ's body. But one may wonder if the leaders of Mosaic have adequately accounted for the complexity that is present in their midst or adequately questioned the problems of a model that draws so eagerly on the promises of globalization.

The deceptive promise of globalization is that it seems to highlight diversity, giving individuals access to surface-level knowledge about cultures distant from their own with the click of a mouse. Yet, Michael Budde points out the dilution of real differences that global culture industries effect. He observes, "Beneath the dizzying array of cultural choices, however, remains the oligopolistic substratum of the global culture industries. For all the surface diversity . . . the dominant culture industries have concentrated decisions in amazingly few centers: Disney/ABC, Sony . . . and the like."[28] As leaders seek to form congregations that truly honor ethnic histories

---

25. Marti, *Mosaic*, 160. This description of Mosaic is based upon a snapshot of the church at the time of Marti's writing, and reflects Marti's perceptions, not those of every member and leader.

26. Ibid, 163.

27. Ibid.

28. Budde, *The (Magic) Kingdom of God*, 94.

and cultural distinctions, they do well to heed Budde's warning, lest they content themselves with superficial changes in worship style, while ignoring the disciplines of confession, repentance, and justice-seeking love that the task of forming many members into one body requires. Mosaic may excel in these practices, but Marti's account of their philosophy of ethnicity raises the question as to whether it is adequate to the task of genuine reconciliation.

The affiliation-based, pragmatic perspectives of Hollinger and others account well for the reality that North Americans today often inhabit multiple circles simultaneously, finding identity and belonging within various subcultures. Hollinger praises the "willingness of the postethnic to treat ethnic identity as a question rather than a given."[29] Hollinger's model, along with Appiah's critique of some of the unintended consequences of multiculturalism, seeks an understanding of ethnicity that is more fluid and dynamic than highly bounded historical constructs. Yet it may leave behind accountability to the past and a solid basis for community. Anselm Min echoes that need in his evaluation of postmodernity. He argues that postmodern discourse has rightly brought issues of justice and liberation into a new light through its recognition and appreciation of difference, but it has been weaker at articulating a basis for connection. Min argues for a theology of *the solidarity of others*, explaining, "Solidarity of others . . . is my way of deconstructing and sublating postmodernism . . . Otherness is critically negated in its absolute claim, transcended into the solidarity of others, and preserved in its proper meaning in that solidarity."[30] Hollinger's postethnic perspective also seeks a basis for solidarity in our common concerns. His vision allows for a great deal of personal choice in the matter of ethnic affiliation, though it is not entirely clear on what basis one might make those decisions. He concludes, "Boundaries are necessary. A post-ethnic perspective understands that. Which boundaries, and where? We are all left with the responsibility for deciding where to try to draw what circles with whom, and around what."[31]

29. Hollinger, *Postethnic America*, 106.
30. Min, *Solidarity*, 82.
31. Hollinger, *Postethnic America*, 172.

Critique of Affiliative, Choice-Based Models

Hollinger's assessment understands identity primarily as a matter of freely chosen self-definition. Identity is something individuals construct, using the tools they find most useful and attractive.[32] Yet this highlighting of choice obscures other key sociological and theological dimensions of ethnic identity. First, it can be future-oriented to the potential exclusion of the past. It has wings, but may overlook historical roots and the troubling sense of accountability that hovers near those roots. In severing continuity with one's past, one suffers the loss of what Booth calls the *life-in-common*.[33] W. James Booth reflects, "That life-in-common . . . implicates us in a mutuality not only of our present moment but of our shared past as well, our collective memory."[34] Second, it diminishes the awareness that identity is formed in community, not solely or even primarily through isolated individual choices and desires. It reflects what Charles Taylor calls, "the monological ideal" of an identity that is solely generated inwardly and independently.[35] As Rowan Williams cautions,

32. Mary Waters puts forth a similar vision. She asserts, "The ultimate goal of a pluralist society should be a situation of symbolic ethnicity for all Americans. If all Americans were free to exercise their 'ethnic option' with the certainty that there would be no costs associated with it, we could all enjoy the voluntary, pleasurable aspects of ethnic traditions . . ." ("Costs of a Costless Community," 293). The goal of equality argued for here is laudable, and she is right to point out that whites have had much more freedom to self-label than have others, in United States history. Yet the selective nature of ethnicity portrayed here can avoid accountability and hence needed confession and reconciliation.

33. Jurgen Habermas uses the term, *Lebenswelt*, or life-world, to denote the cultural system of interpretation that allows individuals to arrive at shared meaning in communication. He writes, "In their interpretive accomplishments the members of a communication community demarcate the one objective world and their intersubjectively shared social world from the subjective worlds of individuals and collectives" (*Theory of Communicative Action*, 70). Habermas's insights have implications for preachers seeking to communicate in settings with diverse interpretive systems. Here, we work with Booth's concept of the *life-in-common*, which deals more with the shaping power of the shared past for members of a community.

34. Booth writes, "When projects are formed in the present, this behavior is explicable only against the background of the planner's continued existence into the future. We can add to this that to see the group as the subject of imputation, of responsibility for or ownership of its past actions is to locate the trace of a continuity extending back into the past. So (future) deliberation and commitment, and (past) accountability and the boundaries of life-in-common that mark us apart from other groups or individuals all require a certain kind of persistence across time" (*Communities of Memory*, 4).

35. Taylor, *Multiculturalism*, 33.

But we do need to be careful of falling into the trap of regarding "the self" as a spring of action determined by pure will or as a timeless substance operating by pure reason. Both of these myths represent attempts to guarantee that the self remains transcendent of its surrounding, free and (possibly) immortal . . . But it might be truer to say that the self's transcendence is in its memory, precisely in its recollection *now* of another reality, a past reality, both distinct from and part of the present situation. Memory affirms that the present situation has a context; it, like the self, is part of a continuity, it is "made" and so it is not immutable.[36]

Third, it runs counter to the Christian doctrines of creation and election. The narrative in Scripture of God's gracious creating and choosing of humanity teaches us that our lives and identities are *given* to us, to be received from One who is wiser and more generous than we ourselves. From this we can infer that the creator has placed us in ethnic groups to fulfill his purposes. Paul proclaimed to the Athenians, "From one ancestor he made all nations to inhabit the whole earth, and he allotted the times of their existence and the boundaries of the places where they would live, so that they would search for God . . ." (Acts 17:26). William Dyrness discerns well the tension in God's call for humans both to receive and to choose their ethnic identity. He writes, "The Hebrews were people who joined themselves freely to God's project of forming a people that reflected God's purposes and character; their identity was partly received as a gift and partly chosen in their response of obedience."[37] Dyrness contrasts this with an idolatrous *grasping* of identity, such as occurred at Babel. To receive the gift of creation implies that one will seek to love the ethnic group into which one has been born, accepting some measure of accountability for the heritage of its failings, and committing to work for its welfare, while setting that particular welfare within the larger framework of affiliation across ethnic lines, in solidarity with all humanity.

History has seen the pendulum swing from rigidly defining and accentuating ethnic distinctions, to fuzzily obscuring them. One result of globalization, shifting immigration patterns, and cross-ethnic marriage is that ethnic identity today is inevitably more fluid and dynamic. This can either result in efforts to conserve and preserve group identity or in efforts to forge new, hybrid identities, based in centers other than strict conceptions of one's bio-geographical ethnic heritage, as is reflected in Hollinger's

36. Williams, *Resurrection*, 30.
37. Dyrness, *The Earth is God's*, 98.

vision of a post-ethnic America. As those who preach and lead congregations marked by greater diversity, we seek to incorporate the insights of recent scholarship, while retaining elements of the traditional understanding of an ethnic group as a people who share a linguistic and cultural history and a common geographical point of ancestry. Perhaps more significantly, as a problem and opportunity for congregations and preaching, members of a given ethnic group share a common narration of what has happened to them and what they have done. They are formed in part by collective memories of a shared past that give their members security, meaning, and identity. Their ethnic history has the potential to form a tapestry upon which to narrate the story of God's redemption. As Dyrness puts it, "a major function of ethnicity is to locate the search for God, to be that locus in which God might be found and known . . . Ethnicity does provide a lens, an indispensable one as we have seen, in terms of which the grace of God may be seen and grasped."[38] Complicating the concept of a shared history, of course, is the reality that ethnic groups are also in a dynamic process within themselves of negotiating contested narrations, and allowing marginalized voices from within their groups to speak.

Memories held in common shape a group's horizon of action and of belief, on into the present. As W. James Booth words it, "To say that a community is historical is to hold, among other things, that it has a shared past, one expression of which is the narrative of that past, the fruit of the community's will to remember."[39] Societies and their multiple subgroups utilize spatial, ritual, and linguistic frameworks to preserve their stories. They also construct a narrative of those outside their group, all too often portraying them as inferior to themselves and all too frequently as the cause of their suffering. Often undisclosed to those outside their group, these stories serve to distinguish them from other groups and to locate and solidify their identity. At times this functions to equip them to move into the future with a will to cross boundaries and to work for justice for others. For other ethnic groups this narrative process leaves them paralyzed in the past. Collective memories are utilized selectively, for the preservation of a group's identity, and thus they are prone to distortion. As churches become multiethnic, naming the multiple, and often contested, collective memories in their midst is a crucial first step in forming congregations that can hear, honor, and hold carefully painful and joyful ethnic memories, while

38. Ibid., 108.
39. Booth, *Communities of Memory*, 23.

locating them within a larger narrative that makes space for new affiliations to form.

Ethnic Identity Measurement

Erik Erikson defined identity as, "a subjective sense of an invigorating sameness and continuity."[40] Our assumption here is that a healthy ethnic identity is a good that church involvement should foster in its members. In exploring how that identity grows, we will draw from the secular scholarship that has established it as that sense of belonging in, knowledge of, and involvement for the betterment of, the ethnic group or groups with which one perceives common ancestry and shared culture. We will also integrate key theological dimensions such as gratitude, the capacity to confess wrongs done by one's ethnic group(s), the capacity and will to repent and work to redress those wrongs, and an awareness and reception of the grace of God that extends to one's own and other ethnic groups.

Ethnic identity is formed through complex and evolving internal and external processes through which one establishes the boundaries, meaning, and value of one's ethnicity, and chooses behaviors that strengthen or weaken affiliation. It can be measured (albeit imprecisely) by such factors as self-labeling, a subjective sense of belonging, a positive or negative evaluation of one's ethnic group, and levels of involvement in ethnic group activities and political projects. Psychologists and other social scientists have developed several scales, which generally view ethnic identity development as a process that moves through stages from lack of awareness of or outright rejection of one's ethnicity (called pre-encounter in the Racial Identity Attitude Scale [RIAS]),[41] to exploration, (called immersion-emersion in the RIAS, and sometimes characterized by antipathy toward other groups) to resolution, internalization, and affirmation. Other scales have been developed, including the White Racial Identity Attitude Scale, the Cross Racial Identity Scale and the Multi-group Ethnic Identity Measure (MEIM). The MEIM measures levels of *affirmation* (sense of belonging to one's ethnic group), *achievement* (exploration and resolution of ethnic identity issues), and *behaviors* (engaging in practices specific to one's ethnic group).[42] These

40. Erikson, *Identity, Youth and Crisis*, 50.
41. See Helms, *Black and White Racial Identity*.
42. Cokley, "Critical Issues," 226–29.

tools have furthered understanding of the subjective and developmental nature of identification with an ethnic group.

Clayton Alderfer has added an intriguing dimension of identity development with his theory of *embedded intergroup relations*.[43] Its interest is also ethnic identity, but it focuses on the *group* as the primary entity, rather than the individual. Thus it is better able to account for relations between and among ethnic groups. Alderfer notes that for various reasons of a group's internal history and the racism it has faced, a group may become *underbounded*, ill-defined, and overly permeable, causing feelings of abandonment in its members. It may also become *overbounded*, or rigidly defined, granting members little autonomy, and causing fears of engulfment in members.[44] Alderfer also makes the point, often overlooked in other identity scales, that significant positive interaction with *other* ethnic groups is essential to healthy ethnic identity development.[45] Alderfer's insights and those of ethnic identity measurement systems in general, have significant applicability to the consideration of what causes individuals to join (or avoid) multiethnic churches, and what fears and needs must be addressed for them to find wholeness in those settings. It also addresses the complex issue of which immigrant groups, indigenous peoples, or subcultures within African Americans have been most resistant to integration, with ethnic-specificity persisting strongly in religious expression.

While it is true that healthy ethnic identity is forged through strong relational bonds within one's ethnic group and participation in their rituals, political aspirations, and other traditions, new research is showing that crucial dimensions of ethnic identity are formed through positive interaction outside one's own group, and that this is beneficial for the health of the group as a whole. Stella Ting-Toomey has developed an *ethnic identity negotiation* theory, wherein she argues that the more secure individuals' self-identifications are, the more they are open to interacting with members of other cultures. The more vulnerable they feel, the more anxiety they feel in those interactions. She notes, "The more individuals need inclusion, the more they value in-group and relational boundaries. The more individuals need differentiation, the more distance they place between the self and others."[46] She concludes, "Individuals' resourcefulness in negotiating

---

43. Alderfer, "Embedded Intergroup Relations," 238.

44. Ibid, 245.

45. Ibid.

46. Ting-Toomey, "Communicative Resourcefulness," 74.

identities is affected by effectively managing the security-vulnerability and inclusion-differentiation dialectics."[47] For Ting-Toomey, identity formation is a dynamic and evolving process that is accomplished in large part through discourse.

William Gudykunst has isolated *uncertainty* as a pervasive aspect of communication with strangers. He posits that uncertainty can (but need not) lead to anxiety, and that in general people seek to avoid anxiety in intercultural interactions by reducing uncertainty, through making proactive predictions of the stranger's behavior and retroactive explanations of observed behavior. Humans also tend to reduce uncertainty and its accompanying anxiety by simply avoiding those who are not like them. But Gudykunst posits that the willingness to risk, to step out into areas of cultural uncertainty, ultimately lowers the anxiety one feels in those settings. He writes, "An increase in uncertainty avoidance will produce an increase in the anxiety strangers experience when interacting with members of other groups."[48] Gudykunst's insights about risk and growth in cross-cultural communication points to a particularly promising aspect of multiethnic church life, that when it is thriving it can prepare its members to relate confidently and effectively in society.

CULTURE

Culture is the term whose history is arguably the most complex, because much of it operates beneath the surface of the conscious awareness of a given culture's members. Jaegwon Kim asserts that those who study culture are attempting to, "interpret and transmit to future generations the system of values in terms of which participants in a form of life find meaning and purpose."[49] Relating culture to ethnicity, Joane Nagel observes, "[Ethnic] boundaries answer the question, 'Who are we?' Culture provides the content and meaning of ethnicity; it animates and authenticates ethnic boundaries by providing a history, ideology, symbolic universe, and system of meaning. Culture answers the question: What are we?"[50]

47. Ibid, 74.
48. Gudykunst, "Uncertainty and Anxiety," 142.
49. Kim, "Culture," 185.
50. Nagel, "Constructing Ethnicity," 251.

Culture encompasses the patterns of behavior, beliefs, values, and skills that are transmitted (and transformed) through generations. These processes are found and expressed in behaviors or practices, and are embedded in language, ritual, landscape, media, and art. All of this informs the hermeneutics of everyday life—how members of a given culture process and interpret the world. Here we are concerned with culture for three reasons. First, the study of culture sheds light on the practices and performances that shape and define ethnic groups. We are most concerned with the practices that interpret and commemorate shared past events, and the ways those rituals and narrations may make multiethnic congregational life both richer and more challenging. Second, it has proven fruitful in recent congregational studies to consider local churches themselves as cultures, or at least as sharing by analogy many traits and patterns of cultures.[51] Third, central to the concerns of preaching in general is the interpretation of texts, and scholars in the field of hermeneutics have been listening well to the insights of culture studies, thus understanding more deeply the situated nature of all hermeneutical endeavors. This work serves preachers as we consider how members of different cultural backgrounds can read and proclaim Scripture together. With an eye to these three purposes, this section considers historical and emerging secular understandings of culture, theological inquiry into culture and church, and recent paradigm shifts in biblical hermeneutics.

Secular Conceptions of Culture

The English word's root in the Latin, *cultus*, with its connotations of ground plowed and fields furrowed, points to the way that culture has long been considered the realm of human manipulation or cultivation of nature; culture is what humans do or make with life's raw materials. Kant distinguished the realm of nature, ruled as it is by laws and necessity, from the realm of freedom, wherein humans may exercise choices and utilize creativity and energy to shape their societies. These individual and joint efforts express meaning and value. As we look at these expressions, whether in the artistic, political, or religious realms, we can read the values of a culture. Vanhoozer applies Ricoeur's theory of the model of the text in interpreting human action to argue for reading cultures, looking for their plotlines, theses, and other significant indicators of their interpretation of

---

51. See Ammerman et al., *Studying Congregations*, 78–102.

life's meaning.[52] Yet aspects of this model have been questioned. Dyrness objects to the modern, intellectualist understanding of culture as primarily the expression of ideas. He writes, "[This paradigm] is inadequate both to the rich social and cultural patterns of a culture and to the way individual actors use (or misuse) those patterns."[53] In general, theoretical frameworks that viewed culture as the expression of the ideals and values of a rather tightly enclosed, somewhat static social group have given way to ones that view culture as a dynamically evolving process, as a *tool kit* or *repertoire* that participants draw upon for various ends.[54]

Hegel exemplified the idealist, developmental understanding of culture; in his view culture participated in the movement of world history toward its ultimate end in pure, enlightened rationality. The view of culture as the outworking of ideas was paired with the unitary conceptions of *a people* prevalent among German philosophers such as Herder and von Humboldt.[55] Postmoderns today critique this outlook for its tendency toward what Mary McClintock Fulkerson calls, "cultural holism." She explains, "Cultural holism refers to the notion that cultures are cohesive wholes held together by shared beliefs, symbol systems, or rituals that have a unidirectional causal force."[56] She and others point out that this view tends to assume a people in isolation from other societies, and is inadequate for the ubiquitous and complex interactions that take place between ethnic groups and societies today.

Frank Boaz in the 1920s began to articulate an alternative to the use of the expression of ideas as the central lens for understanding individual cultures, wanting instead to look at intercultural practices and patterns. Clifford Geertz in the 1950s followed Boaz but shifted the discussion to a more pragmatic level. He asked anthropologists and others in the human sciences to view cultures as constitutive processes. Geertz developed the linkage between culture and language, the symbol system that enables us to interpret life and express our understanding of its significance, unlike any other species. As he puts it, "The concept of culture I espouse . . .

52. See Vanhoozer, "World Well Staged?," 6–8.

53. Dyrness, *The Earth is God's*, 82.

54. See Mary McClintock Fulkerson, who also cites cultural theorists such as James Clifford and Ann Swidler ("We Don't See Color Here," 147).

55. Dyrness, *The Earth is God's*, 62.

56. Fulkerson, "We Don't See Color Here," 147.

is essentially a semiotic one."[57] Semiotic systems in Geertz's work may be broadly defined as gesture, ritual, dance, visual art and even patterns of behavior in individuals and institutions. Geertz's work has come under critique in recent years from Marxist and feminist theorists who argue that he is continuing in the Enlightenment understanding of belief as individual and privatized, and that he fails to account for power dynamics and complex class relations that shape the symbolic structures of cultures.[58] The French *Annales* school has been notable in arguing that scholars pay closer attention to the horizontal aspects of culture, the behaviors of common people in ordinary life, than to those aspects found in the ideas of the great (and elite) thinkers of a society.

Theological Perspectives on Culture

While postmodern cultural theorists have shifted the discussion from values and beliefs to actions and strategies, downplaying the search for transcendent meaning in culture, theologians continue to inquire into culture as the *lived religion* that is expressed and furthered within societies. Augustine, in *The City of God Against the Pagans*, began a tradition of exploration of the ultimate ends of civilizations. For Augustine, interpretation of culture involved understanding the *loves* of its members, and whether that love is turned essentially toward God or toward self or the glory of the empire. Theologians since then have continued to draw upon Augustine as they link their understanding of culture to religion. Abraham Kuyper follows Augustine in his understanding of culture as inherently religious and in his view that concrete forms of expression such as film or architecture all reflect a worldview. Herman Dooyeweerd similarly speaks of the "ground motives" underlying societies; these ground motives are either God-affirming or God-denying. He called them the "hermeneutic keys for understanding and interpreting periods and patterns of history and culture."[59]

Numerous other Protestant thinkers, from Schleiermacher to Tillich, have reflected on culture as a religious expression. Tillich saw culture as the

---

57. Geertz, *Interpretation of Cultures*, 5.

58. Serene Jones makes this point, as a critique of Lindbeck's use of Geertz, in "Cultural Labor," 159.

59. Dooyeweerd, *Roots of Western Culture*, cited in Vanhoozer, "World Well Staged?," 17.

form of religion, the outworking of a society's shared ultimate concerns.[60] T. S. Eliot interpreted culture similarly. He wrote, "[We] may ask whether any culture could come into being, or maintain itself, without a religious basis. We may go further and ask whether what we call the culture, and what we call the religion, of a people are not different aspects of the same thing: the culture being, essentially, the incarnation (so to speak) of the religion of a people."[61] Eliot recognized the shortcomings of his strong linkage of culture and religion. He argued against two errors: viewing religion and culture as two entirely separate things and fusing religion and culture completely. For him, the concept of incarnation avoids both errors. Eliot's conception of culture represents a somewhat dated understanding of culture, which presumed a more static, monolithic entity, and yet his insights continue to have merit.

Niebuhr's Typology of Christ and Culture

The modern theologian who gave the most sustained attention to Christian interaction with culture was H. Richard Niebuhr, whose classic typologies in *Christ and Culture* continue to stimulate thought. Niebuhr defined culture broadly as "everything that people do," the observable human behavior that eventuates in the creation of states, economies, family structures, and the arts. He then articulated five postures toward culture that the church has historically taken, across a spectrum from a view of Christ as in radical tension against culture, to that of Christ accommodated fully to culture. Clearly rejecting these extremes, he then outlined three more centrist positions: the view of Christ above culture, Christ and culture in paradox, and the transformationist view. Like any typology, Niebuhr's work simplifies and classifies in ways that both clarify and obscure. Ernst Troeltsch's idealist presuppositions heavily influenced Niebuhr's understanding of Christ, who is conceived and portrayed as a universal ideal or set of virtues, rather than a particular historical person rooted in Jewish culture. Duane Friesen objects, "They [Troeltsch and Niebuhr] both begin by describing a Christ abstracted from his own cultural context and define him in such a way that if one were to have a 'pure' relationship to this Christ, one would by definition stand in opposition to culture."[62]

60. Vanhoozer, "World Well Staged?," 20.
61. Eliot, *Notes Toward the Definition of Culture*, 101.
62. Friesen, "An Anabaptist Theology of Culture," 46.

Branson points out the lack of "conceptual congruence" in the model, since Niebuhr chose to work with *Christ* rather than *church*. Branson notes, "It is the two corporate realities (culture and church) that need to be compared and contrasted. Because of this conceptual confusion, Niebuhr's comments tend toward individualism rather than toward corporate meaning and agency."[63] Culture is similarly conceived as a monolithic entity, which inevitably stands in opposition to the monolithic entity called Christ. Friesen calls for a method of discernment and discrimination by which Christians can respond to cultures in different instances with the choice to creatively work within them, protest against them, or withdraw from them entirely. Niebuhr himself acknowledged that different moments in history call for different stances toward culture. Such a discernment process requires the recognition that the church is itself enmeshed in culture and embodied within history. Niebuhr's insights spurred much helpful critical reflection within denominational traditions regarding their characteristic stances toward culture, but globalization and the shift to postmodernity call for fresh paradigms to bring new understanding today.

Currently, many who are thinking about the nexus of missiology and ecclesiology are paying new attention to culture, as churches that seek to live out the *missio Dei* are learning their need for a deeper engagement with the environment that shapes them even as they seek to shape it. Alan Roxburgh speaks from within the Mission in Western Culture project, a movement that is pressing the church to more creative engagement with its cultural context.[64] He writes, "The church's eschatological vision of the future-present reign of God is universal. But it is always and everywhere lived out in the particular locales of created existence. The created order locates people in specific cultures, and God invites the missional community to cooperate with the ongoing work of God's creating in their particular location."[65]

63. Branson, *Intercultural Life and Adult Formation*, 115.

64. The Mission in Western Culture Project was formed to further the dialogue begun by the writings of Lesslie Newbigin. http://www.allelon.org/projects/mission_western_culture.cfm.

65. Roxburgh, "Missional Leadership," 188.

Congregations as Cultures

One reason the study of culture has fascinated Christians is that they live out their religion within the context of local congregations, and those congregations share many of the features of cultures. As with cultures, shared memories of the past strengthen and at times weaken or even immobilize congregations. Like cultures, congregations are in dynamic processes of development (or entropy). Churches employ place, rituals, artistry, and language to express their values to interpret and narrate their past in meaningful ways, and to forge deeper communion among their members. James Hopewell has studied congregations as cultures, looking at the ways they narrate their values and vision of life. He asserts, "a group of people cannot regularly gather for what they feel to be religious purposes without developing a complex network of signals and symbols and conventions—in short, a subculture—that gains its own logic and then functions in a way peculiar to that group."[66]

A question Hopewell does not address is how a congregational subculture might be formed from the interplay of multiple ethnically based subcultures, each of which brings in its own set of symbols, conventions, and corresponding logic. Kathy Black does consider this. She writes,

> Like the people after Pentecost, creating a shared story with a multicultural congregation is essential. It's harder in today's world, because, unlike after the glow of Pentecost, persons in multicultural congregations don't worship together daily . . . It is still possible . . . to create a true community in the midst of great diversity. It just means that creating a new shared story, a collective memory, takes more time and conscious initiative to develop.[67]

Gospel and Culture:
Inculturation, Incarnation, and Hermeneutics

Some of the most interesting insights into the nature of culture and church have come from scholars in missiology and in hermeneutics. The cutting edge insight for missionary endeavors during the last half of the twentieth century was that of the need to *contextualize* the gospel, allowing it (*gospel* here viewed as a static entity) to take on an indigenous form in each culture.

66. Hopewell, *Congregation, Stories and Structures*, 5.
67. Black, *Culturally Conscious Worship*, 87.

Generally this took the form of European and North American missionaries working to shed the gospel of its Western trappings, working with national Christians to find forms of worship, leadership, and proclamation that reflected their culture. This has involved repentance from systems of power and control on the part of the dominant culture. The incarnation of Jesus Christ has served as model and catalyst for this work. The 1978 *Willowbank Report* of the Lausanne Committee for World Evangelization sparked conversations around these themes.[68] Within Catholicism, inculturation has been a topic of intense discussion since the Second Vatican Council, as evidenced in numerous papal documents and conferences.[69] The "Nairobi Statement on Worship and Culture," which the Lutheran World Federation prepared in 1996, articulated the issues clearly, noting that the gospel message and Christian worship will at different times demonstrate elements that are transcultural, contextual, countercultural, and cross-cultural.[70]

While efforts toward inculturation have shown good faith on the part of missionaries, the response of some Christian movements in post-colonial nations has revealed flawed assumptions on the part of some Western missiologists and missionaries. They have tended to assume that the gospel itself is a pure substance, detached from culture, and movements of contextualization have sometimes been done in condescension to the culture that is "receiving" that gospel. Thus the movement of inculturation becomes unidirectional, rather than a mutually enriching process.

A telling response has been that from some African Christians, whose resistance to the call from Roman Catholic bishops for contextualized worship caught Catholic missionaries by surprise. Teresia Hinga interprets their response: "The Christians resisting inculturation [reject] the idea that they *must* incultivate, and incultivate in a predefined and predetermined way . . . inculturation as a process whose initiative lies elsewhere and whose purpose needs to be explained laboriously by experts, may well be rejected, by the recipients."[71] Peter Phan notes the argument of Michael Amaladoss for a paradigm or term that would improve upon that of inculturation, such as *interculturation*. "He [Amaladoss] argues that the image of incarnation

---

68. Lausanne Committee on World Evangelization, *The Willowbank Report on Gospel and Culture*.

69. See the encyclical letters of John Paul II, *Redemptoris Missio* (1990), and *Fides et Ratio* (1998).

70. "Nairobi Statement on Worship and Culture (1996)," cited in Hawn, *One Bread, One Body*, 177–83.

71. Hingia, "Inculturation," 16.

as the model for inculturation may misleadingly suggest that the gospel is somehow culture-free and needs only to be 'incarnated' in each culture."[72]

Culture and Hermeneutics

Many now acknowledge that the gospel itself has always been embedded in culture. As Claude Geffre puts it, "It is an illusion to imagine that in the beginning there existed a chemically pure Christianity that would inculturate itself progressively in other cultures."[73] Geffre too notes the danger that the term *inculturation* could imply that the church could return to an essence of Christianity if only it could free itself from its cultural blinders. While it is essential to pursue self-conscious critique of one's own culture, the aim cannot be to arrive at an ability to interpret Scripture and approach God in worship in a way that is "unfettered" by culture. Rather, the goal must be an approach of humility that embraces one's historical particularity, acknowledging that even as it blinds one to some things it gives a privileged vantage point for others. The New Homiletic, with its turn to the listener and sustained attention to the varied lived experiences of those listeners, reflects this broader shift toward culturally aware approaches to truth and meaning.

Evangelical traditions have been particularly captivated by the quest of modernity for unassailable foundations on which to place the objective truths of the gospel. James K. A. Smith notes that in the minds of many evangelicals, hermeneutics is a necessary evil. "Interpretation . . . is [viewed by evangelicals as] a result of the Fall, is itself a fall—from the intelligible to the sensible, from immediacy to mediation, from understanding to distortion, from reading to interpretation."[74] He cites, among others, Rex Koivisto's work, *One Lord, One Faith*, in which Koivisto calls readers to separate out their denominational and cultural traditions from their reading of Scripture. Koivisto asserts, "Only when we have separated out what is traditional, can we be allowed to hear the crisp, unadorned voice of God ringing out from Scripture alone."[75] In contrast to this pursuit of certainty, Smith develops a creational hermeneutic, based in part on the belief that finitude is part of humanity's created nature, not a result of the fall.

72. Amaladoss, "Beyond Inculturation," 7.
73. Geffre, "Christianity and Culture," 335.
74. Smith, *Fall of Interpretation*, 17.
75. Koivisto, *One Lord, One Faith*, cited in Smith, *Fall of Interpretation*, 42.

Drawing on Derrida's work with the mediated nature of language itself in *On Grammatology*, Smith argues that much is gained when readers give up the expectation of purity in interpretation. The ensuing posture would place them in humble interdependence upon others in a wide interpretive community. He notes, "Following from such a construal, interpretation is not a violation of purity but rather a way of connection, a way of being-with that is essential to be(com)ing human."[76] If pastors and preachers can teach their congregations to receive diversity as a gift for interpretation, they will find that its presence creates a new space for fresh insights.

CONCLUSION

This survey of the history of inquiry into race, ethnicity, and culture has surfaced several broad shifts in understanding and approach to them. Here we will summarize two shifts in scholarly discourse and then notice two features of society today, hinting at their implications for multiethnic congregation formation. The first shift has been the movement from a view of cultures and subcultures as unified within themselves and fairly static across time, to one that views cultures as interwoven and emerging processes. Tanner has pointed out that a major flaw of the modern period was that observers of culture failed to incorporate historical processes, and so took snapshots of cultures, freezing them in time. This led to an accent on differences between cultures, which were each considered as internally consistent, clearly bounded units. Rather, she notes, "[Culture] forms the basis for conflict as much as it forms the basis for shared beliefs and sentiments. Whether or not culture is a common focus of *agreement*, culture binds people together as a common focus for *engagement*."[77] This shift in understanding has run concurrently with the change from a scholarly emphasis on the high culture of the elite to a privileging of observable practices in everyday life.

The second shift has been from an emphasis on culture and ethnicity as inherited givens of history, to one that views ethnic identity as a matter of individual choice, based in chosen affiliations, shared political projects, and preferences often based in personal taste. Recent theories of culture tend to de-emphasize the past or roots of a culture, and this loss comes at a cost. They also leave little room for discussions of transcendent truth, with

76. Smith, *Fall of Interpretation*, 129.
77. Tanner, *Theories of Culture*, 57.

their emphasis on shifting meanings that are produced in a dynamic and ever-changing process of negotiation.

These conceptual developments add needed complexity to consideration of the task of coming together as a multicultural society or congregation. The task for leaders involves more than merely understanding several broad tendencies and traits of cultures that are different from one's own, so as to avoid committing offensive behavior. As multiple ethnic groups gather in congregational life, each group brings numerous strata of lived experiences, hopes, needs, and interpretive frameworks, reflecting family and communal histories of immigration and/or struggles for civil rights, economic and educational status, etc. Adding to the complexity is the reality that multiple communities of memory may exist within each ethnic group.

Several observers of contemporary culture lament the loss of the capacity to sustain a sense of the past in its members.[78] Danièle Hervieu-Léger has noted this loss, with its implications for religious life. She writes, "One of the chief characteristics of modern societies is that they are no longer societies of memory, and as such ordered with a view to reproducing what is inherited . . . Change, which is a function of modernity itself, has resulted in modern societies being less and less able to nurture the innate capacity of individuals and groups to assimilate or imaginatively project a lineage of belief."[79] She attributes this to the rise of the autonomous individual, the proliferation of the image and the accompanying overabundance of information, and the fragmentation of various social structures, including the family.

This vacuum gives urgency and focus to the task of preaching today. As societies become less and less ordered as communities of memory, church members are losing the habit and skill of remembering at all. This has serious implications for their ability to hear, appropriate, and transmit the memory of the biblical narrative. Preaching that fosters the capacity to remember well is crucial to the formation of communities that can enliven

78. For example, Stanley Hauerwas writes, "[I]f . . . an ethic of virtue depends on a particularly strong claim and commitment to the historical nature of human existence, and if the specification of individual virtues and their relation derives from the traditions of a particular community, then we develop some inkling of why many currently feel so morally lost. As individuals we express a lack of common history or community sufficient to provide us with the resources necessary for us to make our lives our own" (*A Community of Character*, 125).

79. Hervieu-Léger, *Religion as a Chain of Memory*, 123.

and honor both Scripture and the diverse experiences and heritages in their midst.

A second observation about society today is that the themes of identity and belonging have emerged as central preoccupations, both in religion and ethnicity. Understanding of the ways ethnic identity and religious beliefs and affiliations reinforce and at times contradict each other is crucial to understanding why ethnic specificity persists so strongly in congregational life in many cultures. As Hervieu-Léger argues,

> The particular attraction that operates between what is ethnic and what is religious springs from the fact that the one and the other establish a social bond on the basis of an assumed genealogy, on the one hand a naturalized genealogy (because related to soil and blood), and a symbolized genealogy (because constituted through belief in and reference to a myth and a source), on the other . . . (Ethnic and religious revival in the West) . . . offer the same sort of emotive response to the demand for meaning and personal recognition which the abstract nature of modern societies with their meritocratic from of government makes ever more urgent; the religious and ethnic strain compete or combine in re-establishing a sense of "we" and of "our" which modernity has at once fractured and created a nostalgia for.[80]

This raises the challenging question, central to the concerns of this book, of whether ethnicity is something the church should reinforce, challenge, or obscure. History has shown the potential for harm in the tight overlap and mutual reinforcement of ethnic and religious passions as they have played out in, for example, Northern Ireland and the Balkans. Too tight a mutual reinforcement leaves little room for prophetic engagement with culture and constructive dialogue between church and culture. Yet, ethnic-specific religious communities have functioned positively to preserve ethnic values and identity for countless immigrants in United States history. Native Americans faced forced assimilation and denial of their culture, all of which was linked with indoctrination into Christianity. The sparseness of Christian faith among America's indigenous people today is in large part a legacy of that severing of ethnic identity from expression in faith, and the forceful imposition of religious adherence. Among African Americans, examples can be found of Christianity bringing both cultural loss and preservation, but in general the mono-ethnic black church has

80. Ibid., 157.

been a powerful contributor to the preservation of a vibrant ethnic heritage and to healthy identity formation.

This chapter has considered arguments, such as those of Gerardo Marti, that the sense of belonging on the basis of ethnicity should be subsumed and superseded by a form of belonging based solely on baptism, church membership, and shared mission. It has found those arguments lacking in their theological integration of the doctrines of creation and incarnation. They also tend to strongly dichotomize Christ/church and culture. The next chapter considers arguments that church involvement should reinforce ethnic belonging and identity through a tight overlap of the two, with church serving as a vital repository of ethnic memory and heritage. This argument has merit, particularly given the history of racism and effacement of ethnic identity that many minority groups have endured throughout this nation's history. Yet it can imply that those who choose to affiliate with a multiethnic congregation (or with a homogeneous church made up of members of a different ethnic group than their own) are in denial about their ethnic identity or are refusing to stand in solidarity with their culture. Ethnic identity is an important value in the mix, but it should not be allowed to trump all other values. A preoccupation with the ethnic identity of the individual can reflect the modern preoccupation with the individual and his or her independently generated sense of self. This emphasis does not square with biblical understandings of identity formation, with their focus on identity as a gift and an image imprinted by our Creator, which is nurtured through membership in family, neighborhoods, communities of faith, and encounters with others who are radically different. While there are costs and losses involved in integration, ethnically diverse congregations can by God's grace become places that foster healthy ethnic identity in their children and adults and can prepare them to interact with others in their increasingly diverse communities. The following chapter examines the theological bases for that assertion.

2

The Theological Basis
for the Multiethnic Church

In this chapter we will explore theological dimensions of multiethnic congregational life, beginning with the doctrine of the Trinity. The deepest basis for unity across cultures is the nature, actions, and purposes of God. God's triune nature supplies our supreme model for reconciled life together. That life together is made possible as communities of faith pursue two core practices of the gospel, hospitality and repentance. As we build a theology to fund life together amidst diversity, we must listen well to those who question the viability, and feel acutely the costs, of ethnic integration in local churches. Finally, we'll look at ethnic diversity in church through the specific lens of understanding ethnic groups as communities of memory and the church as a new community of memory whose proclamation and practices of the gospel must honor and hold, and may even heal, the brokenness in all our stories.

Few Christians today argue against the idea that the church, as the worldwide communion of God's people, should strive to be as ethnically diverse and as deeply reconciled as possible, and that this will be the church's glorious future (Matt 8:11; Rev 7:9, 21:26, etc.). Questions remain though as to whether diversity is biblically mandated for the present, and whether it is mandated or desirable for every local congregation. We still hear arguments that, "heterogeneity is to be the norm in the universal church . . .

while homogeneity is to be the norm in the local church—is this not the more biblical model?"[1] Similarly, Rick Warren writes, "The easiest people for you to reach for Christ are those who are most like you." He continues, "Explosive growth happens when the type of people in the community match the type of people that are already in the church."[2] We will address the limitations of this line of reasoning shortly.

Some argue that the racist history of dominant groups within North America leaves minority groups in need of multiple, ethnic-specific settings for cultural preservation, and that church is one such crucial setting. Others, from a more pragmatic point of view, contend that heterogeneity is not even a desirable goal, since it works against the creation of social cohesion.[3] Others fear that many popular articulations of the vision for intercultural congregational life are far too simplistic, failing to bring a value on confession and repentance or an ability to speak prophetically regarding North America's racist history. That history continues to result in unjust denominational power dynamics, such that movements toward integration often end in assimilation by absorption. Some churches resolve the complexity of shared worship and communal life too quickly, making glib appeals to our common humanity that obscure the beauty, joy, and pain in particular ethnic histories. Here, I want to offer theological resources for those churches that have discerned that they are called to pursue greater diversity and to embrace the arduous ministry of racial reconciliation.

TRINITY

Let's begin with the triune nature of God. Contemplation of the Trinity takes us straight to the heart of all that the church proclaims and worships. It is in the Trinity that Christians find their most profound and true model for human nature and behavior. Humanity is created "after God's likeness," and so is most whole when its patterns of daily life and congregational life reflect the dynamic, self-giving, and creative relationships within the Trinity. Jürgen Moltmann makes this point as he comments on Jesus' prayer in John 17. He writes, "Here the unity of the Christian community is a Trinitarian unity. It *corresponds* to the indwelling of the Father in the Son,

---

1. McIntosh and McMahan, *Being the Church*, 120.

2. Warren, *Purpose Driven Church*, 176–77.

3. Ibid.

and of the Son in the Father. It participates in the divine triunity, since the community of believers is not only fellowship *with* God but *in* God too."[4]

Two primary streams of tradition are animating the discussion today. The Western tradition is rooted in an Augustinian emphasis on God's oneness in nature and purpose. Karl Barth did much to revive interest in God's triune nature, particularly seen through the lens of Christology, in the twentieth century. Lesslie Newbigin has applied the dynamic of Christ being sent by the Father into the world to the church's mission today. He asserts, "The Church is the outward form of the continuous work of the Spirit in re-enacting Christ's coming among men."[5] He summarizes, "The Church's mission to all the nations is a participation in the work of the triune God."[6]

The other stream that is drawing much attention today is from the Eastern tradition, with its focus on the social nature of the Trinity, the *perichoresis*, defined by Randolph Otto as, "a complete mutual interpenetration of two substances that preserves the identity and properties of each intact."[7] John Zizioulas explains that in the Trinity, "Being a person is fundamentally different from being an individual or a 'personality,' for a person cannot be imagined in himself but only within his relationships."[8] The church is called to reflect the image of God as it calls members to lives of mutual interdependence.

But we do hit limits when we look to Trinity as a model for humanity. For example, the doctrine of *perichoresis* offers the compelling image of mutual indwelling, which appeals immediately to those seeking a pattern for intercultural church life that preserves difference within unity. Yet we need to proceed with some caution. As Miroslav Volf puts it, *perichoresis* applies to human relations only, "in an analogous rather than a univocal sense. As creatures, human beings can correspond to the uncreated God only in a *creaturely* way."[9] Finitude and sin limit our capacity to give ourselves in love fully to one another as the members of the Trinity do, without risking loss to our identity and integrity.[10] The Eastern Orthodox

---

4. Moltmann, *Trinity*, 202.

5. Newbigin, *Trinitarian Faith*, 49.

6. Ibid, 50.

7. Otto,"Perichoresis," 368.

8. Zizioulas, *Being as Communion*, 105.

9. Volf, "The Trinity is Our Social Program," 405.

10. Nonna Verna Harrison makes this point in "Human Community," 353.

theologian, David Bentley Hart, recognizes this as well, warning, "For if we forget this interval (or gap), we not only risk lapsing into either a collectivist or solipsistic reduction of human relationality—exclusively outward or inward—but we are likely to adopt either a tritheistic or a unitarian idiom when speaking of God."[11] Recognizing these limits, Christians still rightly find in trinitarian relations both norms and resources for the church's life together and its engagement with its particular cultural context. Here we will learn from three thinkers who are working with Trinity and its implications for the nature and mission of the church in the world. They are Hart, Gary Deddo, and Scott Frederickson.

While Hart never directly addresses ethnic reconciliation, his profound grasp of trinitarian dynamics offers at least two clear principles for that endeavor. First, he addresses the way intra-trinitarian relations of infinite diversity, fecundity and mutual delight come to expression in creation. He writes, "The Christian God creates out of that *agape* that is the life of the Trinity: God not only gives being to difference, but elects each thing in its particularity, is turned toward it and regards it, and takes it back to himself without despoiling it of its difference."[12] This is a powerful insight for congregational life, as we seek to become places where every individual is deeply seen, known, and treasured in his or her particularity. Trinitarian doctrine establishes as normative the need to honor and even delight in difference, while being careful that it not be subsumed, by design or by default, into the dominant culture in a given church.

Second, Hart radically redefines human personhood in light of the way members of the Trinity are persons-in-relation. He agrees with Barth that the modern, Western understanding of the human person as an "isolated, punctiliar, psychic monad"[13] has severely impoverished the term *person* for trinitarian discussion. But, unlike Barth, who for that reason chose in general to avoid reference to *persons* in his discussion of Trinity, Hart argues instead that we should, "take the language of Trinitarian dogma as an imperative to think the concept of the person anew, from above, in a distinctly Christian way."[14] Humans are fully persons only when they are persons in communion, with God and with humanity. As God works salvation for us in Christ, he restores our lives from ones marked by isolation

11. Hart, *Beauty of Infinite*, 172.

12. Ibid, 192.

13. Ibid., 170.

14. Ibid, 171.

and efforts to dominate others to lives lived out in joyful interdependence, marked instead by movements to serve and bless others to interdependence, expressed in movements toward and for others.

Gary Deddo has given specific, sustained attention to the way the ethnically reconciled church becomes a sign of God's triune nature and God's kingdom. He asserts, "Within the matrix of these intersecting relationships we are called to order our lives under the commanding grace of God so that in our relationship with others the truth concerning God's relationship to all humanity comes to light."[15] Trinitarian resources for church life act to call congregations forward and to hold them to account. Deddo warns of two dangers in ethnic identity development and multiethnic congregational life. He writes, "If the norm for the shape of covenantal communion is the communion of Father, Son and Spirit . . . then both unity by absorption and diversity by autonomy must be rejected."[16] He goes on to say, "Since humanity was created for being in a communion that reflects and so glorifies the triune communion . . . resisting reconciliation is not just a violation of an abstract commandment; it is resistance to the essence of who we are and who God is."[17] As the church looks to the model of self-giving love between the Father, Son, and Holy Spirit, it finds rich resources for relating with one another in the midst of difference.

Scott Frederickson draws from both Trinity and Christology in arguing for a dialogical relationship between church and its cultural context:

> It is this "mutual interpenetration" that best explains the relationship between a missional congregation and its context as they coincide together in space and time. The God of Jesus Christ, in the power of the Spirit, has created and redeemed this coinciding. The very incarnation of God into the Son and the resurrection of the Son to God is the way Christianity claims the context. This means that a Missional congregation and its context are related. The missional congregation claims the reality of the context (the Incarnation) while not being subsumed wholly beneath it, in order to show the context a deeper reality (the Resurrection), namely, that God is constantly at work in the world.[18]

---

15. Deddo, "Persons in Racial Reconciliation," 60.

16. Ibid, 63.

17. Deddo, *Gospel in Black and White*, 65.

18. Frederickson, "Missional Church," 49–50.

God desires that trinitarian unity extend outward toward humanity, and God accomplishes that in the incarnational movement Christ makes to embrace humanity. That movement in turn enables our movement toward one another. As the authors of *United by Faith* reflect, "When we gather together in multiracial congregations we are implementing what has already been realized through Christ's death on a cross."[19] We are caught up into the unity of Father, Son, and Holy Spirit in our baptism into Christ's death and life. The Holy Spirit breathes into humanity a new capacity for unity, as is seen most strikingly at Pentecost. This same unity is that which God is crafting in the church today, through the work of Christ (Eph 2:15–16).

Trinitarian Implications for the Early Church

How did the early church wrestle with the implications of trinitarian unity as it integrated diverse ethnic streams? One thing we notice right away is that difference was simply not a problem that the early followers of Jesus solved through separation. The practices for negotiating difference advocated in the New Testament bear this out. In Acts and in Paul's correspondence with churches struggling to navigate cultural differences such as circumcision and eating meat sacrificed to idols, the striking fact emerges that, in light of Pentecost, difference is to be welcomed and that the tensions it brings must be settled through practices of love, submission, and grace. Mark Lau Branson say it well: "There was no pastoral strategy to lessen relational tension in the church by creating cultural or economic subdivisions."[20]

Some have argued that Paul, in a reaction against the ethnocentrism and exclusionary practices in his native Judaism, gained a vision of universal humanity that eradicated cultural specificity. This is the perspective of Jewish scholar Daniel Boyarin, who understands Paul's teachings in Romans, 1 and 2 Corinthians, and Galatians 3:28 as a movement toward a "universal human essence," and hence an "eradication of Jewish identity."[21] This is an interesting critique. But Charles Cousar sees Paul's navigation of cultural difference as more complex than does Boyarin. He sees Paul arguing the cause of non-Jews in Galatians, yet calling Gentiles to humble recognition of their place within the Jewish salvation history in Romans. Paul affirms ethnic and cultural distinctions in 1 Corinthians and Romans yet

19. DeYoung et al., *United by Faith*, 155.

20. Branson, *Intercultural Church Life*, 92.

21. Boyarin, *A Radical Jew*, 56 and 47.

argues against making them the basis for exclusion in Galatians 3:26–29. Noting the range of responses Paul makes to complex ethnic issues in 1 Corinthians, Cousar comments, "Rather than being driven by the vision of a unified humanity in which differences are suppressed, Paul seems more like a pastoral theologian urging a community of God's people to be sensitive to diversities that exist among them and to keep in proper perspective matters that are not definitive for the life of the community."[22]

Can the shape of congregational life be crafted to reflect the trinitarian celebration, honoring of difference and while imitating Trinity's movements to ensure unity? It is clear that the early church strove to do so. Yet Protestant church history in the United States has shown a particular propensity to settle disputes through separation, which has sharply compromised its imaging of Trinity in its shape and practices. One early marker of that trend was the day in November, 1787 when Richard Allen and Absalom Jones walked out of St. George Methodist Episcopal Church in Philadelphia, tired of the view from their segregated balcony pew. While their integrity and courage was laudable, the exclusionary practices that made it necessary were a repudiation of trinitarian unity. In the years that followed, several denominations split over slavery. Separation along ethnic lines became entrenched in American church practice to the point that W. E. B. Du Bois concluded, "No other institution in America is built so thoroughly or more absolutely on the color line."[23] The problem is by no means in the distant past.

Ethnic division in the North American church reflects neither Trinity nor New Testament practices. The metaphor Paul found most expressive of the unity and diversity that characterizes the church was that of the human body (1 Cor 11–13). The honor given to each part, and the way the body works together in unity, reflects the honor each member of the Trinity gives the other in the New Testament (Mark 1:11; John 14:26, 17:1), and the way each member cooperates to accomplish one purpose, whether in creation or in the redemption of humanity. Hart grounds the church's life in Trinity when he encourages us to, "see in the communality and interdependency of the church, the peaceful participation of Christians in one body, a true if vastly inexact image of how God is forever a God dwelling in and with, a God who truly takes delight and is truly at peace; the unity of the church

---

22. Cousar, *Many Voices*, 52.
23. DuBois, "Color Line," 169.

somehow reflects the way in which God is one."[24] When the church func-tions as a body, it offers itself to the world as a visible and attractive sign of the kingdom, and thus as a sign of the very nature of the triune God.

HOSPITALITY

The body metaphor expresses well the unity and diversity that Christ in-tends for the church. Another root metaphor that expresses God's heart for all humanity is the banquet table. From God's gracious provision of food for the first humans, to the eschatological banquets described in Isaiah (25:9) and Revelation (19:9), God's intention is clearly to welcome people into communion with God and with each other. We reflect God's nature when we welcome one another in the same way that Christ has welcomed us (Rom 15:7). Yet in our fallen nature we are more prone to a prideful grasping of what we desire, as the story of Babel starkly demonstrates (Gen 11:1–9).

A table is ideally a space in which discourse and exchange take place in ways that bring honor to guests and host. Babel served the opposite func-tion: while a table brings people closer together, a tower requires distance to appreciate. It was a monument to human achievement rather than the work of God. Babel, in its search for a human-made, monolithic unity, is the essence of inhospitality. While table fellowship makes intimate dialogue possible, Babel epitomized the destruction of the capacity for hearing God or one another.

In the next chapter of Genesis after the Babel narrative, God graciously continued to speak, and found a hearing in two faithful listeners. Abraham and Sarah provide an excellent paradigm for hospitality in the Hebrew Bible. Their lives demonstrated the paradoxical truth that the best path to-ward becoming hospitable lies not in establishing a secure home into which one may welcome others but in the willingness to be displaced, as one is called to set out on pilgrimage. Babel results in an unwilling scattering of humanity, with rebellion and division as its source and end. Abraham and Sarah undertake an obedient journey motivated by trust in God's promises. While the tower builders were making a name for themselves, Abram and Sarai let God give them new names.

God's call to Abraham in the narrative that follows marks the begin-ning of a long, slow arc toward God's ultimate intention to make a new

24. Hart, *Beauty of Infinite*, 179.

home for humanity. At the center of hospitality is the emptying of self to make space for the other. It is thus not surprising that among Abraham and Sarah's first acts along their displacing journey is the offering of hospitality to three strangers. Abraham is the recipient of hospitality from Melchizidek as well (Gen 14:18). In fact, Abraham's ultimate place in God's economy of hospitality is not as host but as honored guest at a banquet table that is set for all the nations, as Jesus prophesies (Matt 8:11), and welcomed child of the One who is preparing a home for him (Heb 11:13–16).

Abraham's example of both giving *and* receiving hospitality serves as a model for leaders of multiethnic churches. For a long time, the prophetic call to the dominant, white majority church was to "make room at the table" to welcome blacks, Native Americans, and immigrants without judgment or elitism. While this prompted needed repentance from exclusionary practices, the paradigm is one-sided and flawed. Aspects of it still speak to the necessary response of welcome that churches must make toward recent immigrants, but the metaphor risks perpetuating power dynamics of superiority and control on the part of the majority culture, as that group construes minority people as guests and therefore passive recipients of the largess of their white hosts. Michael Hawn describes the unspoken drive toward assimilation in many churches that seek to welcome minority people without making any changes in their communal life. He writes, "A sense of *noblesse oblige* may separate the strangers from the church when worship or décor or non-inclusive leadership announces, 'We are glad to do things for you, but you are not really one of us.'"[25] Kathy Black introduces the concept of *reciprocal assimilation*, which is a key to the construction of what she calls the *culturally conscious* congregation.[26] A more adequate paradigm of hospitality, then, is a spirit of welcome coming as a gift that all receive from God, prior to and as they extend it. It appropriates the vision of God's gracious, lavish hospitality, an invitation to which we all respond, and a grace we all receive with gratitude and humility.

In the Old Testament, God calls Israel to empathetic and gracious inclusion through the command to remember their enslavement with humility. The writer of Exodus used that history as the basis for the call to justice and generosity toward the aliens in their midst. "You shall not oppress a stranger; you know the heart of a stranger, for you were strangers in the land of Egypt" (Exod 23:9). Christine Pohl notes, "Embedded within

25. Hawn, *One Bread*, 8.

26. Black, "Promises and Problems," 142–43.

the covenant between God and Israel was Israel's identity as an alien and its related responsibility to sojourners and strangers . . . this alien identity . . . also provided an experiential basis from which Israelites could know the feelings and needs of sojourners and powerless people living in their midst."[27] God intended that memories of displacement would form a well from which God's followers would draw compassion, empathy, and the courage to extend themselves toward the stranger.

Lavish hospitality is evident throughout the ministry of Jesus Christ, from the very act of incarnation, with its intent of making room for humanity in God, to his teaching and acts. His parables were replete with the imagery of banquets, welcome-home parties, and wedding feasts. He redrew the lines of belonging and family membership, away from boundaries drawn on the basis of birth, status, or strict adherence to a moral code, and towards obedience to his will and willingness to enter God's kingdom as a child.

Jesus was a disturbingly unpredictable guest, illustrating well that hosts can expect to be troubled and transformed in the very act of offering hospitality. While the abundance he brought to the wedding at Cana was gladly received, the tension he introduced into other settings, where he upset hierarchies and challenged exclusion, was less enthusiastically welcomed (Luke 7:36–50; 14:12–14; 11:37–52). He taught a revolutionary form of hospitality to his followers, promising them that as they welcomed the least, they would welcome him (Matt 25:31–46). He also taught them how to receive the hospitality of strangers with peace and blessing (Luke 10:5). He graciously received gifts awkwardly given, from an anointing with perfume to an anointing with tears (Luke 7:36–50; John 12:1–8). He crossed ethnic and gender boundaries to drink water with a Samaritan woman (John 4). His own hosting of the Last Supper reflected his deep sense of the abundance of his Father's resources, which gave him freedom to serve with abandon to the end (John 13). The cross formed his ultimate act of hospitality. Volf captures this well: "First, on the cross God renews the covenant by making space for humanity in God's self. The open arms of Christ on the cross are a sign that God does not want to be God without the other—humanity—and suffers humanity's violence in order to embrace it."[28]

27. Pohl, *Making Room*, 28.
28. Volf, *Exclusion and Embrace*, 154.

This movement of hospitality continued, albeit imperfectly, in the life of the early church. On the day of Pentecost the Holy Spirit threw wide the doors of the embryonic church to all the nations gathered in Jerusalem. In Acts 10, God gave Peter a vision of inclusion of the Gentiles. The process of welcoming Gentiles was not without tension, as is evident in Acts 11, and in Peter's own difficulties with participating in table fellowship with them, noted by Paul in Galatians 1. Cousar notes the strength of the verb *pro-slambano*, used in Paul's exhortation to welcome one another in Romans 15:7. He observes, it means "to receive or accept into one's society, into one's home or circle of friends. It connotes more than merely tolerating or indulging the other person with his or her cultural features; it entails accepting, giving space for, and respecting the distinctiveness of the other."[29] When the church perseveres in the difficult process of making room for strangers, those acts of hospitality may serve as signs and foretastes of the kingdom of God and as instruments of it.

REPENTANCE

It is more fun to talk about hospitality than repentance any day. Hospitality inspires appealing metaphors, whereas prophetic calls to repentance often inspired acts of violence toward those who proposed them. Yet, due to our fallen nature, hospitality often only happens when an act of repentance takes place. Welcome is unfortunately not our knee-jerk, reflexive response to the other. Hospitality is the joyful practice that only becomes possible as Christ's followers repent of exclusive ones. Craig Dykstra notes the powerful connection between repentance and community:

> If, in repentance, I give up self-establishment and self-sustenance, I also become freer to see others as they are because I am less captive to the need to distort them for my own purposes . . . Repentance is becoming unself-conscious in a way that allows me to become receptive to the world. The persistent need of the unrepentant ego to establish and sustain itself builds up indestructible walls between ourselves and the world . . . But in repentance, we are able to accept and respect the inexhaustible particularity of others and shape our attitudes and actions to their fundamental needs.[30]

---

29. Cousar, *Many Voices*, 56.
30. Dykstra, *Vision and Character*, 93.

Jesus inaugurated his ministry by proclaiming the intimate connection between repentance and belief (Mark 1:15). Repentance prepares the way for the reception of good news and the welcoming of God's presence, as is apparent in John the Baptist's ministry. In John's understanding, the very process of conversion was marked by confession of one's sins and receiving God's forgiveness. Evangelical Christians have a strong tradition of valuing individual repentance and the confession of their sins to one another, building on the doctrine of the priesthood of all believers. Yet the evangelical church in North America has focused on individual reconciliation with God, often failing to extend that value to reconciliation with neighbors from whom one is estranged. Or, it may make the human connection on an individual level, but it often fails to recognize institutional and historical forces that sanction and perpetuate the effects of sin. Douglas Sharp argues,

> Repentance of the sin of racism entails not only acknowledging the forms and expressions of racism in our personal and sociocultural worlds but also denouncing them, turning away from them and refusing to express them or be drawn into their expression by others . . . We cannot give up our personal sin and still live neutrally, passively and agreeably with the sin embedded in our shared world . . . our repentance must lead to restoring what our history and way of life have taken from others.[31]

Emerson and Smith's research on white North American Protestant priorities finds that members of these churches tend to see the presence of racism, when they see it at all, as taking the form of individual prejudiced attitudes and relational distance, rather than that of unjust institutions and systems. When white Protestants were asked to cite top issues of concern for Christians, only 4 percent named racism as an issue. The interviewers observed that, "As far as they knew they themselves had never engaged in racism. Moreover, they did not believe America's institutions to be racist."[32]

Marti, while coming from a multiethnic congregation, evidences a similar lack of mention of the need for repentance in church life; he uses the word only once in his book. In part this reflects the highly malleable, self-constructed, future and project-based conception of identity at Mosaic Church. For example, Marti describes the way leaders at Mosaic utilize their own ethnic identity in forging connections with newcomers and establishing moral authority. They ask themselves, "Is my ethnic identity a

31. Sharp, *No Partiality*, 287–88.
32. Emerson and Smith, *Divided by Faith*, 88.

help or hindrance in accomplishing my goals? Ethnicity is expressed if it serves instrumental ends. If ethnic identity is a hindrance, it is obscured in favor of other social statuses."[33] This pragmatic strategy has clearly been successful in attracting and incorporating numerous young people of various ethnic backgrounds. It appeals to a generation that wants to believe that it has moved beyond the issues of race that were so painful in the Civil Rights era. The approach is in some ways a new iteration of principles from the church growth movement, where the emphasis on the mission of making individual converts took precedence over the vision of building a reconciled, diverse community of disciples.[34]

As was noted in the previous chapter, one thing this conception of ethnicity and congregational life lacks is a sense of history, and particularly the ethical implications of a group's history. Ethnic identity is more than an instrument one picks up at will or a feature of one's personality, such as extroversion, that one may draw upon at a party but must downplay during a silent retreat. Members of ethnic groups have pasts, and those pasts have propelled them into present situations in which they may benefit from the privilege that accompanies their ethnicity or suffer oppression due to it. James Nieman and Thomas Rogers write, "An ethnic group holds in its common memory a set of substantial experiences that are larger than any single member. The work of remaining in that group requires claiming that history and being accountable to it as the lens through which one's own life is understood."[35] The call to shoulder responsibility for the effects of the past is highly unwelcome among some white Americans, and hence the vision of a church rooted solely in future-oriented paradigms of ethnicity can be alluring.

33. Marti, *Mosaic*, 167.

34. On this point, see the writings of C. Peter Wagner and Donald MacGavran. This book does not analyze this movement in detail, but would argue that while Wagner and MacGavran intended to further the growth of the church, their ecclesiological, trinitarian, and eschatological foundations were weak. They borrowed heavily from contemporary marketing strategies, which blinded them to key components of the gospel. For a thorough evaluation of the movement, see Shenk, *Exploring Church Growth*. Strong critique comes from C. Rene Padilla, who asserts, "The use of the homogeneous unit principle for church growth has no biblical foundation. Its advocates have taken as their starting point a sociological observation and developed a missionary strategy; only then, *a posteriori*, have they made the attempt to find biblical support." ("The Unity of the Church," 301).

35. Nieman and Rogers, *Preaching to Every Pew*, 26.

W. James Booth calls us to acknowledge that, "our memory ties us to our past-in-common: we have a sense of a past that is ours, politically, even though we had no hand in its events."[36] Reflecting on the shame we feel as a nation regarding slavery and the pride we feel regarding aspects of our actions in World War II, he writes, "Shame and pride here are indices of an identity in which my biography is interwoven with that of the community in which I am embedded, uniting me thereby with its past, present, and future."[37] Nehemiah and Jeremiah, among others, evidenced the capacity to mourn the sins of their people, confessing on their behalf, and acknowledging the cost in their ancestors' legacy (Neh 1:4–7; Jer 9:1–3). One of the ministries of preaching is its task of witnessing truthfully to aspects of the past that listeners would rather forget; in so doing preaching shapes people who are capable of telling that truth themselves. Branson reflects that, "We bless our churches as we help them tell stories of truth and love, grace and justice."[38]

LOCAL CONGREGATIONS AND ETHNIC DIVERSITY

Our theological exploration pursued just three of the myriad streams feeding the argument for the church being a locus of ethnic reconciliation. Christians are in essential agreement that as a worldwide body, the church should be moving toward maximal diversity and reconciliation. But should every local church strive to be ethnically diverse to the extent that demographics make that pursuit at all feasible? Those who strenuously argue this case must recognize the various losses that are potentially involved, the complexities that are added, and the history of racism that makes integration particularly difficult for members of certain ethnic groups in this country. In highly homogeneous, geographically remote communities, the call to reach out across ethnic lines will take a vastly different shape than it does in dense urban centers. Ethnic-specific mission church models may also reach recent immigrants, who face language barriers, more effectively than some multiethnic models. Arguments against diversity in congregational life have some validity and offer needed critique of a naïve embrace of diversity. After hearing those arguments, we'll consider some of the problems through the lens of the contested collective memories that

36. Booth, *Communities of Memory*, 41.

37. Ibid, 42.

38. Branson, *Memories, Hopes, and Conversations*, 58.

are present when members of many ethnic groups attempt to form one community.

Arguments for Homogeneity

Advocates of congregational homogeneity such as Rick Warren and others informed by the church growth movement have often argued that uniformity is a more realistic, expedient, and effective interim strategy prior to the *eschaton*. From a pragmatic standpoint, this argument has some empirical data to support it, if the goals of church growth are limited to numerical growth and social cohesion. Emerson and Smith note the sociological realities that tend to lead to ethnic sorting, such as the need for social solidarity that is present in any organization. They write, "In a pluralistic market, and given that most people seek the greatest gain for the least cost, internally diverse congregations are typically at a disadvantage . . . The cost of producing meaning, belonging, and security in internally diverse congregations is usually much greater . . ."[39]

However, they and others argue that sociological realities and principles should not have the last word in determining the church's vision. Padilla critiques the homogeneous unit principle of church growth, writing,

> Because of its failure to take biblical theology seriously, it has become a missiology tailor-made for churches and institutions whose main function in society is to reinforce the status quo . . . What can it say to a church where a racist "feels at home" because of the unholy alliance of Christianity with racial segregation? . . . Of course, it can say that "men like to become Christians without crossing racial, linguistic, and class barriers." But what does that have to do with the gospel concerning Jesus Christ, who came to reconcile us "to God *in one body* through the cross"?[40]

Padilla points to two of the problematic ends that result when a church has been birthed through the means of whatever marketing or growth strategy is currently viewed as most expedient. First, it will lack the capacity to speak prophetically to society or to individuals. Second, its soteriological foundation is based entirely on an individualistic understanding of souls being saved, to the neglect of a soteriology of the church as a body (Eph 1:14; 2:11–22). Such a highly individualized soteriology will

39. Emerson and Smith, *Divided by Faith*, 145.
40. Padilla, "Unity of the Church," 301.

inevitably diminish its vision for life together. When the measures of vital congregational life are limited to those of rapidly increasing membership and a preponderance of members who evaluate their experience of church positively, then the means to achieving that end can be borrowed with confidence from sociological principles and marketing strategies. But when more robust, biblical ends are desired, then these means are shown to be inadequate to achieving them.

Ray Anderson urges pastoral leaders to view practical theology as *Christopraxis*, where the end is fully integrated into every consideration of the means. Drawing on Aristotle, he writes,

> The *telos* of something is its final purpose, meaning, or character. *Praxis* is an action that includes the *telos*, or final meaning and character of truth. It is an action in which the truth is discovered through action, not merely applied or "practiced." In *praxis* one is not only guided in one's actions by the intention of realizing the *telos*, or purpose, but by discovering and grasping this *telos* through the action itself.[41]

Church growth strategies must incorporate as their most determinative *telos* the transformative nature of the *eschaton*, which by its very nature disrupts and informs every aspect of present life, including congregational practices. As theologian James Smart puts it, "Eschatology is the vision of the future that gives direction to the present and confidence to take the next necessary step toward a future goal."[42] The more churches reflect the ultimate shape of the eschatological body of Christ the more they will participate in the joy and blessing of the life that is coming.

Applying an eschatologically informed praxis to preaching, Thomas Long highlights the New Testament image of the preacher as herald (*keryx*), who brings a word from God's future that challenges and undermines the reigning ideology of the present. Long writes, "In essence, then, it is the duty and delight of the preacher to announce the future, to say to the ears of those who will hear what the eye has not yet seen."[43] Not only is this true for preachers, but the congregation itself by its very shape and practices proclaims a word to the world, as Dietrich Bonhoeffer has argued. He writes,

---

41. Anderson, *Shape of Practical Theology*, 49.

42. Smart, *Old Testament in Dialogue*, cited in Long, "Preaching God's Future," 196.

43. Long, "Preaching God's Future," 202.

The community is therefore not only the receiver of the Word of revelation; it is itself revelation and Word of God . . . The Word is in the community in so far as the community is a recipient of revelation. But the Word is also itself community in so far as the community is itself revelation and the Word wills to have the form of a created body.[44]

Congregations, by their very life together, announce the in-breaking of the *eschaton* upon current reality as they experience together the joyful vitality that deeply reconciled community brings.

Another line of reasoning sometimes heard in defense of homogeneity is that all local churches inevitably fall short of reflecting the eschatological vision of the church in some areas. This is not an argument *against* pursuing agendas of diversity and reconciliation, so much as a rationale for prioritizing other goals that are perceived to have greater urgency, usually consisting in the salvation of individual souls. In making this argument some will note that their denomination as a *whole* represents a broad spectrum of ethnicities and that this is sufficient. Branson addresses the argument that local churches need not reflect biblical norms for the universal church by building the case that the local church *is* the church, in the discourse of the New Testament, and thus the place in which we live out all the commands of promises of God.[45]

In building the case for every local church to take seriously its call to be an agent of racial reconciliation, it is important to note that some geographical locations will make ethnic diversity within a local congregation much less feasible than others. Living out this calling for a homogenous community may take on different shapes in acts of advocacy for justice for oppressed people across the globe or in a nearby city. Preaching and other leadership that celebrates the biblical vision of a diverse church will prepare them to integrate their membership in the increasingly likely event that their community becomes more multiethnic. The authors of *United by Faith* account well for the rapidly changing face of immigration in the United States when they write that congregations in racially isolated areas "should educate themselves as though next year their community will diversify."[46]

---

44. Bonhoeffer, *Christology*, 60.

45. Branson, *Intercultural Church Life*, 64.

46. DeYoung et al., *United by Faith*, 143.

C. Michael Hawn makes another point in response to arguments that a strategy targeting specific types of people or ethnic groups will be more effective or successful. He notes that churches that target a specific ethnic or age group often find that homogeneity is more difficult to achieve and sustain over time than they had assumed.[47] Factors of socioeconomics, life experience, and marriage across ethnic lines inevitably complicate the picture. Thus, every congregation must wrestle with how to honor, celebrate, and navigate diversity, whether it is of ethnicity or of income level, political views, or generation-based worship preferences. This negotiation provides rich opportunities for character formation in areas such as respect, humility, and the capacity to gracefully embrace and value experiences and perspectives that are different from one's own. This is not an area where white North American Christians have historically excelled. The authors of *Against all Odds* conclude this at the end of a thorough analysis of several congregations that have wrestled with ethnic diversity. In a summary of their findings they note, "Whites are more likely than racial minorities to leave interracial religious organizations if their particular preferences and interests are not being met."[48]

First-generation immigrant communities may form another exception to arguments for integration, particularly when the language in their country of origin was not English. The need to hear a sermon and to express worship in one's first language is significant, particularly in the initial year of entry to the United States, when the effort to adapt to one's new culture is exhausting. Ethnic-specific churches can provide a needed respite from cross-cultural effort (and unfortunately from the racism immigrants often face daily). However, immigrants do have other needs, which homogeneous immigrant church populations cannot meet as well. They often need to learn English, they need to get to know Americans from various cultures, and they will eventually need a church to which they and their children can invite their neighbors. Advances in technology are making it more and more possible for churches to offer simultaneous translation easily and affordably. Other transitional settings within the multiethnic church can provide a haven for recent immigrants, such as prayer groups and Bible studies offered in several languages, English as a Foreign Language classes, and occasional worship songs sung in the languages represented throughout the congregation.

47. Hawn, *One Bread, One Body*, 7.
48. Christerson et al., *Against all Odds*, 168.

While not biblically mandated as a measure of faithfulness for every local church, ethnic diversity was normative in the New Testament and is a goal toward which most local churches should strive, to the extent it is feasible in their location, as an expression of the unity Christ brought and as an opportunity for growth and healing. Yet it crucial that we recognize the losses involved and complexities added as congregations diversify. Everyone involved faces losses, such as the loss of ease in communication and the loss of a base of familiarity or common stock of memories that facilitates a sense of belonging and intimacy. But those who have experienced marginalization or oppression in society face more profound losses, and feel them more acutely. They wonder whether predominantly white Protestant churches have the will to do what is necessary to truly become one body, rather than simply assimilate minority members into their midst. Let's listen to four of the concerns they have raised.

Costs of Integration

First, ethnic-specific minority congregations in the United States have traditionally served as greenhouses for healthy ethnic identity formation. They do this through worship and rituals that celebrate and affirm their culture, through leadership structures that honor their cultural styles, and through preaching that includes them in the story of God's redemptive work in history. They see the church as a haven from the voices that deny value to their members, through overt racism or calls for conformity to the majority culture. Their congregations function as places to preserve and transmit memories of God's faithfulness to them, and of their participation in God's mission. Marvin McMickle, a black pastor and homiletician, is particularly concerned that, for blacks who join predominantly white churches, their children will not grow up with knowledge of the rich heritage of faithful obedience of their predecessors.[49] His concerns echo the argument of practical theologian Johann Metz, that narrative plays a crucial role in bringing into the present the collective historical memory of both suffering and freedom, doing so in ways that promote action toward justice in the present.[50] The following chapter explores the ways the New Homiletic, with its highlighting of context, has made space for the telling of local narratives, interweaving them with the narrative of Scripture. As was noted above in

49. McMickle, *Preaching to the Black Middle Class*, 39–50.
50. Metz, *Faith in History and Society*, 109–11.

the discussion of ethnic identity development, one limitation of the ethnic-specific church is that it does not often afford opportunities to build that identity through positive interaction with the other, which is increasingly understood to be an essential part of strong identity development.

Second, many from ethnic-specific (minority) congregations fear the loss of a center of advocacy for justice that could ensue if their members were to join a predominantly white congregation. McMickle notes the role the African American church has traditionally played in numerous socio-economic realms, from credit unions to financial backing of the United Negro College Fund. He rightly wonders if white churches that experienced a large influx of blacks would use their economic resources to further such projects. As he puts it, "The issue is not black membership; the issue is the ministry a white church is willing to conduct in response to the presence of its black members. A failure to make such an adjustment is a clear indication that the black member is simply being further assimilated into white society and is being further cut off from the black community."[51]

A third concern has to do with whether congregations that are initially predominantly white and seek to be ethnically diverse are willing to engage in the costly practices that are required for a diverse community to become a truly integrated, reconciled community. All who enter a congregation come with some need for healing and repentance in the area of ethnicity. They may need to confess to stereotyping assumptions they have made or ways they have enjoyed the privilege afforded them on the basis of their ethnicity at the expense of others. They may need to tell the story of genocide in their country of origin or the marginalization they have experienced in the United States. If members of congregations want to truly know and love each other, they will take the time to tell and to hear those stories.

Robert Vosloo, a South African theologian, raises the issue of time and the hurried approach to relationships that can mark those who have suffered relatively less. He writes,

> We often fail to take or make time for the other. One sees this in the haste of some people to get involved with building a new future without wanting to linger on the injustices of the past, while others, who have experienced hurt due to this past, want more time to search for the truth and hear the confession of the injustices. This leads to a collision of time-worlds that fuels exclusion and violence. Over and against this one can envisage a God who has

51. McMickle, *Preaching to the Black Middle Class*, 135.

taken time into the Triune life—thus enabling people to receive
the gift of time and to find time for reconciliation.[52]

The question of reconciliation turns on diverse members displaying
a willingness to look at and discuss the past, to assume some measure of
responsibility for the history of their own ethnic group, and to listen well to
the pain and anger of others. In a drive-through consumer culture, we want
our church involvement to be delivered to us quickly, and the time cost of
these conversations is too steep for many.

Fourth, proponents of ethnic-specific congregations note the precision and power with which a sermon in that setting may deliver a word of
encouragement or challenge to its members. McMickle asks, "Will white
churches preach a gospel message that seeks to comfort their black members as they contend with racism and injustice in their daily lives? Will
white churches challenge their black members to assume an active role in
addressing the array of social, educational, and economic issues that continue to have a negative impact on those black people who remain locked
in the inner cities?"[53] Charles Foster and Theodore Brelsford also note the
complexity of delivering and receiving words of exhortation across ethnic
lines. They describe a congregation in which the white pastor often seeks
to speak prophetically into the social and economic situation of black men,
noting, "For both groups this encounter with difference is confrontational
and unsettling."[54] While McMickle's rhetorical questions regarding the possibility of preaching to a socioeconomically diverse audience tend to imply
a negative response, Foster and Brelsford note the challenge but still assert
that such preaching is possible and desirable.

CONCLUSION: IMPLICATIONS FOR PREACHING

Having proposed theological reasons for congregations to pursue ethnic
diversity and unity, and addressed some of the costs of that endeavor,
this chapter's conclusion begins to consider the task of preaching toward
greater integration between members of different ethnic groups. It first
makes some general observations about the complexity of the task and then

52. Vosloo, "Reconciliation," 39.

53. McMickle, *Preaching to the Black Middle Class*, 135.

54. Foster and Brelsford, *We Are the Church Together*, 110.

proposes three questions that preachers can ask of their congregations as they prepare sermons.

First, in any congregation preachers alternate between using words that address the entire congregation and words that will find a hearing for a more select subset of their listeners. In those moments preachers are asking some to listen directly and some to overhear. Here preachers fill a kind of inverse image of an orchestral conductor, who at times calls forth the sounds of all those present and at time those of a select few. In an inversion of the conductor's task, preachers are rather appealing to the *ears* of a select few and at times sounding notes that resonate with the whole symphony. Ideally their preaching will act as a musical score that sparks conversations between the sections directly addressed and the whole orchestra. When chosen well, these specific, targeted words can heighten the capacity for empathy between those directly addressed and those who at that moment are listening in on the message. While a white woman may not identify directly with a challenge from a black pastor to a black male to provide faithfully for his family, she may see within herself tendencies toward consumerism and covetousness, as she considers her own financial practices while overhearing.[55] This leads to a greater capacity to see the family resemblance between them, which in turn could enable her to find her place in a much larger family. Here preaching fulfills its call to re-member a sometimes disparate and divided body, as it grows together into Christ (1 Pet 2:4; Eph 2:22).

When does the pastor earn sufficient trust with the congregation (and cultivate it between members) so that painful, and even joyful, stories can be told? Calling forth or telling testimony prematurely can be damaging. Bitterness is evident in the psalmist's voice as he recounts the demand of his captors in Babylon to, "sing us one of the songs of Zion!" (Ps 137:3). This is a cruel version of the orchestral conductor image used above, where an exploitative conductor demands sounds from instruments not ready or willing to yield their songs. As preachers seek to spark new conversations about ethnicity in their increasingly diverse congregations, the sermon will prove to be a highly effective flint stone, but one that can harm as well as heal. They will need to listen carefully to the Holy Spirit and to their congregations for clues regarding the timing, form, and setting in which to tell those stories. Preachers endeavor to tell particular, highly contextualized cultural stories but also to tell the story of the gospel in ways that transcend

---

55. As noted above, the dynamics of a white pastor delivering such a challenge could make it difficult to deliver well, though with the right level of shared lived experience it could be possible.

all cultures and that shape a counterculture. This tension, and the various homiletical theories that address it, is the theme of the next chapter.

Second, the necessity of learning the secrets and hidden histories of other ethnic groups resonates with a tension inherent in the nature of all preaching. By its nature as proclamation, preaching is highly public; it is not about keeping secrets but about making the gospel plain. And yet, at the heart of the truth it makes plain is the mysterious, unspeakable, and hidden nature of God. So preaching participates both in *revealing* secrets and mysteries, and in protecting them. This dual nature of preaching makes it uniquely capable to speak of ethnic pain and sin in ways that honor, connect, and heal. Pastors who dwell amidst multiple subcultures also live in a tension of openness and hiddenness. They both guard secrets in their priestly work of bearing our members' sorrows, and they cultivate a community that is worthy to bear those secrets together. In a climate still deeply divided over race and ethnicity, North America needs spaces where it is safe to tell dangerous and painful memories and where others desire to hear them. It matters that those stories are told, and that they are told *in church*, where disparate people are gathered into one by baptism and Eucharist, and where by God's grace they are being built together as a place and an agent of transformation.

Preaching and the Memories of Diverse Ethnic Groups

How can preaching help members of various cultures put their pasts to work in ways that draw them forward into the future with hope and with the will to work for justice and reconciliation? Preachers, as narrators and interpreters of texts and of life, find themselves in complex relationships with the past(s) of their congregations. All churches stand in a relationship to the biblical past in that they are constantly interpreting ancient texts and locating themselves within the tradition of Israel and the church throughout history. And all congregations struggle to narrate their *common* past in ways that allow them to imagine the future fruitfully, as Branson's work has shown. He discusses the way congregational narratives can become decoupled from the gospel story. "When a church assumes stories without retelling and reentering them, there is little energy to power congregational life and there are no resources for raising a new generation or welcoming neighbors."[56] The task of reading and interpreting Scripture together, and letting it interpret our lives, is vital to a congregation's health.

Multiethnic churches have an even more complex challenge in integrating the gospel narrative with the relatively more recent pasts of multiple communities of memory. While diverse churches that focus on project identity (such as joining together to convert as many as possible) would tend to downplay the recent past of their members, a more thorough understanding of culture demands that its members reckon with that past and its pain. Here preachers must serve as *remembrancers*, to use a classic term for the role of historian as custodian and vocalizer of the community's memories.[57]

This calling draws upon the strong biblical tradition of preachers as *witnesses*. Thomas Long has integrated the work of Paul Ricoeur into his excellent study of the requirements of the witness. The task of witnessing faithfully forms a key component of our examination of preaching and memory. Preachers must ask three questions of their congregations as they prepare to witness in ways that help them to remember well together. Not all of these questions need to be asked in formal discussion with members; some may take the form of an imagined dialogue in the mind of the one preaching that week, as he or she prepares.

First, it would be highly profitable for preachers to ask their members, "*What do you want us to remember with you?* What are the aspects of your ethnic heritage that you fear will be lost as you join to worship with us?" Ethnic groups as communities of memory have their particularized sets of godly heroes and faithful role models, and they often go unnoted in white churches in the United States. Listening to the answers to this question is a type of long-term sermon preparation that is important but never urgent. Yet it serves other functions beyond the sermon event, as it sets the pastor in the midst of the congregation as a sensitive and engaged ethnographer. Leonora Tubbs Tisdale offers excellent suggestions to prepare preachers for the work of ethnography in their congregations.[58] The moment of listening may also offer opportunities for priestly consolation as painful memories are shared. Asking this question well is predicated upon knowing part of the answer already, through reading and in other ways educating oneself about

---

56. Branson, *Memories*, 54.

57. Burke, "History as Social Memory," 97.

58. Tisdale, *Preaching as Local Theology*, 56–91.

history, so as to avoid the syndrome in which minority people constantly fill the wearying role of the educators of naïve inquirers.

This line of questioning may draw on the model of *Appreciative Inquiry*,[59] which Branson has adopted for use in congregations. While his work in *Memories, Hopes, and Conversations* does not deal specifically with ethnic memory preservation, the thrust of his line of questioning, with its emphasis on positive memories and narration of the past faithfulness of God, is easily applied to the telling of ethnic histories, in addition to congregational ones. Adapted for learning about an ethnic group within one's congregation, the Appreciative Inquiry questions could include:

- What are the ways your ethnic background enriches your discipleship?

- What are some of the ways that your people have been faithful to God and have blessed the church throughout history?

- What is most important to you about your ethnic heritage, and what values, stories, traits, and traditions are you most eager to pass on to your children?

- If you could make three wishes for the people who share your ethnic background, what would they be?[60]

This dialogue process would be enriched if it were expanded from a conversation between a pastor and one member to one that took place in small group settings throughout the congregation. While this line of questioning would be particularly appropriate among minority members, it is also desperately needed among members of the majority culture, since they often fail to reflect on themselves of members of an ethnic group that has a history.

The second question preachers must ask of their members is, *"What are you (and other members of your ethnic group) all-too-eager to forget?"* While the first question would tend to elicit stories of pride, and allow the pastor to serve a more joyful role of helping the entire community to celebrate the goodness in particular ethnic stories, this question calls forth the dimension of suffering inherent in the witness' task. Long notes that, "What the witness believes to be true is a part of the evidence, and when the truth

59. Appreciative Inquiry is an organizational development philosophy and process that seeks to improve performance through a method of asking questions that enable individuals to envision positive futures for their organizations or communities. See Whitney et al., *Power of Appreciative Inquiry*.

60. Adapted from the questions in Branson, *Memories*, 12.

told by the witness is despised by the people, the witness may suffer, or even be killed, as a result of the testimony. It is no coincidence that the New Testament word for witness is *martyr*."[61] It is crucial for authentic reconciliation that members of all ethnic groups acknowledge the painful part they have played in oppression of others, and the other societal and individual sins that have characterized their cultures.

Here one biblical model is Paul's strategy in addressing the Gentiles, in Ephesians 2:11. From one perspective on ethnic reconciliation, Paul's words in Ephesians seem singularly insensitive, intended to perpetuate shame. He writes, "So, then, remember that at one time you Gentiles by birth, called 'the uncircumcision' . . . remember that you were at that time without Christ, being aliens from the commonwealth of Israel and strangers to the covenants of promise, having no hope and without God in the world" (Eph 2:11). Why does Paul insist on dredging up this painful past? Why call it to mind? It is for Paul an essential part of the narrative of their salvation and their contemporaneous membership in the church. It calls them to ongoing humility, as they must continue to acknowledge that they did not accomplish their new status as members on their own. This leads in turn to gratitude and worship, and prevents taking their story for granted. It also calls them to merciful and gracious hospitality, in the same way Israel's reminders of their enslavement often prefaced calls to show kindness to the alien in their midst.

The third question a pastor must ask, both in imagined dialogue and in moments of pastoral care, is, "*What does this congregation, and the individuals within it, need to cease to call to mind?*" Here Miroslav Volf's careful wording is more helpful than the simpler term, "to forget." The argument for ceasing to call to mind does not advocate an erasure of memories that would entail loss of essential identity, but rather a gracious putting away of memories, both of pains suffered and of wounds inflicted.

Victims do the former in imitation of and in response to the gracious act of God toward them in "remembering their sins no more" (Isa 43:25). As Volf puts it, "If God's reconciling self-giving for the ungodly stands at the center of our faith, then nothing stands in the way of opting for grace, with its pain and delight of forgiving and ultimately releasing the memory of suffered wrongs."[62] This movement comes as the fruit of a process of naming those painful memories truthfully, integrating them into the wider story of

61. Long, *Witness*, 47.
62. Volf, *End of Memory*, 209.

God's redemption and, finally, of receiving the gift of a new capacity to let them go. Perpetrators also let go of self-recrimination for the wounds they have inflicted on others, as the end of a process of repentance and receiving of God's forgiveness and that of those they have harmed.

In nurturing the capacity for forgiveness in a congregation through proclamation, the preaching team must tread carefully. They must be careful not to move the process too quickly, heeding the warning of Vosloo about the time that reconciliation takes. White people in North America are particularly prone to wanting to move on from the past prematurely, much like the white South Africans Vosloo described above. Like midwives, preachers watch for the right moment when forgiveness is ready to be born in the oppressed and when the moment is right for oppressors to receive forgiveness, even to the point of no longer calling it to their minds and no longer letting it define their identity.

This chapter has sought to examine the challenges and opportunities that abound when churches seek to become more ethnically diverse. Today, in a striking reversal of our long history of segregation, many churches see a form of ethnic diversity as a selling point, touting it on their letterheads and billboards. Yet some have embraced diversity as a goal without a clear understanding of the complexity that accompanies it or a clear theological and biblical basis for it. The result can be a superficial integration that falls short of becoming a culturally conscious church, one that functions as a sign, foretaste, and instrument of God's kingdom through practices of reconciliation and healing. This chapter has put forth a theological rationale for the ethnically diverse and reconciled church, using the doctrine of the Trinity and the habits and disciplines of hospitality and repentance. It has begun to explore the place of memory in the formation of ethnic identity, with an eye to how congregations that incorporate members of various ethnic groups need to learn to interact with those memories on multiple levels. The chapters that follow explore in more depth the question of how preaching, as part of its proclamation of God's good news to all people, can shape communities of memory capable of confession and repentance that fosters reconciliation. How can preaching augment practices of justice and healing within congregations, and outward toward society? The challenge is made more complex when multiple, contested narrations of the past are given voice, and yet the potential for transformation is greater for that very reason.

3

Models of Preaching Text and Experience
The New Homiletic and a Homiletic
Informed by Postliberalism

We have argued for the value of ethnic diversity in congregations, drawing from theories of ethnicity and culture, and from biblical and theological sources. Along the way we have named some of the complexities and difficulties involved in becoming fully integrated, reconciling communities. This chapter turns now to the specific role preaching may play in that endeavor. Ethnically diverse churches require a homiletical theory adequate to fund preaching that can shore up some of their instability, exploit their strengths, and further their flourishing. Toward that end this chapter considers the contributions of the New Homiletic and the critique of it found in postliberalism, particularly as that has been applied to preaching in the writing of Charles Campbell.

Multiethnic churches face two overarching needs, if not more than homogeneous churches, then at least in different ways. These needs have been addressed directly by few homileticians. First, the congregations that are growing more diverse need to attend to and give voice to the cultural expressions, memories, gifts, and hermeneutical vantage points of all those in their midst. Second, these congregations need intentional formation into communities of character that are deeply committed to the practices that make unity possible: hospitality, repentance, reconciliation, and mutual submission. Preaching plays a crucial role as it inspires and challenges congregations to live out this vision of community. It would oversimplify matters to assert that the New Homiletic offers more resources to perform the first task, of naming diverse experiences, and that postliberalism is more equipped to perform the second, that of forming united congregations. But this generalization does accurately read the strengths of these schools of thought. After we examine the goals and limitations of the New Homiletic and of postliberalism, we will consider some theological perspectives that synthesize their approaches to text and experience.

All congregations need to learn to narrate the past faithfully. They must tell both the shared narrative of their congregational life and tap into the particular histories of their members. This can happen with less intentional effort in an ethnically homogeneous setting, as preachers access a ready stock of references for shared humor, shorthand references that all understand, and easily accessed illustrations. It requires more intentionality in a multiethnic one. When pastors articulate well the experiences of various ethnic groups, whether from the pulpit or in other congregational settings, they guard against the erasure or even denigration of cultural heritage and identity that too often happens when assimilation is the implicit pathway for the entrance of minority persons into a community.

How should that narration take place in the pulpit? What are the desired ends, and what are the risks, of the potent yet vulnerable narration of painful, shameful, or joyful pasts? This raises a broader and much debated question in homiletics, that of the parameters within which preachers narrate *any* human experience in the pulpit. In wrestling with these questions, homileticians and theologians have engaged the discussion that has taken place among linguists and philosophers about the priority of language and experience, which turned sharply when Martin Heidegger and others began to argue that experience arises from language rather than preceding it. This has led to consideration of the role of shared language in articulating and even permitting or giving rise to religious experiences.

Homiletical discussion in the last thirty years has also sought to reply to and reframe Barth's dismissal of human experience as a point of contact for the revelation of God.[1] The New Homiletic has labored from numerous angles to recover a place for human experience in the sermon, and

1. Barth, *Preaching of the Gospel*, 12. See Rice's responses in *Interpretation and Imagination*, 14 and 60–63. See also Craddock, *As One Without Authority*, 57.

homileticians committed to postliberalism have offered a radically different vision of the priority of language, the biblical text, and human experience.

Here, we will assess each theoretical framework for its methodology in ordering and naming human experiences with reference to the biblical text. We will consider the assumptions about culture and the nature of humanity in each approach and the potential ability within them to form and unite congregations and to proclaim the agency of God. While there is much to appreciate in the vision of Hans Frei, George Lindbeck, and others who have shaped the postliberal perspective, I will argue here that its deficiencies render it inadequate as a sole foundation for a homiletic of cultural diversity. In constructing a homiletic that honors, celebrates, and narrates multiple cultural memories faithfully, we need more nuanced dialectic between experience and language, and between human, earthly experience and the knowledge of God. The thought of John McClure and Nicholas Lash moves promisingly in that direction.

THE NEW HOMILETIC

The New Homiletic is a fairly wide tent, encompassing a range of theological, rhetorical, and even sociopolitical theories and strategies. And, as Dale Andrews notes, the designation itself is something of a misnomer, since little in its strategies and emphases has been received as new to African American preaching, nor to other more oral cultures.[2] This discussion is thus primarily a review of paradigm shifts within the academy and their effects on mainline Protestantism and, less directly, on evangelical preaching. Several themes and concerns distinguish it from the milieu out of which it arose. Let us begin by setting it in its historical context.

Historical Context of New Homiletic

The decades of the 1960s and 1970s brought a crisis of confidence in the pulpit. Church attendance in many denominations was in decline, and societal assent to the authority of the preacher was shaken, due in part to widespread questioning of authority in general. The modernist assumptions that had undergirded exegetical methods and sermon structures were eroding. Traditional modes that had served well since John Broadus' classic

2. Andrews, "New to Whom?," 1–3.

text, written in 1898,[3] no longer seemed efficacious. Many such books advocated a rather dispassionate dissection of a text, from which one distilled a thesis and its sub-points. One then ordered them into a deductive presentation, utilizing Hellenistic rhetorical principles to persuade by means of logic, supplementing with illustrations only as a kind of ornamentation.

A more recent impetus for the rise of the New Homiletic was that two other movements in preaching had run their course and lost steam. The therapeutic model, which Harry Emerson Fosdick pioneered, had sought to use the pulpit as the setting for large-scale pastoral counseling. A strain of prophetic preaching, which William Sloane Coffin exemplified, used preaching to voice the concerns of the social gospel, civil rights, and pacifist movements of the 1960s and 1970s. It thrived for a time, but left some congregants and pastors alike weary of relentless calls to action. Preachers were in search of new ways to engage their congregations on Sundays.

The New Homiletic also saw itself in part as a correction to the dim view of human capacity to move from natural experience to a spiritual encounter with God, found in the writings of Karl Barth. While recent scholars have engaged in a retrieval of Barth's vital contributions to preaching,[4] many at least early in the development of New Homiletic theory were reacting to his articulation of the nature of proclamation. Barth, for reasons that made sense in his historical context, was eager to protect the revelation of God from the realm of human experience. In part, his concern arose as he saw a faulty line of thinking in liberal German theologians, whose work inadvertently lent credence to totalitarian states. In protest to an overly anthropological strain in the liberal projects of his day, Barth stressed the infinite qualitative difference between God and humanity and elevated the role of divine agency in proclamation. He portrayed the preacher as a herald who announces news that comes from above and outside the realm of what can be discerned through reason or experience. He downplayed the roles of cultural and congregational context[5] and of the personality or rhetorical

3. Broadus, *On the Preparation of Sermons*.

4. Willimon, *Conversations with Barth*; and Webb, *Divine Voice*, 20–25.

5. Of course, Barth is famous for his statement that pastors and indeed all Christians should have, "The Bible in one hand and the newspaper in the other," which goaded pastors to pay attention to context. However, it seemed that in Barth's understanding the newspaper provided the focus for *application* of revealed truth, which was discerned largely apart from context. No authoritative single source has been found for this Barth quote. It is thought to be from a lecture and not any published work. A *Time Magazine* piece on Barth published on Friday, May 31, 1963, states, "[Barth] recalls that 40

skill of the messenger. Though Barth was himself a masterful rhetorician, as William Willimon puts it, "He evinces a Platonic suspicion that language is a dispensable container for the truth that language is meant to express, rather than an integral part of the truth itself."[6] As Barth expressed his ideal, "[Preaching] must be a selfless human word . . . the less it obtrudes itself in its own solidity between God and the hearer . . . the better it will be."[7] This obscuring of the personality of the messenger leads Andre Resner to conclude that, "Those who followed Barth's theology tended toward a homiletical Docetism, i.e., a discussion of the Word of proclamation apart from its physical embodiment in the preacher."[8] In addition to diminishing the role of the preacher, Barth's confidence in the agency of God to accomplish all the work of proclamation had the effect, at least in the eyes of many homileticians, of emptying the listener of any active role in the sermonic process.

Characteristics of the New Homiletic

In many ways the heart of the New Homiletic can be described as a turn toward the listener, a turn that views the listener as an active partner and therefore crafts sermons that facilitate listener engagement. Richard Allen and Thomas Long have summarized the New Homiletic in these terms.[9] We'll look at six aspects of the turn toward the listener: Buttrick's phenomenology of how speech forms in consciousness and his accompanying theory of sermon movement, a shift towards inductive reasoning, a revival of narrative form, the use of imagery, a concern for a more inclusive conversation with the congregation (particularly with marginalized voices), and explorations of ways to perform the text or sermon.

years ago he advised young theologians 'to take your Bible and take your newspaper, and read both. But interpret newspapers from your Bible" (Princeton Theological Seminary Center for Barth Studies, http://libweb.ptsem.edu/collections/barth/faq/quotes.aspx?menu=296&subText=468).

6. Willimon, *Conversations with Barth*, 250.

7. Barth, *Church Dogmatics* I.2, 764.

8. Resner, *Preacher and Cross*, 62.

9. Allen, "Turn To the Listener," 166–96; and Long, "How Shall They Hear?," 167–88.

1. Sermonic Movement

H. Grady Davis laid the groundwork for the shift to a more dynamic understanding of the sermon structure in 1958 with his book *Design for Preaching*, where he argued that the sermon should have an organic sense of movement. He likened the sermon to a tree that grows and develops over time.[10] This conception of the sermon as an event in time has proven critical to every subsequent aspect of the New Homiletic. David Buttrick further developed the sense of sermonic movement, rooting it in a phenomenology of the way humans perceive reality and the way that language functions in the hearer's consciousness. Like a camera, Buttrick understands the mind to focus on images in sequence. Thus he urges preachers to construct each sermon as a series of logically connected moves, with both variety and continuity. A sermonic move is a module of language that forms in consciousness to pattern new understanding. In shaping each move, preachers seek to employ vivid language, imagery, and illustrations, with one goal in mind: "With images interacting we *imitate human consciousness* in order to serve faith-consciousness."[11] Buttrick is concerned to *name* God in ways that lead to transformation. He worked against modern conceptions that portrayed language as representing or precisely corresponding to reality. Buttrick labored hard to understand the way the listening mind operates, and not only at the individual level. One of the more fascinating aspects of Buttrick's proposal is that he saw the power of language to shape communal or shared consciousness as well, though he did not develop in depth the implications of this for the formation of congregational character and mission.[12]

2. Inductive Movement

Another aspect of the turn toward the listener is the shift toward inductive reasoning. While deductive reasoning flows from a general principle to its specific implications of that principle, inductive reasoning moves from specifics to generalizations, from concrete experience to abstract principle.[13]

10   Davis, *Design for Preaching*, 24.

11.   Buttrick, *Homiletic*, 167.

12.   Buttrick, *Homiletic*, 92 and 248–49. Charles Campbell calls Buttrick's understanding of communal formation "esoteric," lacking the "enacted dimension of the community" (Campbell, *Preaching Jesus*, 228 n. 29).

13.   Richard Eslinger has a strong critique of deductive preaching. He writes, "Deductive preaching has exemplified a minimalist and often arbitrary relationship to biblical

Fred Craddock articulated the need for this shift in his works *As One Without Authority* and *Overhearing the Gospel*. Craddock based his strong call for inductive method in the doctrine of the incarnation, in which the invisible God became tangible, visible, and concrete.[14] To differentiate his project from traditional strategies, Craddock asserted, "Sermons that move inductively, sustaining interest and engaging the listener, do not have points any more than a narrative, a story, a parable, or even a joke has points."[15]

Craddock has been keen to infuse a sense of anticipation on the part of listeners, drawing them into a powerful experience with the text. Craddock brought this sense of a dynamic encounter with the text from his engagement with the New Hermeneutic school of thought, which Gerhard Ebeling and Ernst Fuchs developed at Tubingen.[16] Their emphasis on the text as a Word-Event, and indeed of the linguistic nature of all existence, shaped his understanding of the sermon as an experienced event. Craddock also draws upon the philosophical and linguistic insights of Ludwig Wittgenstein and J. L. Austin to argue for the capacity of language to constitute and shape reality, and for the performative capacity of words.[17] Craddock is also concerned to create a more dialogical relationship between preachers and listeners, and to shorten the distance between the two.

Through induction, Craddock has sought to create a space in which an independent experience may occur within the listener, giving him or her freedom to respond at will. It is not only freedom, but also *agency* that Craddock's method intends to give to hearers. He hopes that his methods will cause them to be active participants in crafting meaning, rather than passive recipients of knowledge.[18] Thus for Craddock assertions in sermons should be more implicit than explicit, more suggestive and connotative

---

material throughout its history . . . Deductive preaching's use of Scripture . . . most often constitutes genuine misuse" (*The Web of Preaching*, 16).

14. Craddock, *As One Without Authority*, 52.

15. Ibid., 81. (Of course stories and jokes have points, which makes them "so much more interesting" for the listener, as Neal points out to his new companion Del in the movie *Planes, Trains and Automobiles*.)

16. Ebeling writes, "But the sermon as a sermon is not the exposition of the text as past proclamation, but is itself proclamation in the present—and that means, then, that *the sermon is EXECUTION of the text*. It carries into execution the aim of the text . . . *Thus the text by means of the sermon becomes a hermeneutic aid in the understanding of present experience.* When that happens radically, there true word is uttered, and that in fact means God's word" (*Word and Faith*, 331).

17. Craddock, *As One Without Authority*, 28–29.

18. Ibid., 54–55.

than denotative. A crucial theological basis for Craddock's work lies in his high view of humanity's capacity to perceive and encounter divinity, as he follows Paul Tillich and Rudolf Bultmann in looking to human experience as a significant source of knowledge of God.[19]

3. Narrative Dimensions

Proponents of a New Homiletic have also sought a new way to grasp the narrative quality of life, and of Scripture itself, and to privilege this over linear, rational argumentation in the sermon. Again, H. Grady Davis set this in motion with his insight that most of the gospels' ideas are conveyed in story form. He wrote, "We overestimate the power of assertion, and we underestimate the power of a narrative to communicate meaning and influence the lives of our people."[20] Eugene Lowry further developed the concept of the narrative form as a homiletical plot, which highlights the drama of a text by delaying the sermon's meaning. It moves toward creating and then accentuating a conflict, discrepancy, or "homiletical bind," that requires resolution. More than any other homiletician, Lowry has labored to shift the enterprise of preaching from *doing space*, where one orders ideas and constructs linear arguments, to *doing time*, a conception in which one orders experiences of life under law, and then narrates the dramatic shift to life in the light of the gospel. In his model the sermon unfolds like a well-told drama or novel does, with twists and turns and sudden reversals. Richard Eslinger notes, "It is in the notion of the homily's *torque* . . . that Lowry makes a distinctive contribution."[21] Lowry is not concerned so much with the telling of stories, whether as illustrations or as the centerpiece of a sermon, as he is with conceiving the sermon as a whole in the form of narrative. He writes, "the term *temporal sequencing* serves best and may refer either to *source* (narrative text) or to *presentation* (narrative discourse)."[22]

Numerous homileticians have elaborated on the concept of the sermon as story and of preachers as storytellers. Edmund Steimle, Morris Niedenthal, and Charles Rice assert that humanity lives by story. Our stories connect us, give meaning to the events of our lives, and allow the sermon to

19. Ibid., 12.

20. Davis, *Design for Preaching*, 158.

21. Eslinger, *Web of Preaching*, 51.

22. Lowry, *The Sermon*, 24.

reflect the "blood and soil of actual life."[23] Steimle argues for an interweaving of biblical story and our story, and for sermons to embody the characteristics of a good story, while preserving a place for propositional truth to play a significant role. Steimle draws upon the New Testament hermeneutical work of Amos Wilder, who highlighted the significance of the parables for creating worlds of meaning for their listeners. Rice has emphasized the importance of the nonbiblical narrative as well, finding in great literature extended metaphors that communicate truth and connect with listeners' experience. Like Craddock, Rice saw the typical preacher of his day as too distant and authoritarian, and sought through storytelling a strategy that built a sense of connection. These authors also share a preference for locating meaning, and the sermon's persuasive power, in narrated experience rather than in rational argument.

One question that arises in the quest for preaching that forms congregations into highly committed communities is the capacity story has for building cohesiveness and strengthening group identity. While stories can have great power to unite listeners, James Thompson raises the concern that, "Stories may shape communal identity, but ultimately the cohesiveness of the community requires the *interpretation* of the communal story."[24] Multiethnic congregations may need to create more spaces for tentative voices to articulate disparate stories and for patient listeners to validate them, before a communal story emerges that resonates for all. It will take time to release and then hear the voices that can narrate the struggles and instances of redemption to which all members bear witness from their distinct locations. But leaders of ethnically diverse congregations also do well to heed Thompson's warning, teaching their members to interpret their experiences through the texts and doctrines of the church tradition.

4. Image

A fourth dimension of the New Homiletic has been a recovery of the value of imagery and imagination in preaching. In some historical traditions of preaching, the preference for unadorned logic was accompanied by a suspicion of imagery as deceptive at worst and disposable at best.[25] While not

---

23. Steimle et al., *Preaching the Story*, 174.

24. Thompson, *Preaching Like Paul*, 12, italics mine.

25. Eslinger notes, "The history of the relationship between homiletics and imagination theory has been more than rocky or unstable. At times, the two have remained

displacing reason, the New Homiletic in contrast privileges imagination and narrative for their capacity to provoke an experiential encounter with text and meaning.

The scholarly study of the use of image in preaching draws in part on the hermeneutical principles of Paul Ricoeur, who taught that imagination has the power to give form to human experience, and that it is the way we redescribe reality. A central premise in Ricoeur's work is that it is the symbol that gives rise to thought.[26] Ricoeur asked, "How do humans access truth?" He noted that traditionally we have answered that we do so through concepts. Ricoeur shows that we access truth through imagination as well. He asked, "For what are the poems of the Exodus and the poem of resurrection . . . addressed to if not our imagination . . .?"[27] Margaret Miles has also highlighted many strengths of imagery, such as its social availability, polyvalence, and affective capacity.[28]

Key homileticians advancing the use of imagery in preaching include Charles Bartow,[29] Patricia Wilson-Kastner, Thomas Troeger, and Paul Scott Wilson. Wilson-Kastner has underscored the theological basis for the use of image in the incarnation. In the incarnation, word became flesh, visible and tangible. Preaching that focuses its words on the concrete, specific, and ordinary imagery of daily, earthly life imitates God's incarnational movement. Within a thorough survey of the use of imagery in the Hebrew Bible and in Jesus' teaching, she notes that images have focusing power, and that in that act of focusing a space is made for an encounter with God.[30] She urges that images should appeal to the senses, be open-ended, and multi-dimensional. She also works with the linkage of imagery to the liturgy, reminding preachers that proclamation is a sacramental act.[31]

Paul Scott Wilson has worked with the ways in which image and logic complement one another in homiletics. He makes the distinction that, "Logic is primarily unidirectional or linear, moving step-by-step to a specific purpose or intent. It finds meaningful connections between ideas primarily on a temporal axis of cause and effect. By contrast, imagination

---

alienated or estranged, through long periods in the tradition" (*Web of Preaching*, 246).

26. Ricoeur, *The Symbolism of Evil*, cited in Thompson, *Preaching Like Paul*, 13.

27. Ricoeur, "Toward a Hermeneutic of the Idea of Revelation," 117.

28. Miles, *Image as Insight*, 10–12, 35–39.

29. See Bartow, *The Preaching Moment*, 33–46.

30. Wilson-Kastner, *Imagery for Preaching*, 21–23.

31. Ibid., 95–102.

finds a meaningful connection between ideas that have no causal relationship. Imagination not only brings two ideas together, it also perceives a
unity between them, or, to use Coleridge's words, it 'reconciles' them as
a new identity . . . This perception of unity is not random; it is an act of
discernment, a means of knowledge."[32]

Thomas Troeger urges preachers to attend to the character of their
articulations of reality as they arise from the preachers' historically condi-
tioned imaginative construction of the world. Troeger sees the use of image
as in tune with the postmodern preference for authenticity over authority,
and he sees it as moving the sermon in the direction of a corporate event.
He writes, "The recent focus of homiletics upon narrative and imagery
can be seen as nothing less than a corporate awakening in the church to
the need for 'mobilizing a shared awareness of the experiential grounds to
which one's theological concepts appeal for their very meaning.'"[33]

5. Conversational Models

A fifth aspect of the New Homiletic has come from insistent voices around
the New Homiletic table who argue that the shifts toward inductive, narrative, and image do not go far enough towards two of their central concerns:
shortening of the distance between preachers and congregations, and hearing from voices on the margins of church and society. They urge a further
shift, in which the sermon is neither crafted in isolation nor delivered as a
finished product, but instead is a collaborative interpretive project. It may
or may not take on the actual shape of a conversation, but always it is intended to spark conversations.

Included within this endeavor would be those who are seeking to
broaden the range of people with whom the sermon is in dialogue, literally or imaginatively. This would include the work of some liberation theologians, Kathy Black's work on behalf of the deaf community and other
minority groups, and those who are giving the clergy tools to interpret
their congregation's unique cultures, such as Leonora Tubbs Tisdale, Joseph
Jeters, James Nieman, and Thomas Rogers. These highly contextualized
models move from a wide range of lived experience, seeking to enhance re-
ceptivity for distinct listening groups through calibrating modes of preaching to accommodate the modes of perception of various listeners. For

32. Wilson, "Beyond Narrative," 136.

33. Troeger, *Imagining a Sermon*, 92.

example, Tubbs Tisdale critiques the emphasis on the fine arts in narrative homileticians such as Rice, arguing that this approach may not reach local congregations whose worldviews and daily life do not resonate readily with the sensibilities of the fine arts. Instead, she urges pastors to understand preaching as folk art that practices a local theology in close conversation with the meaningful symbols and language of its context.[34]

O. Wesley Allen has pressed preachers hard in the conversational direction, arguing that even McClure's collaborative model of sermon preparation in *The Roundtable Pulpit* does not go far enough. Allen wants us to view congregational conversation as a form of proclamation as well. Lucy Rose's work also sought a more profound shift in the conception of the relationship between clergy and laity, as well as shifts in assumptions about the neutrality of language, and a change from focus on questions of truth to a greater concern with questions of *meaning*. While she praised aspects of the New Homiletic, she saw it as still ensconced in classic formulations of preachers as authoritative senders and congregation members as passive recipients of the message.[35] Rose placed preacher and congregation together on one side of a gap, from which they embark together on a journey that has text and its mystery on the other side. She viewed preaching as a tentative proposal that invites counterproposals. "It is a wager on the part of the preacher, a genuine yet humble confession of faith that acknowledges its particularity and self-interest and seeks the corrective and confirmation of others' wagers."[36] Rose's methodology accounted for context with utmost seriousness and articulated an egalitarian view of clergy and laity relationships. However, some scholars are concerned that her preference for questions of *meaning*, which arises primarily if not exclusively out of human experience, over transcendent truth,[37] may remove the capacity of the sermon to proclaim any normative lens through which to interpret that experience. David Lose writes, "Robbed of its assertive character, of its ability to advance propositions about truth and reality, confession ceases to be performative."[38] The performative nature of speech, and specifically of proclamation, brings us to our sixth aspect of the New Homiletic.

---

34. Tisdale, *Preaching as Local Theology*, 122–24.

35. Rose, *Sharing the Word*, 78.

36. Ibid., 107.

37. Ibid., 131.

38. Lose, *Confessing Jesus*, 133.

6. Performative Dimensions

The performance stream that feeds the New Homiletic draws from the springs of theater, genre studies, the liturgical movement, and recent philosophical work with the performative nature of language. Homileticians such as Charles Bartow, Jana Childers, Clayton Schmit, and Richard Ward urge preachers to grasp the drama of the incarnation, the dramatic tensions within life, and those within scriptural texts. They understand the interpretation of texts to be inseparable from performance. Performance is hermeneutical and hermeneutics is performative.[39] They argue that the sermon should draw upon the rich resources of the entire liturgical event, with all the drama, energy, and movement that it holds. They call preachers to attend to genre, seeking alignment between form and content.

This alignment between the form of the text and that of the sermon has been pursued in the homiletical work of Richard Lischer and Thomas Long. They seek a sermon that embodies the text, doing what the text does,[40] and so facilitating a deep encounter with the text for listeners. In seeking to craft words that perform texts, they draw upon J. L. Austin's speech-act theory. Austin distinguishes *constative* speech, which states facts and describes reality, from speech utterances that have performative effect. *Locutionary* speech states and observes; it is simply the act of saying something. *Illocutionary* interactions perform an action *in* their saying, as they illicit a response. *Perlocutionary* speech acts actually effect change *by* being spoken.[41]

Austin's theory of the performative power within speech resonates with certain theological understandings in the New Hermeneutic school regarding the event-ful nature of texts. Gerhard Ebeling's conviction that the sermon is an execution of the text fuels the hope of preachers that their sermons can have a transformative effect. Ebeling asserts that, "Whatever precise theological definition may be given to the concept of the word God, at all events it points us to something that happens, *viz.*, to the movement

---

39. Cosgrove and Edgerton summarize performance theory well. They write, "The process of preparing to preach is a series of performances, each leading to the next, and finally to the preaching event itself. Interpretation is eventful and embodied: the preacher performs the interpretation, and those present interpret the whole performance. The listeners, in turn, will perform their understanding in speech and action" (*In Other Words*, 24).

40. See Lischer, *The End of Words*, 82, and Long, *Preaching the Literary Forms of the Bible*.

41. Austin, *How To Do Things With Words*, 8.

which leads from the text of Holy Scripture to the sermon."[42] Clayton Schmit applies this conviction about the text's power to preaching and other liturgical proclamation, noting that it is the power and presence of God that completes the performance of our words. He writes, "The performatory power of the words we speak in worship stems from what God has accomplished through the Word in creation."[43] Performance theorists have been explicit that the goal of proclamation is to create an event, experience, or encounter that may lead to transformation.

Initial Evaluation of the New Homiletic

What are the primary contributions of the New Homiletic, in a quest for a homiletic that furthers the flourishing of multiethnic churches? While few of its scholars have devoted extensive energy specifically to the integration of culture and ethnicity with homiletical concerns,[44] the New Homiletic brings critical resources to the table for those who seek to take cultural location seriously. This is primarily because it has worked so hard to evaluate and reformulate preaching from the perspective of the individual listener. Yet it has its detractors, both sympathetic and oppositional. While Campbell raises a set of concerns that flow specifically from his postliberal framework, other scholars have also offered corrections or alternate perspectives to the New Homiletic. We'll hear from them briefly first and then interact with Campbell's concerns.

James Thompson warns that inductive and narrative preaching works best where listeners are well informed of their Christian heritage already. He is also concerned that the emphasis on literary form and technical aspects of the sermon can draw away from attention to theological content.[45] He would grant more authority to preachers than Craddock would, so that the sermon can make the ethical demands upon its listeners that many texts do.[46] Richard Lischer agrees with these concerns, adding that sermons weighted too heavily toward story can lead to "salvation through introspection." He cautions, "The critical evaluation of our sermons entails

42. Ebeling, "Word of God and Hermeneutic," 85.

43. Schmit, *Too Deep for Words*, 48–49.

44. Most notable has been the work of Nieman and Rogers, *Preaching to Every Pew*; Jeter and Allen, *One Gospel, Many Ears*; and Tisdale, *Preaching as Local Theology*.

45. Thompson, *Preaching Like Paul*, 12.

46. Ibid., 13.

... analysis of the many ways our pulpit stories have been transparent to the needs of the ego but opaque to the claims of God's righteousness."[47]

Long raises the concern that the eagerness to see sermons engender an experience can make an idol of experience, and that a powerful narration of one's own or a fictional character's life experience can "swamp" or replace the gospel story.[48] Here, Long begins to name one of the central concerns of postliberals: the biblical story may be eclipsed through a privileging of the human story, which is often narrated in individualistic terms. Craddock's inductive movement begins with the human story in ways that can threaten to be more memorable and meaningful than the biblical story.

A different problem with Craddock's inductive movement surfaces when we take congregational diversity into account. Craddock, leaning on Tillich, appeals to *common* human experiences, seeking points of identification, common ground from which to name theological truth. John McClure notes, "This idea of interchangeable experience pervades modern homiletics and is fundamental to the New Homiletic."[49] While humanity has much in common at the core, when some in a congregation have lived through genocide in Cambodia or endured years of overt racism and others have lived in relative ease, the degree of interchangeability of experience is lessened. Preachers must use care in assuming that their experiences of life are normative. Rose, discussing the dangers in appeals to common experience, writes, "These dangers include a blindness to conflicting experiences and a resultant imperialism than names as 'common' or 'human' what is particular and limited."[50] The potential to grow into a vibrant community that is capable of identifying with a broad range of experiences and of standing in solidarity with others is greater in diverse settings than in more homogeneous ones, if those experiences can be named with care, and those habits cultivated with diligence. That practice may simply be more complex than the process Craddock articulates.

SUMMARY OF POSTLIBERALISM

A different critique of the New Homiletic comes from postliberalism. While it was George Lindbeck who first used the term, *postliberal*, he would

47. Lischer, "The Limits of Story," 36.

48. Long, *Witness of Preaching*, 44–45.

49. McClure, *Other-Wise*, 51.

50. Rose, *Sharing the Word*, 128.

credit the New Testament scholar Hans Frei with seminal insights that led to the concept's development. Both sought a theory to explain the loss of Scripture's formative authority, the church's accommodation to culture, and one that would offer a strategy for cultivating Christian identity, rooted in the centrality of Jesus Christ in the life of the church.[51] Clifford Geertz's paradigms for understanding culture, Peter Berger's sociological inquiries into plausibility structures, and Ludwig Wittgenstein's concept of the language game were key theoretical building blocks for Lindbeck. Here, in summarizing the goals and methods of postliberalism, three aspects stand out: its nonfoundational premise, its conception of religion as a cultural-linguistic system, and the concept that the biblical narrative absorbs the world (*intratextuality*). After a summary of these elements, we'll focus on Campbell's application of postliberalism to homiletics.

1. Nonfoundational Premise

Postliberals are consciously working within a postmodern framework in their eschewal of universal philosophical foundations to legitimate or defend Christian faith. Foundationalism may be described as the presupposition of modern, Enlightenment era Western philosophy that every non-basic belief must build upon a universally compelling belief, a first principle, which needs no external, prior support. This is rooted in Descartes' search for an absolute certainty, which was universally self-evident and was not tied to any contingencies of history or religion. Theologians since the Enlightenment (and indeed from much further back) have sought to establish the Christian faith upon empirically verifiable propositions. In contrast to the emphasis on reason and logical proofs, various liberal Christian theological projects have sought to translate or correlate the tenets of Christian faith with the psychological, aesthetic, and spiritual longings within the broader culture. Friedrich Schleiermacher's apologetic appeal to Christianity's cultured despisers through a universal feeling of absolute dependence, and Paul Tillich's search for the presence of God in the depths of human experience, both represent appeals to different types of foundations within their contemporary cultures. David Tracy represents

---

51. Alister McGrath makes this summary in "An Evangelical Evaluation of Postliberalism," 35.

those from the Chicago School who articulate the *correlationist* or revisionist strategy from the liberal Protestant tradition.[52]

Postmodern thinkers object to the quest for philosophical foundations. They argue that the confidence that marked that quest ignored the interpretive process inherent in all perception, and the many ways statements that assert universal truth may be used to legitimate privilege and power. Postliberal theologians similarly object that foundationalism obscures the radical particularity of the Christian faith. They designate extrabiblical theories and universal human experiences as foundations, and insist that the biblical text does not need such external validation. One difficulty here, as Jeffrey Goh points out, is that Lindbeck's system is itself built on the foundation of the revelational authority of the biblical text. He cautions that, "Philosophical nonfoundationalism . . . would hardly accept as 'foundationless' any appeal to the relational authority of a religious tradition as Lindbeck has done."[53]

The refusal of postliberalism to engage with various foundational structures has led some to accuse them of an isolationist sectarianism, imperialism, and fideism.[54] In lieu of philosophical foundations, Lindbeck has posited a closed system that is only fully intelligible from within, on its own terms. When a community makes little attempt to articulate its truth claims in terms that are intelligible to external worldviews or language structures, it becomes difficult for those outside it to interact with and assess its claims, at least on ground that feels familiar. In fact, it becomes difficult for those within it to find the critical distance necessary to evaluate their own beliefs. Postliberalism's strong appeal to the community of interpretation for authority leads to a circular reasoning, wherein the truth of the gospel rests in its function as true for the community. This in turn may lead to a sectarian refusal to engage culture.[55] In fact, readers of Lindbeck credit him with a strong desire to enter into conversations across traditions; indeed ecumenical dialogue has been one of his central concerns.

---

52. See Tracy, *Blessed Rage for Order*, 32ff.

53. Goh, *Christian Tradition Today*, 256.

54. See Clark, "Relativism, Fideism and the Promise of Postliberalism," 107–20.

55. See Allen, "Two Approaches to Theology," 41.

2. Cultural-Linguistic Approach to Religions and Doctrine

As Lindbeck looked out at current religious expression in American Protestantism, he concluded that theories of religion fit one of three models.
The first he called the cognitive-propositional model, which emphasizes
doctrines as articulating truth claims about reality. The second is the
experiential-expressive approach, which focuses on doctrines as, "non-
informative and non-discursive symbols of inner feelings, attitudes, or
existential orientations."[56] Neither of these views accounted sufficiently
for one of Lindbeck's initial questions, which was the variability of doctrine within faith traditions that are seeking and even finding ecumenical
common ground. He proposed a third alternative, the cultural-linguistic
model. In this model, he asserted, "The function of church doctrines . . . is
their use, not as expressive symbols or as truth claims, but as communally
authoritative rules of discourse, attitude, and action."[57] From here he developed the idea of doctrines as having a *regulative* function. They describe
the grammar of the language game that is played within a given tradition.
Thus he proposed that doctrinal statements are second-order assertions.
Lindbeck explained, "They acquire enough referential specificity to have
first-order or ontological truth or falsity only in determinate settings . . .
[such as] adoration [and] proclamation . . ."[58]

One grasps the significance of conceiving a faith tradition as a cultural-
linguistic community more fully when one sees how Lindbeck understands
the shaping function of language itself. The experiential-expressive model
would posit that there exists within humanity a universal, pre-linguistic
experience in search of language. Lindbeck counters that it is language that
makes experiences possible, as it creates a world within which to live. The
use of this language, "is a communal phenomenon that shapes the subjectivities of individuals rather than being primarily a manifestation of those
subjectivities."[59]

Some have objected to Lindbeck's cultural-linguistic model of religions, and particularly its application to the Christian faith. At times
Lindbeck analyzes the rules of language games in a way that makes little
reference to the God who gives breath and power to human speech. The

56. Lindbeck, *Nature of Doctrine*, 16.
57. Ibid., 18.
58. Ibid., 68.
59. Ibid., 33.

language system model can deny God's prevenient grace through God's presence beyond and before language. Language learning is viewed as an entirely human task. In Lindbeck's writing, the miraculous, God-initiated dimension of conversion and regeneration is minimized. This results in a reduction of the process of conversion to social enculturation. Transformation is replaced by catechesis in a series of grammar and vocabulary lessons and their accompanying habits and virtues. William Placher notes, "Christians . . . need to assert that our Christian speaking and acting all respond to a prior initiative from God, and it is not clear that a cultural-linguistic model which denies the legitimacy of reference outside the world of our language can make sense of anything that precedes our speech and action."[60] Willimon's incisive critique of postliberalism is simply stated: "The major missing element in Lindbeck's analysis is *agency*."[61] Adonis Vidu points to this deficiency as well, arguing that, "From the point of view of the Christian narratives, being a Christian does not speak so much about the person who becomes, but about the God who saves."[62] Belying this lack of agency, the nature and work of the Father and the Holy Spirit are both strikingly absent from the discussion in both Frei and Lindbeck.

3. Intratextual and Narrative Understanding of Scripture and Life

The concept of intratextuality is central to Frei and Lindbeck's proposal. What takes place *intra* the text is reality, or humanity's experience of all of life, as well as the rational interpretation of that experience. The text becomes a framework of meaning that is ever extending. For Lindbeck, "Intratextual theology redescribes reality within the scriptural framework rather than translating Scripture into extrascriptural categories."[63] Communication with those outside the Christian faith tradition, then, does not involve translation or correlation to the language or assumptions of the surrounding culture, but rather Christian self-description. It offers an alternative vision of reality, a re-description of the world in biblical categories, and endeavors to make that vision as appealing as possible to onlookers,

60. Placher, "Ricoeur and Postliberal Theology," 49.

61. Willimon, *Conversations with Barth*, 217, italics mine.

62. Vidu, *Postliberal Theological Method*, 188.

63. Lindbeck, *Nature of Confession*, 118.

while always seeking to "reverse the direction of conformation," as Nicholas Wolterstorff words it.[64]

Hans Frei saw the roots of this conformation in the turn in biblical hermeneutics toward the historical and critical study of texts. This led to a quest to ferret out the text's meaning, for which the text itself was relegated to the status of a conduit. Meaning is detachable from the story in which the meaning is found.[65] This in turn resulted in the loss of a biblical imagination, the clouding of a biblical lens through which to view the world and interpret one's experiences. Frei describes this as "the great reversal," or eclipse, wherein, "interpretation was a matter of fitting the biblical story into another world with another story rather than incorporating that world into the biblical story."[66] In contrast, Frei insists that the meaning of the biblical narrative is, "constituted through the mutual, specific, social context, and circumstances that form the indispensable narrative web."[67]

Postliberal readers of Scripture begin with the text, and they use text as a tool with which to find truth that lies within and beyond it. The shape of the narrative shapes and limits our language patterns. Truth is found within it; the text is both sufficient and authoritative. As Frei puts it, "The truth to which we refer we cannot state apart from the biblical language which we employ to do so. And belief in the divine authority of Scripture is for me simply that we do not need more."[68] Postliberals thus urge a return to a premodern, intratextual mode of reading the Scriptures. Here, Lindbeck and Frei both draw upon Barth's confessional approach, with its rootedness in the "strange new world" of the text.[69]

In building his narrative framework, Frei also follows Erich Auerbach, who developed the idea of the realistic narrative that constitutes reality through its intense, dynamic, overarching story. Auerbach contrasts Homer, who creates a world that readers or listeners enter and enjoy for a time, with the biblical narrative. "[The Biblical narrative] insists that it is

---

64. Wolterstorff, *New Haven and Grand Rapids*, cited in Lindbeck, *Nature of Confession*, 47.

65. Frei, *Eclipse of Biblical Narrative*, 6.

66. Ibid., 130.

67. Ibid., 280.

68. Frei, "Response to 'Narrative Theology: An Evangelical Appraisal,'" 22–23.

69. Barth used this phrase in a sermon entitled, "The Strange New World of the Bible," in Barth, *Word of God and Word of Man*, 28–50.

the only real world; [it] is destined for autocracy."[70] It follows then that we fit our lives into its world; we make sense of life on *its* terms. As Jeffrey Goh summarizes Auerbach, "The demand of Holy Scripture is that of an all-consuming communal text that engulfs the whole of extra-biblical history."[71] As Frei puts it, "The direction in the flow of intratextual interpretation is that of absorbing the extratextual universe into the text . . ."[72]

While Frei insists on the primacy of the biblical narrative, he is quick to assert that the narrative is not history, but rather *history-like*. "We are in fact thrown back on the story simply as a story, regardless of whether or not it is well documented."[73] Frei's work here is subtler than this summary accounts for, but it is troubling that, while he has labored hard to avoid the decoupling of meaning from text that he saw happening in higher criticism, he appears to have decoupled historical reference from the narrative. Ricoeur criticizes Frei on his depiction of the gospel narratives as "history-like," noting that, "The question of the referential claims of these stories remains unavoidable."[74] Wolfhart Pannenberg insists that the resurrection must be understood as a historical, actual event. Pannenberg writes, "It is tempting to treat the traditions as stories and in this way to avoid the problem of historical criticism and the question of the facticity of what is recorded, but we can do so only at the expense of the truth claims of the tradition."[75] Laurence Wood credits Frei and Lindbeck with a rediscovery of the biblical text through their emphasis on a realistic reading of the text, but he also asks, "How could he [here referring to Frei] claim to develop a realistic narrative based on the actual exegesis of the events in Jesus' life, death and resurrection as a real story, a real history, and a real account of things as they were perceived?"[76] The narratives represent themselves as realistic depictions of history, not as fiction or as narratives for which factuality is of minor importance.

While Frei and Lindbeck's evasion or dismissal of the question of historicity in their discussion of biblical narrative is particularly troubling for evangelicals, no phrase has caught the eye, nor raised the eyebrow of

70. Auerbach, *Mimesis*, 16.

71. Goh, *Postliberal Vision*, 160.

72. Frei, "The Literal Reading," cited in Lose, *Confessing*, 118.

73. Frei, *Identity of Jesus Christ*, 102.

74. Ricoeur, "The Hermeneutics of Testimony," 44.

75. Pannenberg, *Systematic Theology, Volume I*, 232.

76. Wood, *Theology as History and Hermeneutics*, 154.

theologians, as much as that of the text of Scripture *absorbing the world*. Here, the goal is that disciples, as hearers and followers of the Word, increasingly come to inhabit the one real world that the biblical narrative renders. This can oversimplify both text and culture, representing them as monolithic, static entities. In addition, the possibility that culturally situated persons could entirely inhabit a biblical world strikes many as a denial of the doctrines of creation and incarnation, doctrines which affirm the goodness of this world as gift from God and the place in which we may encounter God. Others object that even if such absorption were desirable as an end, it may also be simplistic to imagine that it is possible. As Miroslav Volf writes, "We can look at culture through the lenses of religious texts only as we look at these texts through the lenses of our culture. The notion of inhabiting the biblical story is hermeneutically naïve because it presupposes that those who are faced with the biblical story can be completely 'dislodged' from their extratextual dwelling places and 'resettled' into intratextual homes. Neither dislodging nor resettling can ever quite succeed; we continue to inhabit our cultures even after the encounter with the biblical story."[77]

The charge of naïveté comes with relation to how one determines what constitutes the tradition and how one will therefore interpret the text. Ronald Allen notes, "Postliberals sometimes speak blithely of Christianity as if it is a univocal phenomenon. This bypasses one of the most exciting and vexing emphases of recent Christian discussion: pluralism in the Bible."[78] The Bible itself does not emerge from one culture, but from a complex of cultural traditions, and it does not speak univocally on many topics.

A related problem of textual interpretation stems from postliberalism's diminishment of the power of *experience* to correct and nurture the tradition. In so doing, Lindbeck and Frei have left little room for voices from the margins that may alter practices and beliefs, and sharpen the lenses through which the whole church interprets texts. Goh warns, "The danger . . . is that the status quo in the cultural-linguistic system of Christianity perpetuates the illegitimate exclusion of experiences from certain sectors of the church which heretofore have had no voice."[79]

The model of text absorbing world also presupposes rather modern notions of culture as static and monolithic, and demarcates the boundaries

---

77. Volf, "Theology, Meaning and Power," 51.

78. Allen, *Two Approaches*, 41.

79. Goh, *Postliberal Vision*, 447.

between Christian and secular culture too sharply. John Howard Yoder's concern with Niebuhr's characterization of culture, noted in the previous chapter, applies here as well. Culture is complex, not monolithic, and therefore we cannot respond to it with wholesale affirmation, rejection, or even paradox or synthesis. As Miroslav Volf asserts, "There is no single correct way to relate to a given culture as a whole, or even to its dominant thrust; there are only numerous ways of accepting, transforming, or replacing various aspects of a given culture from within."[80]

CAMPBELL'S POSTLIBERAL HOMILETIC

Charles Campbell has done the most work to apply postliberalism, and Frei's hermeneutical principles in particular, to homiletics in order to fund his critique of the New Homiletic. Campbell would like to see three moves occur in homiletical practice today, moves that would spring from a rejection of assumptions that he sees underlying the New Homiletic. These desired shifts in understanding of the goal of preaching may be summarized as: from the sermon provoking an individual encounter to the sermon producing congregational formation, from narrative focus on plot to narrative centered on the character of Jesus Christ, and from the sermon as transformative event to the sermon as catechesis in language, virtues, and habits. After an evaluation of Campbell's thought, we'll hear a synthesizing proposal from McClure regarding text and experience, noting its resonance with the work of Nicholas Lash.

Campbell at times seems to transpose Lindbeck's three models into a hierarchy of evolution in religious development. While Campbell voices appreciation for some of the intentions of the New Homiletic, and wholly approves of its movement away from a methodology rooted in cognitive-propositional approaches to faith, he views it as stuck at the experiential-expressive level, with all its modernist, individualistic, and anthropocentric baggage. Campbell puts forth a model of preaching within what is, in his view, the highest and best paradigm of faith, the cultural-linguistic model.

80. Volf, "Theology, Meaning, and Power," 63.

1. From Individual Experience to Congregational Formation

The first move Campbell is eager for is a movement away from viewing the goal of the sermon as the creation of an individual encounter with God, or even with text or with the realities of life, and toward seeing the goal of a sermon as the faithful narration of text and the formation of a faithful community. In Campbell's critique of appeals to experience, Charles Rice comes under particular criticism, since he most explicitly builds upon theologians who ground faith in human experience or their sense of God, such as Schleiermacher and Tillich. Campbell takes Rice to task for his use of Tillich's theology of culture and Schleiermacher's theory of expression of religious feeling through the arts, and Rice's subsequent assertion that a culture's art and literature evoke recognition of fundamental religious experiences. Here Campbell charges Rice with adopting a *translation model*. The result is that, in Campbell's view, "Human experience and contemporary culture . . . provide the terms within which the preacher makes the gospel meaningful."[81] They set the terms, and thus inevitably have the last word.

Campbell sees more nuances within the work of Craddock, whom he sees as giving a higher place to Scripture as the "church's book." Yet Craddock's inductive method betrays too much confidence in human experience as a beginning point for knowledge of God, and this is suspect for Campbell. Craddock would have preachers move from the particulars of human life to an awareness of how Scripture addresses those situations. Campbell criticizes Craddock for appropriating modern liberal assumptions about the individual and his or her rights, and sees this individualism lurking in the inductive method itself, at least as Craddock employs it.[82] Campbell charges that, "Craddock's use of the 'rights' language of modern liberalism to describe the hearer's role in the sermon further highlights this individualistic orientation."[83] Inverting Craddock's inductive model, Campbell insists that we move instead inductively from the particulars of Jesus' life to an explanation of how that story shapes the church's life.

In reply to Campbell's concerns with individualism in the New Homiletic, while its earliest architects worked somewhat inevitably within a modernist framework, the New(er) Homiletic has brought to the table a strong postmodern critique of individualism, and with it a high level of

81. Campbell, *Preaching Jesus*, 150.

82. Ibid., 133.

83. Ibid. Campbell refers us to pp. 17, 62, 93, and 149 of Craddock's *As One Without Authority*.

awareness of the congregation as a whole. Lucy Rose, John McClure, Ronald Allen, Leonora Tubbs Tisdale, and many others have raised awareness of the different kinds of listeners that are present as preachers proclaim their messages. This has contributed to a new focus on the whole congregation engaging in the sermon. Campbell might counter that greater awareness of diversity of needs among individuals merely makes preachers more skilled at narrating a wider variety of *individual* experiences. This is a valid critique of the New Homiletic, which has tended to focus on individual encounters with text. However, the concern for congregational formation is growing among homileticians who employ various New Homiletic strategies. For example, a strong theme within performance theorists of preaching is that the congregation performs the word together. Jana Childers includes preaching within worship when she asserts, "Worship is about *all* of God's people performing—giving form to—their response to God."[84] Congregation formation is increasingly becoming an explicit goal of many who identify themselves within the New Homiletic.

It is also worth stating that a starting place with the individual does not necessitate an ending point in individualism. Jesus placed tremendous value on individuals as individuals, and not simply for their capacity to join the collective of the kingdom of God. We see this in his teaching, where he portrays a Father who knows the hairs on each individual's head and leaves the ninety-nine sheep for the one. Perhaps especially, we see Jesus' value on the individual in his healing encounters. If he had only been concerned with the formation of a community, individual healings would have been a distraction from the task. He did seek to form those individuals into a body, but one in which each member had a vital role, as Paul grasped so well in his use of the body analogy (1 Cor 12:12–31) for the church.

2. From Plot to Character

Campbell's second desired move would be from what he considers to be an anthropocentric narration of the plot of a sermon to a christocentric narration of the unique identity of Jesus. In urging a shift from plot to character (that is, to a focus on the central character of the narrative, Jesus Christ) Campbell critiques Lowry's now classic *loop* for its initial starting point in human needs. He contends that questions that begin there inevitably yield anthropological answers. Thus, narrative preaching that begins

84. Childers, *Preaching as Theatre*, 123.

with common experiences tends to reduce Christology to soteriology. He cautions, "An analysis of the human situation shapes the understanding of what salvation can mean, and then Jesus Christ is provided as the answer to that soteriological question . . . Jesus gets absorbed into human experience and loses his unique, unsubstitutable identity."[85] Here Campbell makes the excellent point that in recent preoccupation with narrative form, some preachers have emphasized plot at the expense of character, subsuming the identity of Jesus into the needs and contours of human experience. His concerns form a valid critique of many sermons fueled by narrative paradigms. The critique applies as well to the recent trend in evangelical "seeker-targeted" preaching, which, while not necessarily narrative in shape, often begins with human need, with God conveniently supplying the answer to every longing and tension within.

However, in rectifying this tendency, Campbell follows Auerbach, Frei, and Lindbeck in an overcorrection that reveals significant holes in their theological fabric. Campbell and the postliberals go further than simply reversing the flow of interpretation from experience to text. For them, text absorbs and even trumps experience. The only faithful option becomes leaving one's lived experience behind and stepping into the newly rendered world of the text. The text, and only the text, is where the action is. Lose protests, "Such a move not only appears remarkably exclusive, bracketing out so much of human experience and existence, it also all but destroys any concern for 'contextual' theology and preaching, as all other worlds and cultures prove only to offer false realities waiting to be incorporated in the biblical world, culture, context, reality."[86] Lose and others see in postliberalism a deficient articulation of creation and incarnation. Lose calls Campbell's vision, "an insidious denigration of created reality, clearly at odds with the Incarnation."[87] Lose makes a solid case for preaching the clear identity of Christ, but it must be the Christ who is at work in the ordinary, temporal world, which has been created with the capacity to bear his identity and to hold forth his presence. We preach to give people eyes to see the work of God in their day-to-day circumstances. This coheres well with Ray Anderson's methodology of Christopraxis, which seeks to discern the movement of Christ in the life of the world and the church.[88]

85. Campbell, *Preaching Jesus*, 39.

86. Lose, "Narrative and Proclamation," 6.

87. Ibid., 8.

88. Anderson writes, "Theological reflection . . . asks the question, 'Where is Jesus in this situation and what am I to do as a minister?' When the Scripture is interpreted

3. From Transformational Event to Catechesis in Habits

Campbell's third desired move would be away from viewing the sermon as an event, encounter, or experience and toward the sermon as catechetical formation of the congregation. Sermons are viewed in large part as "language lessons" that instruct the community in the virtues, habits, and linguistic possibilities of their newly inhabited world. Campbell is eager to note that this extends beyond mere recitation of grammar lessons, but rather includes a jazz-like ability to improvise, or to "go on," as Wittgenstein described well-developed linguistic ability.[89] Oddly, in positing this vision, Campbell's goals for preaching threaten to devolve into the very anthropocentricism he sees in the New Homiletic, though the emphasis shifts from human emotions to human skills and practices. Preaching fuels change in behavior and speech, but the extent to which that change is rooted in the power and goodness of God is limited by the weak sense of the agency of the Holy Spirit.

In his criticism of the emphasis on experience in the New Homiletic, Campbell joins Thomas Long, who, as was noted above, sees a danger of idolatry in the pursuit of extraordinary experiences, and Lucy Rose, who sees danger in making transformation the goal of every sermon. When overemphasized, this goal creates a situation where every sermon ought to precipitate a dramatic turning point or reversal of worldview. Some sermons do this, but Rose notes that others serve the valid function of simply affirming and confirming what is already known and practiced in the congregation. While Long and Rose agree that the emphasis on experience has limits, neither would deny that a real, experiential encounter is one desirable end of preaching.

In contrast, Frei and Lindbeck, and Campbell's application of their work, can seem to downplay any experiential encounter to the point that, in the estimation of James Kay, "Postliberal preaching becomes largely catechetical and ethical in nature; the aim is socialization into the church understood as a community of character."[90] As such, this style of preaching often omits the essential element of *promise*, which is so foundational for

---

in such a way that direction is sought for lives who need to be conformed to the true and healing power of God's Word, we must remember that Jesus is not only the 'author' of Scripture through the power of Spirit, but he himself is a 'reader' and interpreter of Scripture in every contemporary moment" (*Shape of Practical Theology*, 56).

89. Campbell, *Preaching Jesus*, 234.

90. Kay, Review of *Preaching Jesus*, 404.

obedience. Lose gets to the root of this omission, speaking of the lack of reference to the agency of God as the creator who speaks through the created text. McClure echoes this concern, noting the absence of a theology of the work of the Holy Spirit in Campbell's work. He writes, "Without this sense of the Holy Spirit who lives beyond, within, and through the text, it is likely that 'preaching Jesus' will mean 'preaching the textuality of Jesus' or the 'text-Jesus' and not 'preaching the living Christ.'"[91]

THE DIALECTIC OF TEXT AND EXPERIENCE: JOHN MCCLURE AND NICHOLAS LASH

At the heart of this discussion is the relationship of text and human experience, and how preachers give voice to the two. McClure asks of postliberalism the important question, "Is the polarity between the biblical text and experience overstated?"[92] He develops a more nuanced synthesis, arguing that the work of the Holy Spirit during the sermon is to interweave text with experience in the hearts of listeners. Listeners come to understand their faith as both *textualized experience* and *experienced text*.[93] His proposal resonates with that of Nicholas Lash, who responds similarly to Lindbeck's sharp polarization of experience and text. Lash speaks here more broadly than of the biblical text, addressing all the language we employ to describe experience. In a summary of Lash, Paul Crowley notes, "Unlike Lindbeck, Lash is not interested in merely reversing the inner-outer relationship between experience and language . . . Instead, he would claim that . . . all experience is essentially hermeneutical."[94]

Lash's theory of language and experience builds upon Hans-Georg Gadamer's articulation of the hermeneutical nature of experience,[95] and on Karl Rahner's work with the linguisticality of transcendent experiences. Rahner insisted that the two exist not in a correlative, polarized relationship between inner and outer event. Rather, the transcendent experience always exceeds its expression in words, though verbal expression informs the experience.[96] Working with this point, Lash writes, "the accounts that

91. McClure, Review of *Preaching Jesus*, 36.

92. Ibid.

93. Ibid.

94. Crowley, *In Ten Thousand Places*, 105.

95. See Gadamer, *Truth and Method*, 414–17.

96. Rahner, "Theology in the New Testament," 26.

we give, the interpretations that we offer, *make a difference* to the experience itself . . . experience is *modified* by the interpretations that we offer, the memories to which we appeal in the stories that we tell."[97] This point will prove crucial to building our understanding of how societies and the ethnic groups within them narrate events and how that in turn shapes their character and identity.

Lash's view of the dialectical nature of experience and language speaks to the calling preachers have to lead their congregations in the task of understanding and narrating well their memories of the past. This is central to the concerns of the following chapter, which considered how different ethnic groups articulate collective memories. Ultimately we are concerned to explore how proclamation may speak into and may influence that narration in ways that make interethnic reconciliation and understanding more possible. This type of proclamation will involve both of McClure's processes, that of *textualizing* experience and that of experiencing text in new ways. Postliberalism teaches us well how to do the former, but as the sole model, it would prove inadequate to the needs of multiethnic churches. Its method tends to negate and obscure lived experience in ways that do not fully honor culture as created by God.

The New Homiletic has advanced numerous strategies for experiencing text, and recent contributors have worked hard to consider multiple vantage points of historically marginalized listeners. But it stands in need of critique from homileticians like Campbell. His concerns for the centrality of Jesus Christ, the formation of communities shaped by the habits and language of the gospel, and his emphasis on the radical and distinct nature of the biblical text are all important corrections to some strains within the New Homiletic.

CONCLUSION: WHAT DOES ALL THIS HAVE TO DO WITH GROWING HEALTHY ETHNIC DIVERSITY IN MY CHURCH?

Ethnically diverse churches require preaching that furthers a strong sense of social cohesion and commitment, and preaching that names a broad range of experiences, both in lamentation and in celebration. In Campbell we find a strong vision for preaching that furthers the unity of churches, forming the people of God into covenanted communities. Campbell is

97. Lash, *Easter in Ordinary*, 248–49.

right to note the individualist tendencies in both a cognitive-propositional model of preaching and an experiential-expressive one. The New Homiletic, especially early on, has been weak in articulating a vision for the sermon functioning to unite members as one body. The habits and practices of discipleship that Campbell hopes preaching will foster are the very virtues that are crucial to the success of healthy multiethnic congregations.

Postliberalism also offers a mode of locating and transcending painful experiences. While ultimately postliberalism moves too far in its preference for text to the exclusion of experience, it does show us the way text gives us the appropriate context for interpreting our experiences. Our own initial interpretation of it need not be the final word. This has profound implications for ethnic groups whose distorted narratives of the past, both in terms of wounds suffered and wounds dealt, have left them immobilized and isolated. The resulting entrenchment within ethnic narratives is a significant reason that North America's churches remain divided. So a homiletic that could move ethnically homogeneous churches beyond their isolating narratives to ones more situated within the gospel narrative could open significant spaces for new expressions of unity.

The limitations of postliberal theology as an intercultural homiletic emerge when we see its often implicit view of the world in which readers and hearers of the Word actually live. As Volf noted above, the concept of text absorbing the world is naïve, both in its practical impossibility and its assumption that the community encountering the text is comprised of one culture, with a common set of experiences and an essentially similar set of sins and needs.

Postliberalism applied to preaching would inadvertently exact different costs for minority members of a culture than for those in the mainstream of it. For Frei, Lindbeck, and others speaking out of the white, male mainstream, culture is more easily conceived as something to leave behind as an act of repentance and discipleship. The radical movement they envision, wherein disciples step out of their lived world and inhabit the biblical one, makes sense to those who see their world as plagued by materialism, prideful individualism, and imperialism. Through their cultural earpiece, this is the call of the gospel.

For a Filipina immigrant who has experienced marginalization and consistent lack of recognition from the majority culture in the United States, this call to further negate her cultural heritage and denigrate the world in which she actually lives may not constitute an act of repentance so much as a denial of her created worth. There is certainly much created worth and much to repent of in every culture, including those that have not been marginalized. But as she watches her children become mainstreamed into North American culture and longs to see them develop a biblical love for their Filipino culture and follow Jesus as Filipinos, or as Filipino-Americans, the invitation to inhabit the world of the text may not prove to be the transformational practice that it often constitutes for members of the dominant culture.

How then do pastoral leaders preach, when members of both those groups, dominant and marginalized, are in the same room? The difficulty threatens to rival post-intervention Babel as a setting ripe for mutual misunderstanding. How will such congregations affirm and challenge the cultures of origin of recent immigrants, Native Americans, and African Americans, and the subcultures they indwell within this country, while inviting them into a congregation that constitutes in some measure a new culture, with its own values, memories, hopes, and stories? How do they do this for those whose negotiation of culture has been so marked by ease that they are scarcely aware of themselves as having an ethnicity and who may indeed need to repent of that privilege?

Preachers who wrestle with how to unite ethnically diverse congregations must strive to narrate experiences in ways that allow listeners to make connections between their own histories and the radically different histories of some in their midst. This comes through a process of careful listening and of bringing forth and empowering symphonic testimony, drawn forth from many voices throughout the congregation. It comes as preachers locate those experiences within the eschatological purposes of God, inviting congregants to confess to the bitterness and prejudice that may still cling to their narratives of the past, and as preachers seek out and name the redemptive power of God that can be seen in those histories. As Volf writes, "God does not take away our past: God gives it back to us— fragments gathered, stories reconfigured, selves truly redeemed, people forever reconciled."[98] The next chapter explores how individuals and ethnic groups remember their past(s), and how that remembering forms them, as a foundation for a homiletic of shared and redeemed memory.

---

98. Volf, *End of Memory*, 201.

4

Social Memory's Role in Dividing and Uniting

Memory shapes the character and identity of groups; it also conditions the capacity of individuals and communities to hear and interpret Scripture. This is both problem and opportunity as congregations seek to deepen and broaden their diversity. Preachers in those settings will need to strengthen their practices of recognizing, reminiscing, and reminding, consciously preaching out of and into multiple communities of memory. They will honor and celebrate those communities while forging a *third culture* space,[1] a new community of lively memory. As we craft a theology of preaching that furthers the task of remembering together well, we need to take a closer look at how that remembering happens, and how shared memory interacts with cultural and ethnic identity construction. As Richard Terdiman observes, "Of course every culture remembers its past. But *how* a culture performs and sustains this recollection is distinctive and diagnostic."[2] How

---

1. The term, "third culture" is used popularly by two groups: John Brockman, among others, draws on the thought of C. P. Snow to argue for a closing of the gap between literary intellectuals and scientists, in Brockman, *Third Culture*. David C. Pollock and Ruth E. Van Reken, among others, use it to describe expatriate children in *Third Culture Kids*. Here, "third culture" refers to a hybrid culture that honors and draws upon both or many subcultures, that emerges in a shared cultural space such as a congregation. Kathy Black uses it of multiethnic congregations in which, "a 'third' culture emerges out of shared memories that blends elements from each of the cultures present" (*Culturally Conscious Worship*, 90).

2. Terdiman, *Present Past*, 3.

do communities select the events they memorialize, investing some with significance and relegating other events to obscurity? What means do they use to preserve and transmit those memories? What are the ends or effects of those narrated memories in shaping the character of those societies and the individuals that comprise them? In what ways may we understand social remembering as a moral practice that cultivates (or corrupts) virtues, ideally increasing a community's capacity to engage fruitfully with other groups and to request and extend forgiveness? These questions can inform the leadership of ethnically diverse churches and particularly the proclamation that shapes and nurtures them.

We'll begin with a historical overview of memory in general in Western civilization, and then look at the rise in scholarly work on social remembering. Then we'll explore the ways social memory constructs, stabilizes, and perpetuates identity in ethnic and other groups, even as it often simultaneously becomes a site of contestation and struggle within them. A heightened consciousness of the shaping effects of social memory in subcultures within North America problematizes the goal of an ethnically diverse church in useful ways. It may help us to avoid the obscuring of ethnic identity that can happen within some current church growth strategies. By raising awareness of the difficulty of cultures coming together in church, we may point towards a realistic hope for churches to act as third culture communities that honor multiple memories even as they create new shared memories and hopes.

HISTORICAL OVERVIEW

Let's start with an overview of how memory has been conceived, valued, and used, from antiquity to the present. Developments in the material means of preserving and transmitting memories, most notably the shift from oral to written systems, have caused dramatic shifts in the conceptualization and role of memory in society. The focus of this historical review is on memory's role in Western culture, saving Hebrew and early church articulations of the value and function of memory for chapter 6.[3]

---

3. A global review of conceptions of memory would be fascinating as well and will hopefully be included in future work.

Memory in Antiquity

Memory as a concept has proved both fascinating and elusive throughout the centuries. Its consideration has yielded vivid metaphors, from vast storehouses, fields, and palaces, to gurgling digestive systems[4] and cold computer files. These metaphors yield valuable clues as to how a society understands memory to function. Memory's value in societies has waxed and waned over the centuries, reflecting fluctuations in its perceived linkage with history, imagination, language, reason, moral character, and religious devotion. While in general remembering has been treated as an individual's task, we will look for traces of the development of a formally articulated concept of social remembering. First, let's look at five aspects of memory in antiquity.

Mnemonic Strategies for Rhetoricians

In the Classical period, theorists of memory focused on the *means* of memorizing, creating the highly regarded art of mnemonics. With writing the provenance of only an elite few, societies highly prized those who could orally reproduce lengthy epics, myths, genealogies, and national histories. Elite schools of rhetoric cultivated the formal study of the *ars memoria*, advancing sophisticated memory systems. Some of the earliest extant efforts to understand and improve memory came from the Greek poet Simonides of Ceos (c. 556–468 BCE), who connected the various components of lengthy discourses to emotionally evocative images and to logical order. Greek rhetoricians such as Isocrates and Demosthenes, and Romans such as Cicero and Quintilian, focused on imagined places, *loci*, as a mnemonic tool. This strategy continued throughout the Classical period and into the Renaissance. Orators posited mental images of palaces, attaching their ideas to imagined sculptures and furniture in the rooms. They would then mentally "tour" the rooms of the palace as they gave their speeches. Patrick Hutton notes, "The places provided an architectonic design in which the knowledge to be remembered was to be situated . . . The architecture of place, often conceived as a palace or a theater, might be likened to a sacred space with which the mnemonist possessed intuitive familiarity."[5]

---

4. See Augustine, *Confessions*, 10.18.21.

5. Hutton, *History as an Art of Memory*, 30.

For Plato, the images of place used in remembrance were more than a mnemonic technique. Those images expressed transcendent reality. They were directly linked to the ideal forms that they represented. He saw all knowledge as essentially the remembrance of what our souls knew before they inhabited human bodies.[6] Whether the mnemonists' visual techniques were more useful to speakers than the mnemonic devices of the Enlightenment, which were rooted in the logical flow of ideas, is impossible to gauge. Part of what is intriguing here is that their mnemonic practices gave rise to metaphors that contributed to the conception of memory as a static entity, reliably located in the mind of the individual.

Memory's Links to Ethics and Virtue

For classical philosophers, memory was causally linked with ethics and virtue. For example, the playwright Aristophanes linked memory to honesty and integrity when he had his character wryly observe that his memory for debts owed to him was long, whereas his memory for debts he owed was woefully short.[7] Aristotle, who essentially rejected Plato's theory of forms, developed a more empirically based theory of memory. He associated the cultivation of the capacity to remember with the development of virtuous habits and character. Similarly, Pythagoras urged his students to exercise their memories as a means of deepening their "quality of soul."[8] Memory functioned as a moral compass in the literature of antiquity as well. It was Odysseus' memory of home, and his resolution to return to it, that guided him to overcome myriad temptations to forget. Sophocles portrayed Antigone's memory of her brothers' valor in battle and the obligation to bury them with honor as a guiding force in her courageous acts of loyalty.

6. See Plato, *Phaedo*, 263–64. Ricoeur summarizes, "Plato had turned [*anamnesis*] into a myth by tying it to a prenatal knowledge from which we are said to have been separated by a forgetting that occurs when the life of the soul is un-fused into a body— described, moreover, as a tomb [*soma-sema*]—a forgetting from birth, which is held to make the search a re-learning of what has been forgotten" (*Memory*, 27).

7. Aristophanes, *Works*, 181.

8. Gross, *Lost Time*, 28.

Memory as Center of Creativity and Imagination

Classical cultures also valued memory as a primary source of creativity, to a much greater extent than modern cultures do. Modern aesthetics has tended to portray creativity as a process of imagining and producing something entirely *new*, from within the mind or spirit of the individual or from external sources in nature.[9] In contrast, classical culture saw memory as the wellspring of the artistic imagination. That the mythological goddess Mnemosyne (Memory) is the mother of the nine Muses is evidence of this understanding. Premodern societies understood creativity to spring from careful observation of the artistic work of one's predecessors. Reflecting on this, David Gross writes, "If one had no effective memory of the intellectual legacies of the past, there would be nothing to create from, no material for the imagination to work with."[10] This did not imply a rote copying of tradition but rather the extension and flexible reworking of the past. Barbara Misztal observes, "Due to . . . human diversity and the generative use of language and gesture, memory seems to function in these societies in accordance with 'generative reconstruction' rather than mechanical memorization."[11]

Memory and History in Antiquity

History and memory have had a contentious relationship in modern and postmodern scholarship, with memory frequently viewed today as a site of distortion, willful nostalgia, and arbitrary selection, usually in the interests of the elite. History today is often skeptically viewed as the interpretation of events as narrated by the victors. Similarly, recent memory research in psychology, neurobiology, and sociology has emphasized the problem of memory's fallibility. The ancient Greeks and Romans did not suffer nearly as much from such concerns. They understood memories to be imprinted,

9. Wolterstorff notes this shift. He writes, "Around the time of the Renaissance a profound and fateful alteration, localized in the West, began to occur in the consciousness of mankind . . . Artists, rather than following in the footsteps of their masters, began to set out on courses of 'exploration' with no very definite expectations as to the kind of art they would end up producing—and precisely *because* they had no very definite expectations . . . This desire for the innovative, the non-routine, the unexpected, has by now shaped our entire culture" (*Art in Action*, 59).

10. Gross, *Lost Time*, 30.

11. Misztal, *Theories of Social Remembering*, 29.

as in Plato's wax tablet metaphor,[12] with images or likenesses that lived on in their minds. They had a comparably high degree of confidence in the human capacity to store and access those representations, for purposes that included the accurate housing, safeguarding, and recording of history. For the Greeks, the relationship between memory and history was in general straightforward and positive.

Herodotus saw himself and fellow historians as the guardians of memory, in particular the memory of the great deeds of heroes. Chronicling their bravery granted them an ongoing life that persisted beyond their physical existence on earth. Classical poets and historians memorialized their heroes in epic poems and in etchings on *stele*, the inscribed or sculptured stones that were inserted into the faces of buildings, not only to perpetuate their fame but also to bear witness to their courage in ways that would inspire their fellow citizens to similar acts of heroism and patriotism.

Memory in Ancient Popular Culture

While it is easier to find ready evidence for the formal study of memory in elite society, one also discerns the presence of a lively ethnic memory in oral forms such as storytelling. Jacques Le Goff notes, "In societies without writing, collective memory seems to organize itself around three major interests: the collective identity based on myths, and more particularly on myths of origin, the prestige of the leading families that is expressed by genealogies, and the technical knowledge that is transmitted by practical formulas that are deeply imbued with religious magic."[13] In the minds of ancient people, the past was fused with the present, which proceeded from it in an unbroken line. The past was the source of myths of creation and origin, memories of which fostered social cohesion and perpetuated the political order. Those social groupings tended to be rigidly defined and thus communal memory more simple. Misztal contrasts this with today when she writes, "Since modern societies offer individuals the possibility of belonging to many groups and a choice of different sets of identities, social memories in those systems are not exclusive but multilayered and overlapping."[14] In ancient cultures, the identity of a given individual was

12. See Plato, *Theaetetus*, 191c–198d.
13. Le Goff, *History and Memory*, 58.
14. Misztal, *Theories of Social Remembering*, 30.

tightly connected to his or her membership in a group and to that group's collective memory.

Medieval and Renaissance Periods

The medieval period displays continuity with ancient culture in that societies still highly valued and essentially trusted memory. Indeed, it was manuscripts, not minds, that were viewed as vulnerable to decay and loss. Written texts were assistants at best to the primary sources, which consisted of the minds of well-trained scribes and bards. It remained laudable to be able to recite one's genealogy, and to take instruction from the past. However, significant shifts occurred in the role and conception of memory. Memory was "Christianized" throughout much of Europe. The church calendar and the visual cues of architecture and frescoes imprinted and shaped in the laity a liturgical memory of God's acts of salvation in history. Faithful disciples memorized details of the lives of saints and martyrs. Even the spatial imagery for the *loci* of memory in rhetorical parlance shifted from that of palaces and storehouses to that of abbeys and cathedrals.

Another shift was that with the rise of moral philosophy, with its complex logical systems of reasoning, the most ardent practitioners of the *ars memoria* were Neoplatonist philosophers rather than the rhetoricians and bards of epic poetry of ancient times. In the Renaissance, mystical philosophers continued to see in memory a path to spiritual enlightenment, even vesting memory with magical powers. Like Plato, they held that certain mnemonic images directly expressed transcendent reality. The Italian philosopher Giordano Bruno took Platonic concepts in an esoteric direction, seeing revelatory correspondences between the stars and all other knowledge, which he placed in concentric circles on a "wheel of memory."[15] As Hutton writes, "In such a conception, the role of the *mnemonist* took on added importance. Not only did he practice a skill but he also assumed a priestly status as an interpreter of the nature of reality."[16] Yet, despite the elevated status of memory among the Neoplatonists, in general the perceived value of memory was declining, due to the rise of the scientific pursuit of knowledge, with its emphasis on systematic classification. Thinkers

15. Ricoeur observes, "The revenge of Platonic, and especially Neoplatonic, reminiscence over the Aristotelian psychology of memory and recollection is complete, but at the price of the transformation of reasoned speculation into mystagogy" (*Memory*, 65).

16. Hutton, *History as an Art of Memory*, 31.

increasingly viewed knowledge as an open and expanding set of facts, rather than a finite set whose memorization could be within the grasp of a well-trained mind. Improved means of printing also meant that individual memorization was no longer as necessary. Memory was "exteriorized" into encyclopedias and books.[17]

The view of the past itself was shifting as well, from one in which the past was carried into the present with a strong sense of continuity, with the goal being the replication of it, to a view that appreciated the distinctness of the past from the present. As the written word was increasingly used to preserve historical memory, through archives, libraries and the capacity to print books, educated people came to perceive the past as an entirely different realm. Rather than being the task and duty of all citizens, the study of the past was delegated to historians or antiquarians. Though the Renaissance and the Reformation were both movements of retrieval and recovery of past intellectual and theological traditions, they were both also present and future-oriented movements that questioned and weakened long-cherished traditions. Memory was losing ground as the *sine qua non* for shaping character, accessing creativity, and building nations.

Enlightenment and Modern Periods

With the emergence of modern culture, several factors contributed to a loss of esteem for memory in some areas, and yet there arose a growing role for it in others. In the Enlightenment, the role of reason eclipsed that of memory in the pursuit of science, to the point that memory was seen as actually impeding openness to new ideas. Francis Bacon expressed concern that excessive reliance on memory hindered discovery, initiative, and independent thought.[18] Descartes similarly cautioned that memory was not a reliable guide for ethical behavior or reasoning.[19] Gross summarizes, "In fact, mental residues of old sensations and opinions, marked as they necessarily are by ancient biases and prejudices, were said to block the free exercise of reason . . ."[20] Thinkers and social architects valued tradition itself less as the pursuit of progress became paramount. Modern understandings of what constituted a virtuous person were changing in concert with society's

17. Olick and Robbins, "Social Memory Studies," 115.
18. Bacon, *Advancement of Learning*, 14–15.
19. Descartes, *Discourse on Method*, 7.
20. Gross, *Lost Time*, 99.

devaluation of tradition, leading to a deflation of the value of memory for forming character. The person who placed too much focus on remembering the past was deemed to be closed to new ideas. Gross writes, "A certain amount of *tabula rasa* . . . came to be seen as beneficial, for if the mind does not continually open itself to fresh impressions leading to new associations, the individual unavoidably becomes confined within his own past and thus incapable of successfully coping with the demands of modern life."[21]

The Industrial Revolution and its resultant urbanization brought the loss of traditional sites of social memory that had been localized in village life. This was all to the good in the eyes of urban planners of the nineteenth century, such as Le Corbusier.[22] He envisioned urban settings with no references to the past, which he considered a "danger to life."[23] Freud reinforced this line of thinking, arguing that compelling "mnemonic symbols" in cities would cause unhealthy attachments to the past. On the other hand, perhaps in a nostalgic longing for a more rooted society, memory experienced a popular reprise in the nineteenth century, with the revival of neo-Gothic and neo-Renaissance architecture, renewed interest in genealogies, history, and in collecting antique items. Significant literature also celebrated memory as a force that shaped identity and fostered the imagination, most notably Proust's *Remembrance of Things Past*.

Memory in Modernity

The modern period, with its accelerated rate of technological and intellectual change and revolutionary upheavals in power structures, brought enormous changes in how societies related to their pasts. The rise of capitalism and industrialization contributed to a changed social structure. This displaced the storytelling practices and cycles of life that had been built around shared calendars and commemorative rituals. The nineteenth century brought unprecedented disruption of the very forms and functioning of memory and of the popular conception of history. Whereas prior societies had viewed time as flowing into the present in an orderly and smooth procession, events such as the French Revolution caused a sense of discontinuity between the two. This led to a radical rethinking of the

21. Ibid., 32.

22. The Swiss architect, Charles-Edouard Jeanneret-Gris (1887–1915), came to be known as Le Corbusier.

23. Gross, *Lost Time*, 103.

tasks of remembering and of writing history. Richard Terdiman makes the point that in traditional societies, "objects and people could be said to carry their pasts and their meanings openly."[24] In contrast, in the more complex, urbanized world of early capitalism, memory turned inward, becoming a private possession of the individual, hidden from the view of others.

Two other shifts in thinking about memory happened in the modern period. Both contributed to the development of more recent theories of social remembering. First, the nineteenth century saw a marked increase in the scientific and psychoanalytic study of individual remembering. What previous generations had considered an art, psychologists and neurobiologists began to examine more systematically. Sigmund Freud highlighted memory as he focused on its repression and distortion in psychoanalysis. He put forth the metaphor of memory as an archaeological site, with memories buried under layers of rubble or hidden behind a screen of repression. Because he worked with remembered events and their effects on individual patients, he was less inclined to develop a method for ascertaining the accuracy of recollections of raw data. Subsequent generations avidly sought such methods.

The field of study opened dramatically when the German psychologist Hermann Ebbinghaus applied the scientific method to memory studies in the 1880s. Working with series of nonsense syllables and with human subjects in complete isolation, he created controls for groundbreaking experiments in recall. His work led to numerous studies in the encoding and retrieval of data, studies of retention rates with various variables such as time spent learning the data, and studies of memory distortion among eyewitnesses, etc. This line of research generally reflected an individualistic, positivist, behavioral approach, with a quest for verifiable accuracy.

Ebbinghaus's work shaped perceptions of memory in a decidedly modern direction, since he viewed it as a highly individualistic endeavor and focused on retrieval of data divorced from meaningful events contextualized in lived experience. Still, his work made valuable contributions, and fomented the formal study of memory. Other researchers gave much consideration to constructing typologies of memory, culminating in Endel Tulving's taxonomy of *semantic* memory systems for facts or theories, which create our "knowing consciousness," and *episodic* memory systems for events, which underlie our "self-knowing consciousness."[25] Other

24. Terdiman, *Present Past*, 6.

25. See discussion of Tulving's work in Fentress and Wickham, *Social Memory*, 20.

important research has considered the role of language in shaping memory[26] and the context dependency of memory.[27]

The second shift in remembrance in the modern period was brought on by the world wars, which dramatically impacted the ways that nations engaged in remembering their pasts. Jeffrey Olick and Joyce Robbins contend that the wars brought a loss in the communal capacity for storytelling: "[The] cataclysm left people not only without the conditions for telling stories but without communicable experiences to tell."[28] The war decades left them with experiences so horrific that they defied narration. While storytelling may have declined, new forms of commemoration emerged, with nationalistic goals. Political leaders sought, through calendar, ritual, and myth-making, to foster a corporate memory that furthered the identity and glory of the state. Misztal notes the proliferation of historic sites since World War II, and the fact that 95 percent of the world's museums have been built since the Second World War.[29]

Few single events in human history have so shifted national and societal approaches to memory and historiography as has the Holocaust, which has been called a "crisis of representation."[30] While the needs of nations after World War I had been to further nationalism and even to cement resentment of enemies in order to further future political goals, nations and peoples in the wake of World War II found themselves with more complex and profound needs. They called upon monuments and rituals to ease collective burdens, and also to bear witness to the absent and silent dead, in what societies saw as a responsibility and a debt to remember.

Booth, writing on Holocaust remembrance practices, reflects on this heightened understanding of the moral practice of remembering the Holocaust. "Its governing imperative is a mix of debt to the now voiceless past,

26. See for example Loftus's and Palmer's study, in which they showed participants footage of two cars crashing, and asked them to estimate the speed at which the cars were going when they "crashed" (estimates of 40.8 mph) and asked other participants to estimate how fast they were going when they "contacted" (estimates of 31.8). Loftus and Palmer, cited in Baddeley, "Psychology of Remembering," 54.

27. See Baddeley's work in which he asked deep-sea divers to memorize lists of words while on the beach, and to memorize different lists while ten feet under water. When asked to recall the words, they remembered forty percent less well when trying to recall the words in the opposite environment from which they had learned them (Baddeley, "Psychology of Remembering," 56).

28. Olick and Robbins, "Social Memory Studies," 118.

29. Misztal, *Theories of Social Remembering*, 47.

30. Olick and Robbins, "Social Memory Studies, 119.

to preserve the voice of justice against forgetting or falsehood, and to the needs of continuity in identity."[31]

The increased attention to the psychological and neurobiological functioning of memory, and the impact of the world wars, are by no means the only sources of change in the way our culture understands memory today. The media in its various and emerging forms shapes and consolidates the narration of events. Advances in digital technology have vastly increased society's capacity to access archived data electronically. Globalization and emerging technologies simultaneously open avenues for a greater plurality of narrations to surface, and contribute to the loss of local narratives, which become submerged in the tide of hegemonic global currents. Industrialization and global immigration on an unprecedented scale has caused the loss of place, and the resulting search for other means of preserving memory and narrating identity.

So far we have focused on the intellectual history of the concept of memory, giving attention as well to the state of memory, particularly communal or collective memory, in different periods: the esteem for it, cultivation of it, and the extent to which it has been a shaping and unifying force. Hervieu-Léger has assessed the practices and capacities for remembering in the modern period (which she extends to contemporary society, seeing the terms, "hyper-modern" or "high-modern" as more useful than postmodern).[32] She sees an almost complete collapse of the ordering of society around remembering and transmitting what has been inherited. A number of trends in modernity have weakened what Hervieu-Léger calls the "chain of memory," from the heightened value on the individual, to the pursuit of rational and scientific methods of knowledge of the world, to the rise of mass communication. While readily granting that societies with stronger "official memories" were often characterized by tyranny and oppression, she laments the fragmentation of memory today. She asserts, "The contemporary fragmentation of space, time and institutions entails the fragmentation of memory, which the speed of social and cultural change destroys almost as soon as it is produced."[33]

Her observations form a sober challenge for the church, as it seeks to nurture the capacity to remember well in its members.[34] Ethnic groups

31. Booth, *Communities of Memory*, 94.

32. Hervieu-Léger, *Religion as Chain of Memory*, 165.

33. Ibid., 129.

34. Robert Wuthnow writes, "The church's role as a community of memory is being

within nations struggle as well to foster a sense of continuity with the past in their members, whose affections are pulled in numerous directions. The isolation and fragmentation of modernity leaves many hungry for a sense of lineage and communal identity; the extent to which ethnic membership and church membership may (or even should) meet that desire is one of the more complex puzzles of church leadership in today's multicultural society.

Modern Metaphors for Memory

Accompanying these shifts have been changes in the dominant metaphors that indicate how popular culture conceptualizes memory. Rhetoric in popular culture has moved away from internal metaphors, such as the spacious fields and palaces found *within* the human mind as conceived by Aristotle and Augustine, to external, mechanical metaphors that out-source the remembering process. The analogy of the camera and the photograph prevailed throughout the twentieth century as a dominant metaphor for the way individuals *captured* memories. This focused on the visual dimension of remembering, and showed confidence that memories could be accurately recorded and accessed in a fairly straightforward process.

Today, the dominant metaphor in popular culture for remembering is the work a computer does as it retrieves data through a search for patterns that share common elements. Aspects of this comparison are natural and useful, but the analogy is limited and may distort key features of human remembering, perhaps most notably the human capacity to forget, or to re-narrate events over time. While we frequently speak of computers "remembering," human remembering involves processes of which computers are not capable, such as the exercise of the will and a discursive process that takes place in groups. Edward Casey laments the computer analogy, writing,

> Human memory has become self-externalized: projected outside the *rememberer* himself or herself and into non-human machines. These machines, however, *cannot remember*; what they can do is record, store, and retrieve information—which is only part of what

emphasized by MacIntyre, Bellah and indeed many church leaders precisely at a time when an increasing percentage of the American population includes those not being born and raised in churches . . . In other words, memory is being emphasized because memory is now increasingly problematic. We can raise questions about tradition with greater urgency now than we could have had we lived in the thirteenth century" (*Christianity in the Twenty-First Century*, 47).

human beings do when they enter into a memorious state. The memory of things is no longer in ourselves, in our own discerning and interpreting, but in the calculative wizardry of computers.[35]

Scholarly consideration of memory has shown a marked turn toward understanding memory both as *process*, which highlights its interactive construction in interpersonal discourse and in societies, and as a *practice*, with an ethical dimension. This has arisen in tandem with considerations of culture itself as a dynamic and evolving process, and it has opened fruitful paths of inquiry. Michael Lambek and Paul Antze urge us to, "imagine memory as a practice, not as the pre-given object of our gaze but as the act of gazing and the objects it generates."[36] Viewing remembering as a practice highlights its interpretive and interactive nature—and its vulnerability to distortion.

THEORIES OF SOCIAL REMEMBERING

Early in the twentieth century a few innovative thinkers began to consider the social dimensions of remembering. Their thought echoed and sparked developments in the fields of psychology, sociology, anthropology, and historiography. This section considers the work of sociologist Maurice Halbwachs and, briefly, the psychologists Frederic Bartlett and Lev Vygotsky.

Maurice Halbwachs

If Maurice Halbwachs (1877–1945) was not the first to use the term *collective memory*,[37] he was certainly the first to bring it into contemporary scholarly vocabulary, through his work *Les Cadres Sociaux de la Memorie*, originally published in 1925. Halbwachs was a student of Emile Durkheim, as evidenced by his emphasis on the need for social solidarity and on the value of a shared past in fostering social cohesion. Halbwachs observed the ways that groups constructed memories so as to highlight and perpetuate their particular identity. He explored this in a variety of settings, from the family to nations and religious groups, including the reconfiguration

35. Casey, *Remembering*, 2.

36. Antze and Lambek, *Tense Past*, xii.

37. Olick and Robbins, in "Social Memory Studies," 106, note that Hugo von Hofmannsthal first used the term in 1902.

of maps of the Holy Lands by Christians and Jews. Halbwachs's research in Palestine was critical to the development of his theory that cultures superimpose their memories and religious beliefs onto concrete locales through rites of commemoration. From these studies, Halbwachs drew several fascinating conclusions about the nature and function of memory for groups.

First, Halbwachs observed that individual memory is attached to or embedded in one's membership in social groups. One does not remember in isolation but as part of a family, nation, and society, in a process of actual or imagined mutual verbal construction and elaboration. He observed, "One cannot think about the events of one's past without discoursing upon them. But to discourse upon something means to connect within a single system of ideas our opinions as well as those of our circle."[38] In the course of that discursive process, the presence of the other is crucial to retrieving and making sense of our memories. Halbwachs used the metaphor of crystallization to illustrate the dependence of individual memory on the surrounding community. He wrote, "Just as we must introduce a small particle into a saturated medium to get crystallization, so must we introduce a 'seed' of memory into that body of testimony external to us in order for it turn into a solid mass of remembrances."[39]

Here he made a fundamental departure from Freud's understanding of the self and of memory. Freud perceived memory to be stored in the individual psyche, the access to which was blocked by screen memories and other forms of repression. In a groundbreaking move, Halbwachs expanded the sources and processes of memory to the external and the social world. He wrote, "There is thus no point in seeking where [my memories] are preserved in . . . some nook of my mind to which I alone have access: for they are recalled to me externally, and the groups of which I am a part at any time give me the means to reconstruct them."[40]

Key to this understanding is the concept of *social frameworks*. For Halbwachs, social or collective frameworks attach to space and time in ways that give groups common perspectives, sets of boundaries, continuity over time, and coherent identities. The social framework functions much like the plot summary of a novel; it is the set of essential images of past events, and the relationships linking them that determine the ordering of those images. Halbwachs drew on his work with Holy Land commemoration to

38. Halbwachs, *On Collective Memory*, 53.
39. Ibid., 25.
40. Ibid., 38.

consider how images became localized within physical landscapes. He also noted that individuals might be members of multiple groups at the same time and thus interpret their memories through differing frameworks.

Within families, Halbwachs compared the framework to a suit of armor, which preserves and protects the family.[41] One aspect of the way that remembering happens in families, Halbwachs observed, is by way of a summation of multiple recollections into a prototypical scene. As we remember a specific scene of, for example, our parents' marriage, we reconstruct it, combining elements borrowed from several periods, which may have actually gone before or followed the scene. Rather than letting this human tendency undermine the veracity of our memories, Halbwachs argued that this consolidation of memories into a composite image gives a "gripping abbreviation"[42] that captures the essence of one's parents. Middleton and Brown summarize, "We may consider these shared summative prototypical images as akin to the knots that hold the network of relationships together and through which our individual acts of remembering are obliged to pass."[43]

Halbwachs's insights are foundational for current work being done on shared reminiscing as a process of group identity construction. John Meacham, who has studied the dynamics of group reminiscing, notes, "The points of memories determined by one individual who is constructing a . . . meaningful narrative have little value; value accrues when the lines or meaningful narratives constructed by two or more individuals intersect to yield shared reminiscences that become the basis for further dialogue, shared feelings, and cooperative action."[44] Meacham's metaphor of the lines that individuals draw in the process of discourse, and the points of intersection and meaning that emerge, builds upon Halbwachs' theory that memory takes shape in the process of discourse. As ethnically diverse churches seek to grow in knowledge of one another through becoming communities that make space for reminiscence, the works of Halbwachs and of Meacham both provide intriguing insight into that endeavor.

Halbwachs also pondered the way that the needs of the present influence how groups select events to commemorate. Societies, families, and minority groups within nations highlight events that perpetuate their social

41. Ibid., 59.
42. Ibid., 60.
43. Middleton and Brown, *Social Psychology of Experience*, 40.
44. Meacham, "Reminiscing," 44.

cohesion, their myths of origin, and their values and goals. This in turn perpetuates a common outlook or worldview, giving a group durability and cohesion. He wrote, "Collective frameworks are . . . precisely the instruments used by the collective memory to reconstruct an image of the past which is in accord, in each epoch, with the predominant thoughts of the society."[45] Misztal credits his work as groundbreaking for sociology, writing, "His assertion that every group develops a memory of its own past that highlights its unique identity is still the starting point for all research in the field."[46] It is important to notice here that in Halbwachs' work, not only are groups defined by what they remember, but equally or more importantly, by what they forget.[47] Halbwachs extends this concept to the ways groups survive physical displacement from the land that had served as a reinforcement of social memory for them. In their new locale, they employ a dynamic grafting process of selection and disposal of the elements they find around them, both remaking the new space in the image of their past and adapting to it in ways that expand and reshape their common identity.

Critique of Halbwachs

Some critics of Halbwachs have accused him of sociological determinism, sensing in his writings a collectivist understanding of consciousness itself, such as appears more clearly and prevalently in the thought of Durkheim and Carl Jung. Does Halbwachs conceive of the group as an ontological unit that actually performs the task of remembering? Does he thereby negate the role and active agency of the individual? Some interpreters of Halbwachs argue that he does. Fredric Bartlett saw in Halbwachs's writings a tendency to attach an almost mystical soul to collective memory, though many see this as an early misreading of Halbwachs's work on Bartlett's part. Certainly, Halbwachs sees the individual as only capable of remembering within a collective context, and this was a radical departure from dominant understandings of memory.[48] And, Halbwachs does at times describe

45. Halbwachs, *On Collective Memory*, 40.

46. Misztal, *Theories*, 51.

47. Middleton and Brown assert, "Forgetting is an active process of disposal that is rigorously applied within the collective framework and subtends collective remembering. We might even say it is the central issue in Halbwachs' thought" (*Social Psychology of Experience*, 52).

48. Halbwachs writes, "It is in this sense that there exists a collective memory and

the collective memory as a substantive entity with an existence, which has struck many critics as a quasi-mystical and logically indefensible position. For example, he asserted, "Now that we have understood to what point the individual is . . . dependent on society, it is only natural that we consider the group in itself as having the capacity to remember, and that we can attribute memory to the family, for example, as much as to any other collective group."[49]

Critics have also questioned Halbwachs's odd-sounding concept of individuals that are remembering together as "vibrating in unison." He does sound a little strange: "Often we deem ourselves the originators of thoughts and ideas, feelings and passions, actually inspired by the group. Our agreement with those about us is so complete that we vibrate in unison, ignorant of the real source of the vibrations."[50] While this strikes some as esoteric, others point out that here Halbwachs shows insight into the nature of the individual in society, and the ways that individuals experience the duration of time together. Middleton and Brown comment, "We might say that the time of our own life includes within it others' interdependent durations through and with which we endure. Remembering, then, involves a turning around on these 'virtually coexisting durations.' This is the wider import of [Halbwachs' statement about vibrating in unison]."[51]

Others raise the concern that Halbwachs, in his positing of a collective memory, has made a logical fallacy by extending assertions about individuals to groups without sufficiently noting the differences between the two. Noa Gedi and Yigal Elam state this concern strongly, writing, "All 'collective' terms are problematic—and collective memory is no exception—because they are conceived of as having capacities that are in fact actualized only on an individual level . . ."[52] While it may be that at points Halbwachs overstated his case, his refusal to dichotomize individual and group remembering allowed him to explore in groundbreaking ways the preservation and construction of memories, through discourse, localization, and social frameworks.

---

social frameworks for memory; it is to the degree that our individual thought places itself in these frameworks and participates in this memory that it is capable of the act of recollection" (*On Collective Memory*, 38).

49. Ibid., 54.

50. Ibid., 44.

51 Middleton and Brown, *Social Psychology of Experience*, 227.

52. Gedi and Elam, "Collective Memory," 34.

Some scholars seem to have even gone beyond Halbwachs. Michael Schudson boldly asserts, "I take the view that, in an important sense, there is no such thing as individual memory. . ."[53] Here he may be simply extending Halbwachs' theory that recollection is never purely preserved and accessed from within the interior mental life of an individual. Schudson goes on to argue that knowledge is located more firmly in institutions, cultural practices, monuments, and markers of time than in individual minds, and that memories are expressed in the social construction of language prompted by social interaction. They take shape through social patterns of recall to such an extent that it is difficult to speak of individual memory at all. Schudson's wording may be too extreme. The lines separating individual and communal remembering certainly blur, but they do not entirely fade. It remains important to preserve the role and agency of the individual in interpreting and constructing his or her past, and Halbwachs saw this need as well.[54]

Others have criticized Halbwachs for viewing memory almost entirely as a stabilizing, homogenizing process in the life of social groups, thus overlooking the contested and dynamic process that occurs in social construction of memories. Halbwachs writes, "Society tends to erase from its memory all that might separate individuals, or that might distance groups from each other."[55] One can quickly think of exceptions to this assertion, and those who see social memory as a site of contestation find numerous examples throughout history. Many who draw on Halbwachs's seminal ideas have also distanced themselves from the sense (which may be an oversimplification of Halbwachs) that every member of a given group carries an identical representation of the past.

Bartlett and Vygotsky

Two psychologists, Frederic Bartlett and Lev Vygotsky, also made valuable contributions to the growing understanding of the dynamics of social remembering. Bartlett studied memory as a psychologist, but his work caught the attention of many in the field of anthropology and sociology as

53 Schudson, "Dynamics of Distortion," 346.

54. Halbwachs writes, "While the collective memory endures and draws strength from its base in a coherent body of people, it is individuals as group members who remember" (*Collective Memory*, 48).

55. Ibid., 183.

well. Bartlett worked in conscious distinction from assumptions that were foundational to Ebbinghaus's memory research, with its isolation of the individual from all social variables. He investigated the ways individuals and groups "conventionalize" new material through a process of borrowing, modifying, and adapting it to what is known and familiar. Thus, culture becomes the site of a dynamic, interactive process of the construction of meaning. Middleton and Brown summarize, "Bartlett's concern with the conventionalization of cultural materials aimed to show that access to the past is never direct—it always passes by way of a set of resources that are derived from the broader cultural and social landscape. These resources then inevitably shape and restructure whatever is remembered."[56]

In testing his hypothesis, Bartlett asked people to recall a Kwakiutl story, "The War of the Ghosts," that was deliberately told in a vague and ambiguous way, at least as it would be heard in a British context. He then asked listeners to recall it as fully as they could. As they recounted it, Bartlett noted that they made what he called an "effort after meaning." They omitted, amplified, and explained the unintelligible parts of the story, organizing the elements in ways that reflected their worldview. They deviated from the original story in ways that reflected their existing categories for understanding it. Like Halbwachs, Bartlett stressed that what is excluded in that process, or forgotten, is just as noteworthy as what is selected and remembered.

Another key insight that Bartlett stressed even more than Halbwachs was that we reconstruct the past in a discursive process, in the course of conversation. He wrote, "We discuss with other people what we have seen, in order that they may value or criticize our impressions with theirs. There is ordinarily no directed and laborious effort to secure accuracy. We mingle interpretation with description, interpolate things not originally present, and transform without effort and without knowledge."[57]

Lev Vygotsky was a psychologist working in the Soviet Union in the 1920s. He emphasized that all human interaction is mediated through tools such as language. Individual memory is mediated through symbolic systems in the surrounding culture. As Mary Susan Weldon interprets Vygotsky, "Interpersonal processes and mediational tools are products of sociocultural evolution and so are situated in the larger sociocultural

56. Middleton and Brown, *Social Psychology of Experience*, 29.

57. Bartlett, *Remembering*, 96.

context, in both their external forms and internal forms."[58] With Halbwachs
and Bartlett, Vygotsky saw the crucial role played by language, narrative,
and discourse in the remembering process. Memory is made possible only
through engagement in the social practice of storytelling and other forms
of shared memory construction.

THREE THEORIES OF SOCIAL MEMORY DYNAMICS

Three approaches to the *function* of memory in societies have emerged in
scholarly discourse. The work of Halbwachs, Bartlett, and Vygotsky has
established some of the *means* by which individuals remember in a social
context, and that we may fruitfully and reasonably speak, at least meta-
phorically, of societies remembering together. But, in proposing a homiletic
that shapes practices of remembering well together for ethnically diverse
churches, I argue that the way those societies narrate their memories has in
turn a shaping influence on the quality of their communal life. Those habits
of remembering affect their capacity to interact with other communities
and to hear and interpret Scripture. In building this argument, it is useful
to listen to theorists of social memory who attend to the political dynamics
that are at work as states and their citizens engage in the selection and narration of momentous events. Widely varying schools of thought have arisen
out of debates concerning the relationship between memory and history,
historiography, and political theory.

  While Halbwachs, like most scholars of his time, saw memory as
prone to distortion, in his view history, with its critical distance and objectivity, was an endeavor marked by accuracy. This modern, positivist approach to history, with its assumption of objectivity and accuracy, has lost
ground dramatically in recent decades. Postmodern thinkers have insisted
that all history writing is a hermeneutical endeavor, with the legitimation
of certain sociopolitical goals always lurking nearby. As British historian
Peter Burke writes, "Remembering the past and writing about it no longer
seem the innocent activities they were once taken to be. Neither memories
nor historians seem objective any longer. In both cases, we are learning
to take account of conscious or unconscious selection, interpretation and
distortion."[59] Does that process emanate primarily from the state, from elite
members of society, or from the masses? To what extent do those in power

58. Weldon, "Remembering as a Social Process," 74.
59. Burke, "History as Social Memory," 98.

control the memories of a nation or community, and to what extent do collective memories emerge in a process of contestation?[60] We see starkly differing perspectives on these issues in the presentist approach, the Popular Memories Group,[61] and the dynamics of memory approach.

The Presentist Approach

Presentist understandings of social memory emphasize the way that memories function to serve the needs of the present for those in power. Halbwachs used a presentist approach in his work on Holy Lands topography, arguing that the beliefs and interests of the present determined the view of the past, as exemplified in cartographers' work.[62] Historians working within this milieu have studied the way nations have invented traditions and mythologized heroes in efforts to define national identity and strengthen unity and patriotism. Radical social constructionists would closely align themselves with presentists in their understanding of the social forces at work in defining what we remember. Halbwachs would qualify as a presentist, though the locus of power for him is not always the state. In his Holy Lands work it is religious groups. Historians working within this framework have cited an impressive array of examples of invented traditions used in the formation of national consciousness in modern Europe, modern Israel,[63] and the United States. The movement has raised awareness of the way that ruling elites may manipulate truth. Yet their viewpoint tends to be so cynical as to overlook the *limits* to which actors in the present can manipulate the past. The past is

60. One of the most striking examples of a state's efforts to suppress memory is the *Edict of Nantes*, issued by Henry IV in 1598 to end the French Wars of Religions.
Article 1 reads, "Firstly, let the memory of all things that have taken place on both side from the beginning of the month of March 1585 up to our arrival on the throne, and during the other preceding troubles and on their occasion, remain extinguished and dormant as something that has not occurred."
Article 2 includes this command: "We forbid any of our subjects regardless of their state or quality to retain any memory thereof, to attack, resent, insult, or provoke one another as a reproach for what has occurred…under penalty, for those who contravene this decree, of being punished as violators of the peace and disturbers of the public tranquility" (cited in Ricoeur, *Memory*, 454).
61. This school of thought is capitalized because it is (or at least has been) an actual group, working out of the Centre for Contemporary Studies in Birmingham, England.
62. See Halbwachs, *On Collective Memory*, 193–235.
63. See for example Nachman, *The Masada Myth*, cited in, Rodriguez, "What is 'Historical,'" 4.

not a limitless and endlessly pliable resource, and members of a society are not so easily deceived regarding that past. The presentist perspective may inadvertently fall into paternalism, as it tends to view the many members of society who do not comprise the elite as naïve and docile.

Presentist approaches fall prey to circular reasoning, due to their radical focus on the present as the source of the past. Their skepticism toward those in power is often rightly placed. But their view overlooks the power within people to resist state-imposed narratives, to fight for and perpetuate their understanding of "what happened," and the limits to the malleability of the past.

The Popular Memories Group

The Popular Memories Group shares a strong sense of the politicized nature of memory, but it turns its attention to the local memories of common people. It would hold a less deterministic view of the role of the state and its capacity to manipulate and control citizens. The writings of Michel Foucault have informed some thinkers in the popular memory stream. He developed the concept of the counter-memory, which arises from the marginalized in the oral forms such as song and story, and resists the dominant formulation of the past, with its totalizing narrative. Yet, many in the Popular Memory Group find Foucault, like the presentists described above, to be too pessimistic about the capacity of the marginalized to effectively shape society. The Popular Memory Group sees a more dialectical relationship between "popular" and "dominant" narratives.

Dynamic Negotiation

A third group of scholars, who theorize memory as a process of dynamic negotiation, find both presentist theories and those of the Popular Memory Group too cynical and pessimistic, and the latter too focused on contestation. Misztal writes, "Since the popular memory perspective assumes that conflict is the natural state of society, it dismisses the possibility that the politics of memory can be consensual *and* conflictual."[64] Dynamic negotiation theorists see less opposition between memory and history. While the first two theories focus on memory *distortion* for the sake of stabilizing and

---

64. Misztal, *Theories of Social Remembering*, 67.

legitimating systems of power, the dynamic negotiation school of thought approaches the representation of the past in a more nuanced way. It neither reduces history to the complete invention of a state or a society, nor does it hold that varying interpretations may be completely suppressed by those in power. Misztal notes approvingly, "This perspective runs a lower risk of reifying collective memory as it is aware of the flexibility and ambiguities of memory and because it incorporates conflict, contest, and controversy as the hallmarks of memory."[65] These scholars focus less on commemorative rituals and monuments, which tend to build stability and cohesion, and more on narrative practices, which are more open to a dynamic process of adaptation and interpretation. Stories are told in an ongoing process of negotiation between the hard data of historical records and the vivid impact of wounds suffered, between past and current political goals, and between elite and popular viewpoints.

TENSIONS AND PROBLEMS IN SOCIAL MEMORY STUDIES

Here we will summarize several tensions that have emerged in our exploration of memory. In the course of that summary some initial implications for multiethnic congregations, and the proclamation that shapes them, will emerge. Let's consider four problems of memory.

1. Memory as Individual and Social

A persistent question in any discussion of social remembering is the extent to which one can properly conceive of remembering as happening at a level beyond that of the individual. As the historical survey noted, for most of the centuries in which philosophers have reflected on memory, they have considered it within the framework of the individual, an interior phenomenon within an individual's consciousness. Ricoeur calls this "the tradition of inwardness," which began with Augustine, with Augustine drawing upon the thought of Plato and Aristotle.[66] Ricoeur makes the point that, after all, "Memory does seem to be radically singular: my memories are not yours.

---

65. Ibid., 73.

66. Ricoeur writes, "Augustine is at once the expression of this tradition and its initiator. He can be said to have invented inwardness against the background of the Christian experience of conversion" (Ricoeur, *Memory*, 97).

The memories of one person cannot be transferred into the memories of another."[67] As was noted in critique of Halbwachs, collective memory studies have had difficulty pinpointing with clarity and precision the ways that the emotional and intellectual dynamics of individual remembering can function as an analogy for corporate remembering.[68] Yet, Halbwachs and others have made a profound contribution to our understanding of the ways that societies carry the past together into the present.

2. Memory's Spontaneous and Intentional Qualities

To what extent does memory come to us unbidden, and to what extent is it shaped by intentional practices? Ricoeur (following Henri Bergson) uses the pair of terms, "*evocation and search*"[69] to explore this point. Because our focus here is on memory as a habit or practice, we could overlook the power in spontaneous memory. Memories that we invoke with no conscious effort, such as the procedural habit memories that allow us to start a car, are essential to our capacity to function as human beings. Memories of delightful events in our past that spring to mind unexpectedly and without conscious effort are sources of deep joy and satisfaction, and part of our identity as well. Memories of trauma that emerge unbidden by any conscious process are also a significant, though more problematic, component of our identity. In emphasizing memory as a practice, it is important not to eliminate the power and mystery of spontaneous, unbidden memory.

Yet remembering does also take place through a conscious and sometimes laborious process of searching and recovering. It is winsome to hear Augustine pray, as he recalls his past and its meaning, "O Lord, I am working hard in this field, and the field of my labors is my own self. I have become a problem to myself, like the land which a farmer works only

67. Ibid., 96.

68. Kansteiner writes, "Since the threshold between the individual and the collective is often crossed without any adjustments in method, collectives are said to remember, to forget, and to repress the past; but this is done without any awareness that such language is at best metaphorical and at worst misleading about the phenomenon under study . . . These category mistakes stem from a subtle but decisive confusion of the difference between 'collected memory' and 'collective memory'" ("Finding Meaning in Memory," 185–86).

69. Ricoeur, *Memory*, 26. Here Ricoeur draws on Aristotle's distinction between the *mneme* (the memory as the thing remembered) and *anamnesis* (the process of returning to a memory by calling it to mind), which Aristotle makes in *De Memoria et Reminiscentia*.

with difficulty and at the cost of much sweat . . . I am investigating myself, my memory, my mind."[70] Remembering is both a field we plow with difficulty and one in which we may inadvertently stumble upon treasures and occasionally landmines. Spontaneous memory can be shaped, nurtured, and undergirded by habits formed through catechesis in the community of faith, as we will discuss in chapters 6 and 7.

3. Social Memory as Stabilizing and Disruptive

Some scholars emphasize the ways in which societies remember their pasts to stabilize and preserve their culture and further national goals. Many, including Halbwachs, see the past and its shared remembrance primarily as a source of unity and cohesion for groups. Memory is a fundamental ground of shared identity, an anchor of continuity. The narration of the past involves selection, which inevitably simplifies and narrows perspective. Groups in turn are limited in their outlook or worldview by the scope and plot of those shared memories. Groups are also shaped indelibly by the events themselves, which by and large really happened. For all the malleability and contestation of the past as it is represented in much current discourse, the past has a remarkable intractability to it as well. Survivors of genocide who immigrate to North America have been shaped and united by that event. Their narrations of that trauma will display a high level of internal similarity, as will their ensuing worldviews.

Yet memory does not always function to stabilize. Current scholarship notes the dynamic, contested, and even disruptive nature of social memory. Memory, like culture itself, is best viewed as a process, rather than reified as a static container, as many metaphors throughout its history have portrayed it.[71] Within that process, systems of power play a strong role in determining whose voices will be heard. Memory, whether social or individual, is prone to distortion and loss, and it is also capable of recovery and reinforcement by new generations and by marginalized groups within communities, who unearth and give voice to narrations that challenge the status quo. Not only are groups shaped by their memories, but groups also actively shape and refine their collective memories in ways that discard some meanings and

70. Augustine, *Confessions*, 222–23.

71. This is not to argue that place metaphors have no value, nor to denigrate the fine thinking of Plato and Augustine. Chapter 6 will speak highly of Augustine's contributions, which draw upon classical philosophers.

allow new meanings to emerge. Roles may change, events may be rein-
terpreted, and new characters may enter the plot. The same event may be
narrated in multiple ways within a community. This may strengthen the
community, as it learns to welcome alternate readings of its past, or it may
lead to division as new narrations threaten cherished traditions.

Too much focus on the unifying function of the past for specific
groups can lead to a low view of the possibility of uniting across cultures,
since subcultures are viewed as internally similar and highly distinct, and
thus less interpenetrable. The very presence of dissent within groups may
provoke dialogue beyond that group, as members seek perspectives that
can enlarge their interpretation of their past. Ideally, congregations could
function as third cultures that create a space for this kind of interaction
and mutual enrichment to occur, where the narratives of one ethnic group
could correct, enlarge, and inform those of another. This could allow members of an ethnic group to make choices to narrate their histories in ways
that connect them to other groups. When local and particular stories are
placed within the proclamation of a Christian narrative of creation, suffering, and redemption, they might provoke points of resonance and solidarity between members of diverse ethnic communities gathered for worship.
Preachers in these settings need a homiletic that casts the narratives of
Scripture in ways that resonate with, and inform, the stories represented by
their gathered listeners.

4. Memory's Power to Heal and to Harm

The fourth tension is this: on the one hand, we note that social remembering may serve a healing and strengthening role in the life of a society.
Commemoration can interpret past traumatic events in ways that integrate
the past and articulate a meaningful future. Storytelling and ritual performance can function to welcome and incorporate new members, instilling
in them the story that shapes their community. Remembering together can
be a moral practice as societies seek to bear witness truthfully to the suffering they have endured and inflicted, and to name pain in ways that honor
and grieve with those who have suffered. Courageous testimony of this sort
draws upon and demonstrates the inherent strength within a community
and in turn builds its strength. It is enriching to a community's life to hear
the narration of the joys of the ethnic groups in their midst as well. As
members of various ethnic groups reflect on the values of their group that

they treasure, such as respect for the elderly or generosity with time, those values may be brought into the common life of the congregation, enlarging the collected memory of everyone present.

Yet, history has demonstrated all too often that groups are capable of remembering poorly, distorting events, or perhaps remembering facts accurately but drawing conclusions from them in ways that isolate them, closing down dialogue with other groups, whether families or nations. They remember in order to define themselves in stark distinction from others, to segregate themselves from others and keep enmity alive.[72] States and powerful elites within a society can exert influence toward practices that ignore, actively suppress, and distort social memories. This in turn legitimates oppressive ideologies through nostalgic, mythological portrayals of national heroes, erasure of victims of societal cruelty, and exaggeration of the wrongs done by outsiders. Truthful remembering would constitute a threat to many current social and political arrangements and to some ecclesial ones as well. However, those outside of positions of authority are neither innocent nor entirely powerless in this process either.

CONCLUSION: REMEMBERING TOGETHER IN THE MULTIETHNIC CHURCH

Bearing these tensions in mind, let us begin to consider here some of the challenges and opportunities that arise when diverse groups of people choose to try to remember their past(s) through the framework of the church, a community of memory that does its remembering around an altar, illuminated by the word. One challenge that the study of social memory dynamics brings to the fore is that individuals who have memories that are quite different from the bulk of congregants may find it difficult to find a home in those settings. Such persons will rightly seek ways to honor and integrate their past and to bear witness to it, and if they only perceive that happening in a homogenous church composed of members of their own ethnic group, they will not be likely to be drawn to a multiethnic expression of faith. Many churches, while naming multiethnicity as a value and goal,

---

72. Booth writes, "The ills that memory-identity brings in its train are many . . . The capacity of collective memory to keep alive ancient hatreds, or to be used to cloak newly manufactured ones in the guise of something old, has fueled conflict around the globe. Memory keeps the 'wounds greene' and the embers of conflict growing" (*Communities of Memory*, 177).

have overlooked the shaping power of the past and the ongoing demands of that past on their members. Those leaders who argue that people of various ethnic groups must foreground their unity in the shared project of ministry, obscuring their ethnic identity beneath their shared identity through new life in Christ, may be inadvertently severing people from their pasts in ways that cause loss of meaning and connection. Eric Mankowski and Julian Rapapport describe this pattern well, writing,

> Community and cultural narratives often fail to represent experiences that are part of an individual's personal stories: group norms may suppress or deny these stories and the aspects of identity that they represent. Without the validation of the community or culture through storytelling, these identities may be extremely difficult to experience and maintain. Individuals may attempt to seek out new narratives to support these identities. For example, when their experiences conflict with narratives of the church to which they belong, or when they have an experience that cannot be explained by, or integrated into, their personal story or the narratives of the church, people may seek out a different spiritual community.[73]

The above is a sobering call for congregations to seek out ways to honor and empower the disparate voices within a congregation. It points to the challenge and opportunity present in congregational life as well, to look for the work of the Holy Spirit within those disparate stories, to find ways to name and interpret it through the narrative of Scripture, and to speak a word from the pulpit and elsewhere that brings healing, joins members in solidarity with one another, and fosters faith within them.

We've surveyed the historical development of thought regarding memory and its relative value in societies across time. We've been particularly interested in theories of how societies remember together that have emerged in the past century, most notably in the work of Maurice Halbwachs. Theories of social remembering can inform an understanding of the congregation as a potential space for the dynamic negotiation of multiple contested memories. They can help us understand the potentially transformative roles of preachers and texts in the creation of a third culture where conversation about ethnic groups' pasts is welcomed and heard well. In seeking to integrate the insights gained above with homiletical theory, we note that postliberalism is well attuned to the power of social formation

---

73. Mankowski and Rappaport, "Stories, Identity, and the Sense of Community," 215.

through appeals to a memory held in common, that found in the world of the text. Some voices from within postliberalism would seem to relegate human experience to a place of insignificance in contrast or deference to the univocal world rendered by the scriptural text. This understanding would limit the capacity of the preacher to unearth more current, local, particular memories that may be going unheard in the life of the congregation. Attention to lived experience is a particular strength of the New Homiletic. The theoretical framework described above, that views social memory construction in a process of dynamic negotiation, holds the most promise as a resource for seeing scriptural texts and the narratives of lived experience in a fruitful relationship.

5

Means of Social Remembering

Place, Ritual, and Narrative

Groups utilize a vast array of means to organize, interpret, and even access their memories. Here we will look at three of those means: place, ritual, and narrative. These are the media and processes that hold, transmit, and at times even transform memory within nations and their subcultures. As tools, they are interdependent. Narratives impact rituals and give rise to new ones. Place is vulnerable to loss of meaning when unaccompanied by a remembered and retold narrative. Monuments depend for significance upon dedication ceremonies, which include rituals such as speeches and commemorative moments of silence, to interpret and reinforce their visual power. Narratives are strengthened and perpetuated by landscapes, festivals, and communal habits.

The cross-culturally savvy preacher will hold all this in mind as he or she tells the gospel story in a given context. Congregations narrate their histories through their buildings, informal storytelling, and annual events. All of this may reinforce our preaching, and sadly may at times undermine it. Growing our cultural intelligence quotient will help our preaching to land with greater impact.

PLACE

How do physical landscapes and commemorative objects within the built environment shape and sustain communal identity? Is it possible for monuments to "freeze" meaning in time, or is the interpretation of them a task that each generation must undertake? What is the impact of loss of place on the collective identity of a displaced ethnic group? We'll look at the functions, limits, and often contested nature of landscapes and monuments in creating and preserving collective memory.

The monuments that nations and groups make both reflect and shape their character and moral fiber. They also measure their collective will to bear witness to the past. Alan Kirk highlights the dynamic nature of commemorative practices when he writes, "The semiotizing dynamic of memory is energized by the present realities and crises of the commemorating community. As deep reservoirs of meaning, commemorative symbols seem inexhaustibly responsive hermeneutically to complexity and change in a community's social realities."[1] While Kirk's wording here (which he moderates elsewhere) could indicate a complete lack of tethering to historical reality in commemorative practices, he rightly notes the way that monuments and other commemorative practices are both the fruit of, and contributors to, constructions of the emerging identity of ethnic groups and nations.

Even at the level of individual remembering, psychologists have traditionally overlooked the depth of meaning that persons attach to their physical environments. Edward Casey's phenomenological study of remembering argues against memory research that takes place in sterile laboratories, seeking to isolate the purely cognitive dimension of memory. This disembodied perspective on the remembering process is rooted in modernist understandings of the body and of space as containers within which events occur. In contrast, Casey argues, "our experience *takes place in place* and nowhere else, so our memory of what we experience is likewise place specific: it is bound to place as its own basis."[2]

While Casey offers profound insights regarding place and the memory of individual experiences, two scholars who have contributed much to the role of place for societal or national remembering are Pierre Nora and Jan Assman. Nora identifies land, cathedral, and court as the archetypal *lieux de mémoire*, spaces intentionally designated as sites of memory. Nora notes

---

1. Kirk, "Social and Cultural Memory," 20.

2. Casey, *Remembering*, 182.

the loss of a *milieux de mémoire* in modern culture. The proliferation of sites of memory is in his estimation a response to the loss of real environments of memory, which he understands to be found in customs, folk traditions, and oral remembrance.

Jan Assman points out some of the limits of oral means alone for transmitting societal memories. Oral history in its everyday function (as opposed to epic ballads and other more formalized oral communication) has a limited range through which it may extend over time. Assman estimates that the temporal horizon of informal memory through oral communication does not extend beyond eighty to one hundred years from an event. When a society wants or needs to remember an event beyond that time frame, he argues, it must turn to concrete and formalized means. In contrast to the informality and fluidity of oral culture, texts, buildings, museums, monuments, and other objects exist as "objectivized culture." While some assume that in monument-making the endeavor has shifted from memory to history, Assman wants us to see that, "Objectivized culture [also] has the structure of memory."[3] Monuments, urban landscapes, and sacred sites reflect and render a community's knowledge of itself, in a form that Assman calls the concretion of identity. Groups found their consciousness of unity and uniqueness upon this knowledge, and from that concretion of identity they draw energy that shapes their values and transmits their identity to future generations.

While Assman looks to monuments to give more permanence to memories than oral history does, monuments are vulnerable to loss and decay as well. They may function to displace or "offload" memory, allowing us to escape our debts. William James Booth warns that they may serve, "not as a spur to remembrance but rather as a sequestration of the labors of remembrance."[4] They may become lost or absorbed in the landscape of a busy downtown area or be obscured when relegated to a remote rural site. They may fade in time as well. Each generation must choose whether or not to invest monuments with meaning. New generations may also significantly alter that meaning, by including other dead among those honored, by acknowledging their nation's share of blame more fully than previous generations had done, or by denying it. This is evident in the ongoing contestation of the meaning of Auschwitz for Jews, Catholics, and other Polish leaders.

3. Assman, "Collective Memory," 128.
4. Booth, *Communities of Memory*, 105.

Monuments, museums, sacred spaces, and other physical embodiments of memory have tremendous power to teach, inculcate values, and exhort to action. They can re-narrate a national defeat in ways that redeem its shame.[5] They may foster love of one's country, and may reinforce hatred of one's enemies. They may also reframe conflicts in ways that compel their observers to consider alternate interpretations that may spur movement toward reconciliation or propel other action towards justice. Our own nation's recent struggles to find adequate ways to commemorate some of our most tragic and defining events, whether in Vietnam or in Manhattan, show how powerful monuments can be, and the potential they carry both to wound and to heal. Our national interpretations of those events remain sites of contestation, showing how hard groups will fight to see their narratives of the past to prevail.

What shall those past events teach present and future generations? Whom shall they honor and whom will they vilify? Innocent-seeming monuments are politically and morally charged. Barry Schwartz, a historian who has chronicled the creation of the monuments around the United States Capitol, asserts that, "Commemoration lifts from an ordinary historical sequence those extraordinary events which embody our deepest and most fundamental values."[6] Ideally, they can serve as sites in which those who interact with them find a safe space in which to express their anger, grief, and loss. Yet some monuments err in resurfacing the trauma of the initial event in ways that do not lead to healing. Other commemorative structures gloss over pain in ways that leave some feeling that their part in the struggle was not sufficiently named and honored. The latter perceive that those who held the resources and authority to construct the monument, or to craft the words on the plaque accompanying it, did not acknowledge wrongs done to their people with truth and humility.

While not a permanent monument, a striking example of this contestation occurred in the mounting of a Smithsonian exhibit in 1991, titled, "The West as America: Reinterpreting Images of the Frontier, 1820–1920." This exhibit veered away from traditional renditions of the settlement of the West as a triumph of the pioneering spirit and brought to light the displacement of indigenous peoples, the environmental damage, and the

5. Elizondo notes the monument to "La Raza" in Mexico City and the striking inscription on the site of the final battles between Cortés and the Indian nations: "Neither a defeat nor a victory, but the painful birth of the *mestizo* people that is Mexico today" (*The Future is Mestizo*, 73).

6. Schwartz, " Social Context," 377.

commercialism involved. The reactions of museum visitors and members of congress ranged from praise to outrage, provoking a controversy the Smithsonian had not anticipated.[7]

This study of commemoration has primarily described what *tends* to happen, rather than what could or should happen as societies engage in identity construction through practices such as monument making. Later, we will look at how the disciplines of confession, repentance, and commitment to truth-telling could inform congregational practices of remembering the past, toward both solidarity and prophetic engagement with the ethnic groups in their midst. Whose memories are honored and whose are obscured, by the buildings congregations construct and the banners they hang? While consideration of place may seem peripheral to homiletics, it is a profound way through which communities are shaped and memories acknowledged or dismissed, one that pastoral leaders in ethnically diverse settings do well to bear in mind.

Church leaders must also attend to the implications of loss of place for the social remembering capacities and practices of immigrants to North America (and indigenous people who have been forcibly displaced). Displacement from one's homeland brings an inevitable measure of rupture with the past and threatens to erode identity. The journeys involved in that displacement are frequently fraught with danger and always involve loss, leaving displaced persons vulnerable to despair and a disintegrated sense of self. Commenting on land as a locale of memory and identity, Booth observes, "With the loss of these memory markers, those that form part of the basic fabric of a life-in-common, exiles lose part of themselves."[8]

James Nieman and Thomas Rogers reflect on the impact of displacement for immigrants. They assert, "Displacement separates us from the patterns that have been central to us, the strategies that have helped us mark off who we are . . . Displacement threatens the very core of what culture at its best seeks to provide."[9] Congregational life that reinforces cherished forms of piety from the home country of immigrants can make the church a welcome haven in an unfamiliar land, though there is of course a tension here, as those very immigrants do need to grow and change in how they experience God in their new land. Sermons have enormous power to shape how persons in the midst of loss might reenvision their lives as a journey

---

7. Cornell details this controversial exhibit in, "That's the Story of Our Life," 47–48.

8. Booth, *Communities of Memory*, 49.

9. Nieman and Rogers, *Preaching to Every Pew*, 86.

from loss to hope. Nieman and Rogers urge the use of parallel images of pilgrims and immigrants in Scripture, whose experience of meeting God in their journeys can name and reframe their own. Through such preaching, "Radical disorientation does not become the final word. Instead, the parallel shows a displacement whose end is renamed by God."[10]

RITUAL

Ritual carries immense power to reinforce and shape communal memory. Societies plot memory in temporal dimensions as well as spatial ones. Rituals reenact events in time, intensifying shared values and beliefs, and marking key transitions in human life and in a society's history, through physical performances. Bodies become holders of memories, liminal spaces between mind and place, as they engage in dance and other performances, gestures, and practices.

Rituals tend to be repetitive and stylized. Scholars of social memory, particularly those working in anthropology, have considered a broad range of ritual commemorative practices across many cultures, from calendars to festivals, from styles of clothing to gestures and dance. Paul Connerton argues that theorists of social memory have neglected a crucial aspect of performative remembrance, that of bodily practices. He argues that in our study of ritual, we have paid more attention to the content of the ritual, which builds cognitive memory, and not enough attention to its form. Bodily practices shape *habit-memory*, which has the capacity to inform and perpetuate the cultural memory of performers and observers.[11] He writes, "Habit is a knowledge and a remembering in the hands and in the body; and in the cultivation of habit it is our body which 'understands.'"[12] His insight has implications for the liturgical practices of churches, particularly as they welcome immigrants whose habit-memories of prayer and worship may be different from those they find in North American churches. How can churches encompass and give expression to the native habit-memories of recent immigrants and to the members of other minority groups, while

10. Ibid, 106.

11. See also the work of Bob Sitze, He observes, "In ritual, the brain creates habituated responses, which are the most efficient ways by which humans encounter the vast majority of life's circumstances. Habits are formed when repeated actions are interpreted by mindful reflection" (*Your Brain Goes to Church*, 35).

12. Ibid, 95.

building new habit-memories into the whole congregation? Scholars of intercultural liturgy such as Michael Hawn and Kathy Black have done excellent work to guide churches in this area.[13]

Rituals are inseparable from the body. They are also tightly linked to narrative. Rituals perform the dominant narrative of a community and are often accompanied by explicit verbal narrative. Narratives for their part often rely on rituals for visual reinforcement and performative impact. Stephen Crites writes, "For within the traditional cultures there have been some stories that were told, especially on festal occasions, which had special resonance. Not only told but ritually enacted, these stories seem to be allusive expressions of stories that cannot be fully and directly told, because they live, so to speak, in the arms and legs and bellies of the celebrants. These stories lie too deep in the consciousness of a people to be directly told: they form consciousness rather than being among the objects of which it is directly aware."[14]

Hebrew culture and early church communities abounded in such rituals; believing that they carried *anamnestic* power, the capacity to bring the past into the present in ways that reinforced the narrative of the community. Such rituals were and are thought to transform the experience of the present for participants, as is discussed in more detail in the following chapter.

Calendars link communities with their pasts in ways that set them apart from other communities, through the saints or heroes they honor, the events they mark as significant, and the festivals they specify. Often the festivals that honor significant days involve some form of reenactment, as in the Jewish festival of Purim and the church's enactment of the Eucharist. Significant days tend to mythologize beginnings or origins, as well as endings or transitions for the community. As Kirk observes, "Calendar organizes duration, and so it is the essential scaffolding both for situating and reconstituting memories."[15] Peter Burke, commenting on the prevalence of "memorial days," with their accompanying ritual actions in many nations, observes, "These rituals are reenactments of the past, acts of memory, but they are also attempts to impose interpretations of the past, to shape memory. They are in every sense collective re-presentations."[16]

13. See Black, *Culturally Conscious Worship*, and Hawn, *One Bread, One Body*.
14. Crites, "Narrative Quality of Experience," 69.
15. Kirk, "Social and Cultural Memory," 3.
16. Burke, "History as Social Memory," 101.

How does this happen in church? Ellen Tanouye discusses the role of festivals in the Japanese American church in transmitting identity, values, and traditions from one generation to the next. She notes the joyful nature of festivals, and thus their power to draw in, gather, and incorporate newcomers and young people. The annual *mochi* (rice) festival at the New Year serves as a time for church members to renew their covenant with God and each other. She notes that the pastor's sermon that Sunday "framed the *mochi* event theologically for the people."[17] During the making of rice cakes, elders told children stories about life in Japan and their early years of struggle as immigrants. Festivals are a way to celebrate and perpetuate the values and strengths of a culture, and when they can happen in the context of church, they have great potential to integrate ethnic traditions with faith in ways that honor and reinforce both.[18]

NARRATIVE

We've seen that narrative and ritual are interwoven, giving rise to and reinforcing each other. Narrative here refers primarily to the written and oral myths of origin and identity that describe past events in paradigmatic ways that shape and orient the worldview of individuals and societies and secondarily to the informal discourse regarding the past that occurs in daily interaction.

The role of narrative in social remembering is so pervasive that its themes have been implicitly discussed throughout the discussion of Halbwachs' and Bartlett's theories. When we consider the theological implications of social memory theory in multiethnic settings, the role of narrative will be crucial. That discussion may yield means by which to assess a society's ethnic narrative practices for their level of truthful bearing witness to the past, for their capacity to foster linkage with other ethnic groups, and for the ways they limit their members' interpretative capacities as hearers of Scripture. As Crites points out, "Narrative form is by no means innocent. It acknowledges and informs only what is contained in its own ordering of

17 Tanouye, "Festivals," 186.

18. In a multiethnic church, the number of ethnic-specific festivals it could sustain would be limited. One example of a congregation celebrating the specific culture of one population within it is Altadena Baptist, whose white and African American members work together to host a lecture series and other events during Black History Month (Interview with George Van Alstine, August, 2007).

events."[19] Preaching the narratives of Scripture in conscious dialogue with multiple ethnic narratives can both honor specific narratives and narrate the history of the congregation as an emerging *third culture* that draws its values and practices from Scripture as well as from its cultural sources.

Narratives articulate and shape the social memory of a community. Alasdair MacIntyre observes, "There is no way to give us an understanding of any society, including our own, except through the stock of stories which constitute its initial dramatic resources."[20] Current ethnic identity theory, with its emphasis on construction as a dynamic and evolving process, views narrative as central to that enterprise. As sociologist Stephen Cornell asserts, "Constructing an ethnic identity involves, among other things, a gradual layering on and connecting of events and meaning, the construction of a collective narrative."[21] How do groups select and plot the events that have shaped them? As is true of commemoration through monuments, control of the scope and nature of narratives frequently becomes a site of complexity and conflict. Let's start with a look at one particularly useful diagnostic type of narrative: the myth of origin. Then we will consider key questions: where does the story begin? Where does it end? In what order or sequence did events happen? And of those events, what is highlighted and what obscured?

Myths of Origin, and Other Beginnings

The myth of origin is a specific type of narrative, one that offers a unique vantage point for understanding a community's perception of itself, since it is often tacitly assumed to capture and define the essence of a society. These narratives portray the beginnings of a society, nation, or ethnic group, often through a triumph in battle or other adversity, in ways that demarcate those groups as distinct from others. In his discussion of the French and American revolutions, John Gillis writes, "Conceiving of themselves as standing at the starting point of a new era, revolutionaries on both sides of the Atlantic created a cult of new beginnings and, with it, a whole set of memory practices and sites that were as controversial then as they are today."[22] Congregations similarly sift through the salient features of their

19. Crites, "Narrative Quality of Experience," 82.
20. MacIntyre, *After Virtue*, 216.
21. Cornell, "That's the Story of Our Life," 42.
22. Gillis, "Memory and Identity," 8.

beginning and craft a story that reflects their values and outlook on the world. Minority ethnic groups within a nation do this as well in telling the story of their emergence as a distinct group. These myths do much to shape and define the character of those communities.

In addition to specific myths of origins, how a group chooses the beginning points of various plots within its ongoing history says a lot about its identity. Some disruption of equilibrium instigates the beginning of any new incident. But which disruption was it? It depends who is telling the story. For example, Michael Schudson notes that in the Russian narrative of World War II, the war begins in June 1941 with the German invasion of the Soviet Union. He notes that they could begin the war story in 1939 with the Hitler-Stalin Non-Aggression Treaty, but this is not the part of the story they choose to emphasize.[23] The point at which a nation portrays itself as entering into a larger story is indicative of its understanding of its role in that history, whether as victim or victor.

Narration of Endings

The chosen beginnings of narratives are indicative of a community's character and needs, and the accounts of endings of episodes reveal much as well. The closure of a story can perpetuate a myth of progress or one of decline. Different stories of the same event can conclude on a note of triumph over adversity or can highlight the tragic dimensions of its resolution. The overarching narrative of the West since the Enlightenment has essentially been one of progress, but some nations and peoples tell the same events within the framework of a tragic narrative. Stories of a society's struggles with other societies or nations may end in ways that invite further interpretation or in ways that close down the interpretive process. MacIntyre, describing the way myths inform our conceptions of the future, writes, "There is no present which is not informed by some image of some future and an image of the future which always presents itself in the form of *telos*—or of a variety of ends or goals—towards which we are either moving or failing to move in the present . . . Thus the narratives we live out have . . . a partially teleological character."[24] MacIntyre points to the visional component of stories, as they reveal and shape a community's sense of what constitutes a good person or a good society.

23. Schudson, "Dynamics of Distortion," 355.
24. MacIntyre, *After Virtue*, 215–16.

Plotting and Sequencing

How do the various events in the life of a people unfold meaningfully, and how do they articulate the causal relationships between them? Who benefits from choices regarding the sequence in which they are described? Who should play the key roles? Plotting is essentially a sense-making process, wherein disparate and seemingly random events and characters are associated in ways that give a semblance of internal logic and order, in part through attributing motives to actions, and connecting actions with outcomes. The story of an ethnic group is often the story of its significance within the larger society in which it dwells. Storytellers tend to fit events into classic templates such as comedy, tragedy, or adventure formats. James Wertsch highlights Paul Ricoeur's narrative theory when he points out, "A crucial fact about narratives as cultural tools is that they make it possible to carry out the 'configurational act' required to 'grasp together' sets of temporally distributed events into interpretable wholes or plots."[25]

Plotting is an evolving process for a society. While distance in time from an event may foster distortion and fading of memory, it may also offer perspective, and may grant room for the emergence of multiple perspectives, a discursive space that was lacking to those who directly experienced a traumatic event. Paul Antze and Michael Lambek write, "The meaning of any past event may change as the larger, continuing story lengthens and grows in complexity. As readers we are continuously re-exploring the significance of earlier episodes of the story in light of what transpires later, as we are caught up in the hermeneutic spiral of interpretation."[26]

Cornell argues that the process of plotting narratives comes into play particularly at times of *crisis* for ethnic groups. He writes, "The narrative process comes to the foreground in situations of rupture as groups try to make sense of new problems or opportunities, defend or assert claims, reframe identities, mobilize members for political action, or otherwise rethink who they or others are."[27] Shifting demographics in neighborhoods, changing immigration patterns, and international crises all contribute to the perception within an ethnic group that their identity is at a crossroads.

As was noted in the preceding chapter, theorists of social memory disagree over the extent to which elite and popular forces determine what

25. Wertsch, *Voices of Collective Remembering*, 27.

26. Antze and Lambek, *Tense Past*, xix.

27. Cornell, "That's the Story of our Life," 45–46.

a society emphasizes and foregrounds, and the extent to which the narrated past is invented. But they, along with political theorists, moral philosophers, and historiographers, all agree that the history of any culture is told through a process of selection. As Gordon Allport and Leo Postman's work on rumor transmission demonstrates, selection includes a process of leveling, or loss of some details, and sharpening, accenting the details deemed significant by the teller(s) of the story.[28] From the vast amounts of events that could be narrated, communities formally and informally select the events that they perceive to be significant and emblematic to their identity. As Booth comments on the selection process, "The contours of memory-identity, of recollection and forgetting, are jagged and uneven in the way that an autobiography would be. Some episodes stand out as identity-defining, as bathing all others in their light and investing them with a unifying meaning; some are not relevant."[29] Societies tend to select narratives that attract and hold attention and to edit those stories in ways that represent themselves positively.

Narratives must be interesting and compelling, and selection serves this end. It cuts through unnecessary detail and culls the most salient and interesting events. To capture the imagination of a society, narratives tend to feature appealing protagonists and clear villains. Michael Schudson notes, "Particular works of art or efforts at story-telling may live on in memory in ways that overwhelm less dramatic, less lucid, less epitomized, less narrativized ways of telling the past."[30] He offers the example of the Dutch foregrounding of the narrative of Anne Frank, which portrays the Dutch as resisters to Nazism and overlooks their high level of collaboration with Germany.[31] Even more striking is a study done in 1991, in which Germans were asked to name and discuss important events of the previous sixty years. Narrations of World War II focused on bombings and food shortages in Germany, and only *seven* of 728 respondents mentioned Jews at any point.[32] Michael Kammen makes a similar point about silences regarding painful aspects of history. He has analyzed news media during the two decades after the Civil War in North America, during which time strikingly little was written about the war or its causes. His theory is that,

28. See Allport and Postman, *Psychology of Rumor*, 75–98.
29. Booth, *Communities of Memory*, 52.
30. Schudson, "Dynamics of Distortion," 357.
31. Ibid, 357.
32. Schuman et al., "Collective Memories of Germans and Japanese," 439.

"Binding the nation together again . . . swiftly became the order of the day
. . . amnesia emerged as a bonding agent far preferable to memory." [33] All
three examples illustrate the way selection serves the ideals, interests, and
needs of those narrating the past.

CONCLUSION

Place, time, and narrative interact to give tools to society for its project of
remembering its past. All three integrate the past into the present, showing
how events in history have shaped a group's unique role in the world, given
its members a destiny, or perhaps have all but ruined their capacity to succeed. Monuments, festivals marked on specific cultural calendars, and local
stories all serve to set boundaries and delineate between cultures, since they
tell particular, not universal, stories and commemorate local tragedies or
victories. Yet they can cross boundaries as well. They can speak an intelligible word to other societies, one that builds empathy and understanding.
Garro notes the dialogic and relational goals in a group's narration of the
past, noting, "Recounting past experiences not only conveys information
about events in the world but also tells the listener something about the
kind of person we are. Telling about a past event allows us to relay what
matters to us and to impart how an event takes on meaning for us, [and] to
recreate an event so that the listener identifies with the teller's experience." [34]
Whether that telling takes place through the marking of time, the making
of a monument, or through story, identification on the part of the listener
or observer is a primary goal, desired though often unstated. Societies recount their pasts to shape and inculcate new members, be they immigrants
or younger generations, and to make an internally cohesive society. They
also may use that telling to open their society up to others.

Pastors who approach their congregations, particularly ones that
are new to them, as ethnographers approach cultures, bring a heightened
awareness of the ways cultures commemorate their past. Leonora Tubbs
Tisdale offers help in analyzing all of the categories of ritual, place, and
narrative named above, in one's congregation. Particularly helpful is her
set of questions to ask in plotting the storyline of a congregation. She urges
pastors to ask, "Who are the heroes, and who are the villains, as parishio-
ners recount their congregation's history? Where are the silences, and what

33. Kammen, "Patterns and Meanings of Memory Distortion," 334.
34. Garro, "The Remembered Past," 120.

can they teach us? What are the recurring metaphors and images? What vision seems to unite the members as they move into the future?"[35] Viewing one's congregation as an alien culture and oneself as an ethnographer has potential to invigorate a pastor's curiosity about the history/histories of the people he or she serves and leads. It has pitfalls as well, all the pitfalls of participation and observation that plague anthropology as a field, and in particular the danger of attempting to adopt the stance of an unbiased critic, standing outside and even above one's church.

Social memory studies can help pastors attend to the way that memories influence the listening capacities of all those to whom they preach.[36] This is shaped by the stories listeners bring with them to church. Mark Alan Powell draws on the literary critical term, *social location,* to describe differing interpretations of texts among listeners. What distinguishes his research, and makes it especially applicable here, is that he has worked not only with interpretation but also with actual remembering of texts. For example, he asked one hundred North American seminarians, a broad sample in terms of age, gender, race, etc., to read silently the Luke 15:11–32 pericope of the Prodigal Son and then recount it in pairs. One hundred percent mentioned that the young man squandered his money, while only six noted that a famine came upon the land. Repeating the experiment in St. Petersburg, Russia, he found that only 34 percent mention the squandering of money, whereas 84 percent mention the famine. Powell notes that in 1941, St. Petersburg endured a famine for 900 days, which caused the death of 670,000 people.[37] This detail would register in their minds with much greater force than in the minds of North Americans, for whom the concern was the reckless waste of wealth.

Powell seeks to heighten the sensitivity of pastors to the fact that listeners are engaged in a process of sorting input, prioritizing it, matching it to existing memories and worldviews, and rejecting or forgetting some or much of it. He notes, "They create a meaning that seems appropriate to them with little awareness of the extent to which their social location has

---

35. Tisdale, *Preaching as Local Theology,* 66–67.

36. Brueggemann writes, "The listening is done through certain sensitivities that may distort, emphasize, enhance, or censor, depending on the particular situation of the listening community. The listening community is engaged in a constructive act of construal, of choosing, discerning and shaping the text through the way the community chooses to listen" ("The Social Nature of Biblical Text," 128).

37. Powell, *What Do They Hear,* 11–16.

influenced that process."[38] One clear implication is that preachers need to become aware of their own social location as they attend to and interpret texts. They also need to become adept story-listeners, with ears attuned to the pain endured by individuals. Some of that pain comes from family, career, or physical illness. But an often overlooked dimension is the pain endured while in other countries, where some have endured famine, ethnic cleansing, repressive regimes, or civil war. Many have experienced displacement through immigration, and most have endured subtle or overt racism in North America. These experiences act as filters that sharpen their capacity to hear some texts and dull their capacity to hear others. Those who have grown up in ease, whose ethnicity places them at the center of cultural acceptance, also have sharpening and dulling filters through which they listen and recall. Nearly every listener also carries joyful memories that heighten his or her capacity to hear certain texts of promise and celebration. This diversity of backgrounds and listening capacities makes the preaching task rich and complex. Like the sower's seed of Mark 4, some meaning is inevitably lost. But more meaning is gained when congregations are working hard to listen together. As Justo and Catherine Gonzalez write, "A group of Christians with a particular social, political, and economic perspective, no matter how learned or earnest they are, can never listen to the entire message of Scripture with the same level of challenge, as a more diverse group."[39]

What narratives can connect a community's past to its future in ways that sustain it and provoke growth? What kinds of stories do the members of those ethnic groups need to tell and hear, particularly at times of dislocation? How can preachers connect the biblical narrative to the narratives of pain, dislocation, and oppression that simmer below the surface in their congregations? A homiletic that is conscious of the power of being recognized through story, and the honoring that comes when space is made for reminiscence, goes far to honor the many pasts represented in a diverse gathering. A homiletic of reminding can proclaim God's acts in ways that give new interpretive skills to those who listen, allowing them to incorporate the past into a larger narrative of God's grace and redemption. The preacher can provide key interpretive leadership to the congregation as he or she engages in a process of hearing, sifting, and retelling the various narratives that emerge from within the congregation. When the preacher

38. Ibid, 19.
39. González and González, "The Larger Context," 37.

brings the narrative of Scripture to bear on a particular incident, this can provide an interpretive framework through which other members may view their own story. The next chapter will provide theological resources for pastors as they engage in this task.

6

Theological Dimensions of Memory

So far we have looked at numerous ways memory can lead us astray, muddying the task of preaching and the pursuit of deep reconciliation. Secular scholars and theologians alike tend to focus on the fallibility of human memory,[1] both in its limitations within individuals and in the tendencies of groups toward distortion, repression, and nostalgia.[2] Memory is conceived largely as a tricky problem: it is fragile when it ought to be strong and tenacious when it ought to allow bitter memories to fade. The previous two chapters detailed many of the volatile dynamics afoot in social remembering.

Memory is begging for a second look, one that treats it as good gift. So we will here explore memory from a theological and biblical perspective, building on an overarching premise that remembering is, at least in part, an intentional practice that both reveals and in turn shapes the character and

1. Daniel Ben-Amos writes in defense of memory, "No longer the negative side of history, it is the bond that unites societies, creating images that attain the truth value of a symbol, even if deviating from facts. As such, collective memory becomes the creative imagining of the past in service of the present and an imagined future. For too long the exploration of memory, private and public, focused on its failure to document, maintain, and communicate events as they happened. Memory and the oral tradition that embodied it were regarded as suffering from an inherent failure to keep accurate records" ("Afterword," 298).

2. A striking example of distorted nostalgia in the Old Testament is the Israelite's memory of and longing for the fish and leeks of Egypt (Num 11:5).

spirituality of individuals and groups. We will focus on memory's capacities to further human flourishing—what Paul Ricoeur calls "happy memory."[3] Practiced well, memory grows our relationship with God and situates us rightly with one another.

Scripture portrays the human capacity to remember as a generous gift of God, a capacity that constitutes us as image-bearers of the God who remembers. God is described as at work to strengthen within the people of God specific shared memories and, just as crucially, to build into them the habit of remembering well. This will imbue them with tendencies toward worship and discipleship, and will equip them to engage in mission. After looking at that, we will take up two memory-related issues that arise in the Bible. Memory in Scripture has numerous problematic aspects that this chapter does not attempt to solve, such as the meaning of the Bible's references to God recalling someone at a discrete point in history,[4] the meaning of God forgetting sins,[5] and the seemingly vengeful command to remember and obliterate enemies such as the Amalekites.[6] Two themes that are of

3. Paul Ricoeur notes that in developing his philosophy of memory he is arguing, "against the tendency of many authors to approach memory on the basis of its deficiencies, even its dysfunctions . . . It is important . . . to approach the description of mnemonic phenomena from the standpoint of the *capacities*, of which they are the happy realization . . . Successful recollection is one of the figures of what we term, 'happy memory'" (*Memory, History, Forgetting*, 27–28).

4. This can raise the difficult question of what God's thoughts were toward those individuals and groups "before" that moment in which God recalls their suffering. God's remembrance within these narratives may be interpreted as the moment within finite history in which God takes action. See Noah (Gen 8:1), Rachel (Gen 30:22), the Israelites (Exod 2:24), Hannah (1 Sam 1:19), and Cornelius (Acts 10:4).

5. Though in fact, this chapter's disagreement with Miroslav Volf's advocacy of human and divine forgetting will necessitate some discussion of eschatological forgetting. On one level, the eternal and omniscient God forgetting anything is a logical impossibility. Yet God's merciful forgiveness of sins is portrayed at points in Scripture as so complete that God no longer remembers them: (Isa 43:25, 64:9; Jer 31:34; though see Jer 14:10; Rev 18:5). Edward Blair writes, "To forget . . . something is to let the past fall out of dynamic, conditioning relation to the present" ("An Appeal to Remembrance," 44). Blair's description of Shimei's begging King David for mercy forms an apt analogy to God's forgiving being characterized as forgetting. He writes, "When Shimei entreats King David not to remember his rebellious insults (2 Sam 19:19), he obviously does not expect the king to put them beyond his powers of recall but rather not to let the disloyal deed condition his actions toward the suppliant" (ibid., 43).

6. Exod 17:14–16; Deut 25:17–19. Miroslav Volf points out that at points in history militaristic Jews have used the command to conquer and kill Canaanites as justification for mistreatment of non-Jews. He writes, "The memories of the Exodus . . . properly understood, are not the problem; rather, decontextualized, thinned-out and distorted

more ultimate interest to the topic of multiethnicity in congregational life are the fear of being forgotten, and the salutary place for a kind of forgetting in movements toward healing and reconciliation between members of ethnic groups.

THE GOOD GIFT OF MEMORY

The Bible insistently portrays Yahweh as a God who remembers. Humanity has been given the capacity to remember as an essential way that we reflect God's image. To strengthen and shape lively habits of memory, the biblical writers sought to instill within their hearers enlarged capacities to imagine the past and participate in it. This in turn would lead hearers to give thanks, confess failings with humility, act in faith, discern wisely, and extend justice and mercy to others. While memories often spring to mind spontaneously, remembering is usually portrayed in Scripture as effortful and intentional labor. It involves the cultivation of habits through disciplined recitation, attention to narratives, wholehearted engagement of all the senses in various rituals and liturgies, and the marking of time in holy rhythms. In the New Testament, the church is called to remember through the lens of the death and resurrection of Jesus Christ, which is vividly called to mind in the Eucharist.

Divine Memory

God remembers, always and completely. As Brevard Childs notes in his comprehensive survey of memory in ancient Israel, the verb *zachor*, "remember," appears seventy-three times with God as the subject.[7] God's omniscience extends through eternity. God's being has infinite and eternal endurance and persistence through time, even as God transcends time. God's transcendence does not mean that God stands solely and aloofly outside of or above time. The incarnation makes this clear. As Robert Jenson puts it, "The true God is not eternal because he lacks time, but because he takes time . . . He is not eternal in that he secures himself from time,

---

versions of these memories are" (*End of Memory*, 95). He also asserts that, due to its sanctioning of excessive violence, "On its own, the Exodus memory is not a fully adequate framework for remembering rightly" (ibid., 110).

7. Childs, *Memory and Tradition*, 31. Childs is only counting instances in the *qal* form in this count.

but in that he is faithful to his commitments within time."[8] Commenting on Barth's description of the eternity of the triune God as "pure duration," Jenson writes, "That this duration is "pure" means that it is not broken, that nothing escapes God by receding into the past or not yet having come into reach from the future."[9] Because of this God's nature and actions have continuity and consistency, or what Israel praised as God's *chesed*, "eternal, steadfast love" (Ps 119:89–90; Isa 55:3). Richard Ginn's study of anamnesis notes that, "The recital of the acts of God in the past therefore acts as a statement of belief about God in the present. There was one history because there is one God. There was a continuous history because God has always been God."[10]

The Hebrew Scriptures proclaim repeatedly that God remembers, and is therefore faithful to, God's covenant.[11] Creation itself serves as a "remembrance" or visual goad to memory, as seen particularly in the rainbow serving to remind God of the Noahic covenant (Gen 9). Here, God models and demonstrates the way that creation is intended to function for humanity as a stimulus to memory, and to the faithfulness which that memory catalyzes for humanity. The priests and their clothing serve as reminders to God as well. God commanded Aaron to "bear before the Lord" on the shoulder-pieces of his ephod two onyx stones with the names of the children of Israel (Exod 28:12) as a remembrance for God. The priests understood that reminding God of his covenant and his people was an act of intercession, as is seen in Isaiah 62:6, where those who "remind the Lord" were exhorted not to rest until God established Jerusalem. Closely related to God's remembrance of the testament or covenant is God's remembrance of the land given to Israel (Lev 26:42), and of God's *chesed*, that loving kindness which is the source from which the covenant flows (Pss 25:6–7; 98:3).[12] In Luke, Zechariah celebrates God's remembrance of the covenant as he sees it unfolding in the event of John the Baptist's birth (1:72).

The Scriptures also celebrate that God remembers God's people. Being held in God's remembrance was understood to be necessary for a person's ongoing existence (Ps 8:5). While God holds God's people in remembrance constantly (Isa 49:15–16), God is also roused at key points to heightened

8. Jenson, *Systematic Theology*, 1:217.
9. Ibid.
10. Ginn, *Present and Past*, 14.
11. Gen 9:15; Exod 2:24; 6:5; 32:13; Lev 26:42; Ps 105:8, 42.
12. Clancy, "Old Testament Roots of Remembrance," 42.

remembrance. This fuels God's mercy and compassion toward humanity and is sometimes portrayed in quite subjective terms as occurring in response to complaints and pleas.[13] The plea for remembrance from the man on the cross beside Jesus was for both mercy and persistence, for life beyond his imminent death (Luke 23:42). God's remembering stirs yearning and passion within God (Jer 31:20). The prayers of the Psalter reflect a lively understanding of a God in dynamic relationship with God's people, a God who sees, hears, and notices, and who is deeply moved by that perception (Pss 25:6, 74:2, 89:47). Remembering provokes God to act to save and redeem. As Childs puts it, "God's remembering always implies his movement toward the object of his memory . . . The essence of God's remembering lies in his acting toward someone because of a previous commitment."[14] At key points in redemptive history, when the narrative notes that God remembers God's people, it indicates that a pivotal act of deliverance is about to take place.[15] God's remembrance of Israel's sin also indicates an inflection point in God's relationship with them, a point of judgment and reckoning (Jer 14:10; Hos 7:2). The Israelites, by drawing an analogy based on the forgetful idols that surround them, have forgotten that their God takes note of their sins and bears them in mind, and this has severely affected their patterns of relating toward God and their passion for holiness.

Human Memory in Augustine

Let's step back from Scripture for a moment to bring into the conversation one of memory's most astute champions and critics. Few have pondered and reveled in the gift of memory as thoroughly as Augustine, whose ruminations on this topic are found primarily in book 10 of the *Confessions,* and books 10, 11, and 15 of *De Trinitatis.* Humans reflect the nature of God when they remember, and memory is central to what makes us humans, in distinction from animals.[16] Augustine pondered the powerful means[17]

13. Pss 74:2, 22; 78:39; 89:51.

14. Childs, *Memory and Tradition*, 34.

15. Exod 2:24–25; 1 Sam 1:19; Judg 18:28; Pss 89:50, 105:42–43.

16. Certainly animals have a kind of memory, as Augustine points out. They can return to their nests, and can learn from past experience to avoid dangerous areas. See Augustine, *Confessions*, 10.18. But they lack the capacities of language, reason, and will (especially important for Augustine) required to order and put memories to use towards logical, ethical and spiritual processes. See also Augustine, *The Trinity*, 12.2.

17. The means of recollection for Augustine involved culling through the

by which memory collected and held in its vast storehouse not only past experiences but principles, skills, works of literature, scents, and other sensory perceptions.[18] Memory forms the springboard for any conscious action.[19] To the extent that we have stable natures and continuity of identity over time, that is due largely to memory.[20] It allows us to perceive duration, whether of a single musical note, a syllable,[21] or a lifetime. It allows us to anticipate the future.[22] J. Mourant goes so far as to say that, "For Augustine, memory is essentially duration and a spiritual power that both transcends and spiritualizes space and time."[23]

While Augustine's most famous metaphors for memory were the vast storehouse, the palace, or the open field, he was ambivalent about the aptness of these images, since he acknowledged that memory was not solely a spatial entity. He asked God, "Why do I ask in which area of my memory you dwell, as if there really are places there? Surely my memory is where you dwell, because I remember you since first I learnt of you, and I find you there when I think about you."[24] Augustine also developed the striking analogy of memory as the stomach of the mind (*venter animi*), a depository or holding space that can call to mind affections such as sorrow or joy without feeling that emotion in the present. Since this metaphor is a bit less palatable than those of the storehouse or palace, it has not gained the traction that they have in public discourse. But the stomach image is brilliant in its insight that memories are held, digested, and processed over time, eventually becoming useful to the whole body as nourishment. The image, with its distancing of memory's feelings from the mental sphere,

---

"innumerable images of all kinds of objects brought in by sense-perception." The will directs the mind toward the memory-image (*Confessions* 10.8).

18. Augustine, *Confessions*, 10.8–17 details memory's myriad capacities.

19. Ibid.

20. Augustine believed that memory would be part of our identity even after death (*Trinity* 14.4–5). But he was deeply aware of the complexity of desires and fears that form our identities and make them hidden from full comprehension.

21. Roland Teske cites Augustine's work with memory's perception of the duration of musical notes and syllables in *De Musica 6.5.10* (Teske, "Augustine's Philosophy of Memory," 155).

22. Augustine writes, "For we . . . see some of our thoughts about future things more clearly and more certainly, as thought they were very near; and we do this when we are able and insofar as we are able, by our memory which seems to pertain not to the future but to the past" (*The Trinity*, 15.7.13).

23. Mourant, *Augustine and Immortality*, 155.

24. Augustine, *Confessions*, 10.26.

also evidences Augustine's propensity to radically separate rational from emotional processes. This is reflected as well in his eschatological vision of the memory of evil, which will remain "accessible to apprehension by the mind," but will be "erased from their feelings."[25] Memory of human sufferings will continue; Augustine understands this to be crucial to our eternally singing the praise of God for God's mercy.[26]

Not only has God placed the capacity to remember within us, but God graciously and mysteriously *inhabits* human memory. "You conferred this honor on my memory that you should dwell in it."[27] Yet, memory, marred by the fall and limited by human finitude, cannot take us all the way to God. Augustine pondered the conundrum that he could not find God outside his memory, and yet memory itself had to be transcended in his quest for true life. He longed to go beyond memory to somehow reach out and touch, and cling to God. He prayed, "I will pass beyond even that power of mind which is called memory, desiring . . . to be bonded to you by the way in which it is possible to be bonded."[28] Augustine sought a connection with God at once more mystical and more tangible than memory. Edith Wyschogrod writes, "At the very juncture between the soul and God, Augustine has fallen back upon the most corporeal of senses, that of touch. What better metaphor for contact with the divine? . . . Yet despite this effort to go beyond memory, in a remarkable turnabout Augustine will be unable to transcend it."[29] Finally, after considering all the sins that sensory pleasures can bring, Augustine came to a place of resolution and hope as he reflected upon that most sensory of signs, the Eucharist. He concluded book 10, his masterful rumination on memory, by writing, "I think upon the price of my redemption, and I eat and drink it, and distribute it." Memory brought

25. Augustine writes, "There are two corresponding ways of forgetting evil. The learned scholar's way of forgetting is different from that of one who has experienced suffering. The scholar forgets by neglecting his studies; the sufferer, by escaping from his misery. The saints will have no *sensible* recollection of past evils; theirs will be the second kind of forgetfulness by which they will be set free from them all, and they will be completely erased from their *feelings*" (*City of God*, 22.30, italics mine).

26. Ibid., 22.30.

27. Augustine, *Confessions*, 10.26.

28. Augustine's ambivalence is striking here. He must rise above memory, and yet, "If I find you outside my memory, I am not mindful of you. And how shall I find you if I am not mindful of you?" (ibid., 10.17).

29. Wyschogrod, *An Ethics of Remembering*, 185.

him to the table, where his hunger for something he could touch and taste was at last satisfied.

Aware of memory's limits, Augustine remains its champion. In *De Trinitatis*, he honors and elevates memory, counting it as a one of the three fundamental elements of human nature that composed his psychological analogy of the Trinity, along with the understanding and the will.[30] Here, Augustine relates the will to love, and then relates that love to the Holy Spirit. Augustine understands will-love to be inseparable from desire or delight. He writes, "For without memory the gaze of thought has no object to return to, and without love it has no reason to return to it."[31] While pain or pathological obsession could also form reasons to return to a memory, Augustine's insight is profound. Love catalyzes and directs remembrance, and the practice of remembering fuels love. Augustine's vision of the interplay between love and memory illuminates Jesus' promise, noted above, that the Holy Spirit would remind his followers of Jesus' words. This promise is sent in the context of a discourse on the deepening relationship of love between God and his children, which will issue forth in obedience to his words. Jesus promises his followers, possessed as they are with fallible and faulty capacities for remembering, that the Holy Spirit will enter into such a dynamic and intimate relationship with them that the Spirit will actually speak into their minds—the memory of Jesus' words will strengthen belief in him (John 14:29; cf. Rom 12:2).

Functions of Human Memory in Scripture

Let's get back to Scripture and look at how God worked in the history of Israel and the church to form a community of memory whose identity and values would be shaped by the content and practices of remembering. We'll explore various capacities and disciplines that remembering facilitates for individuals and communities. The first capacity relates to a basic challenge that occasioned the writing of many of the books of the Bible, that of enlivening the memory of past events for a people who had not directly experienced them. The other capacities are qualities of faith and character that memory can strengthen in individuals and communities.

---

30. Augustine develops this analogy in books 10 and 11 of *The Trinity*.

31. Augustine, *The Trinity*, 15.21.41.

1. Memory Brings the Past into the Present

A key motivation for writing Scripture for many of its authors and editors was the need to incorporate hearers into the circle of those who could call that history *their* story. The writer of Deuteronomy[32] faced this challenge as he sought to relate the experiences of the exodus and wilderness years to a generation that could not directly access those events in memory. D. P. Veldsman observes, "It is now [the moment of Deuteronomy's writing] that memory takes on central theological significance as Israel encounters the same covenant God through a living tradition, as an actualization and re-interpretation of redemptive history."[33]

While not explicit in Scripture, rabbinic tradition holds that remembrance should provoke a high level of evocative intensity in each generation. In the words of Maimonides, "Each individual is obligated to envision that he, himself, left Egypt."[34] In some rabbinic understandings, not only are Jews enjoined to envision themselves in the Israelite past, but they are entreated to acquire a perception of history "as an ontical mode of time-in-the-present,"[35] such that they view themselves as currently and historically participating in the exodus from Egypt. Jewish theologian Arthur Cohen puts it this strongly: "The Passover Haggadah commands that every Jew consider himself as though he had gone forth in exodus from Egypt. The grammatical authority of the Haggadah makes clear that this is no meta-phor, whatever our wish to make apodictic language metaphoric. The authority is clear: I was really, even if not literally, present at Sinai. God contemplated my virtual presence there, thirty-odd centuries ago. The fact that history could not prevision and entail my presence is irrelevant."[36]

---

32. We here refer to "the writer of Deuteronomy" for the sake of simplicity, but recognize that many scholars believe Deuteronomy to be the work of multiple redactors over an extended period of time. See Thompson, *Deuteronomy*, 47–68.

33. Veldsman, "Remembering as Socio-Historic Dynamic," 11.

34. Spero cites The Rambam (Maimonides), *M.T., Hil. Hamets u-Matsah* in "Remembering and Historical Awareness," 59.

35. *A Conspectus of the Lectures of Rabbi Joseph B. Soloveitchik: Shiurei ha-Rav* cited in Spero, "Remembering and Historical Awareness," 63. Spero discusses the psychological dangers in certain Jewish practices of the fusion of past and present, as a potential "regression to a de-differentiated state of mind," such as is characterized by mentally disturbed persons, in "Remembering," 64–66. An important regulative parameter becomes the delimited rituals within which such a fusion may occur.

36. Cohen, *Tremendum*, cited in Berger, "Bearing Witness," 3:2,333.

Through narrative, ritual, and multisensory cues, families are en-joined in Scripture to perform the events of the exodus in such a way that they became conscious participants, members who belonged and who were thus constrained to the same level of obedience to the covenant as their an-cestors.[37] Throughout the Hebrew Scriptures, God finds occasion to remind his people that he brought them out of Egypt.[38]

Enfolding chronologically distant groups into an ongoing community of memory was not only a problem for the writer of Deuteronomy but was a challenge and goal for many other writers of Scripture. Philip Esler dis-cusses the strategy of the writer of the book of Hebrews, and specifically his choice of exemplary figures in Hebrews 11. The writer strives to create or reinforce a stock of common memories from the distant past that would locate and frame their recent suffering, and thus deepen and expand their corporate identity as members of the people of Israel and of the church. Es-ler writes, "The previous sufferings of the audience of Hebrews constituted a fertile ground for bringing personalities and events from the history of Israel into living connection with them."[39]

The author of Hebrews is engaged in reactivating the memory of these ancestors, enlisting them as partners in the work of identity construction and event interpretation that the Hebrews community must undertake. Bib-lical authors wanted their hearers to be gripped and shaped by that past. As John Hendrix writes, "At the core of anamnesis is the capacity to take hold of an event or occurrence from the historical past and to allow that event, occurrence or person to take hold of oneself."[40] Danièle Hervieu-Léger connects memory to imagination and hope when she notes, "In the Jewish and Christian traditions, the religious wresting of the past from history is given privileged significance by the core events being magnified in time."[41] Having considered the power of memory to bring the past into the present in significant ways, let's take a look now at several qualities that memory nurtures, according to the writers of Scripture. All are crucial to becoming people capable of participating well in healthy, diverse congregations.

37. Cf. Blair, "Appeal to Remembrance," 44.

38. Josh 2:10; Judg 2:1; 1 Sam 8:8; Ps 81:10; Jer 2:6, etc.

39. Esler, "Collective Memory and Hebrews 11," 159.

40. Hendrix, "Making the Trip," 420.

41. Hervieu-Léger, *Religion as a Chain of Memory*, 124.

2. Memory Fosters Humility

Memory preserves and fosters humility. Humility is nurtured by honest confession regarding one's past, and that of one's nation, culture, or ethnic group. The Scriptures call Hebrew worshippers to engage in a courageous and unsettling level of honesty about their humble origins. This truthful recitation is not something they ever move beyond. It forms a fierce shield against pride or complacency. Within the context of the offering of first fruits, which could become a source of pride in one's own ability to produce and offer up an impressive crop, worshippers are instructed to confess, "A wandering Aramean was my ancestor . . ." (Deut 26:5–10), narrating the story of their humble beginnings and of God's deliverance. The narration culminates in the proclamation that it is God, after all, who gave the land that produced the crop. Thus, as Ginn notes, "Remembrance in Judaism was a pattern of life which transformed chronicle into confession."[42] Humility sets the stage for a life lived in dependence on God as creator, provider, sustainer, and Lord. A more extreme example in Ezekiel involved God orchestrating the people's sudden and distressing remembrance of their sins, which had been buried in denial, and this truthfulness finally yielding the desired fruit of repentance and shame (Ezek 20:43; 36:31).[43]

The gospel writers modeled this type of humility for the early church by writing freely of their most shameful moments of failure to understand their Lord's words or to follow them. Particularly poignant is Peter's denial of Christ, which is ended just as his mind is flooded with the memory of Jesus' words foretelling that denial (Matt 26:75). Paul, who likewise freely confessed his own failings, was also eager for both Jews and Gentiles to remember their guilt and distance from God, prior to entering into the salvific work of Jesus Christ. He reminded Jews in Romans 3 of their shared guilt with Gentiles, and exhorted Gentiles in Ephesians 2:11–13 not to forget the alienation and hopelessness that characterized their past life. This call to remembering was an invitation to difficult and unsettling work, which undoubtedly met resistance.[44] This was a past the Gentiles would no doubt rather forget. K. Lyon, writing on the moral value of bearing in mind those

42. Ginn, *Present and Past*, 15.

43. Ezek 20:43, 36:31.

44. James R. Wilkes discusses the need for courage in remembering truthfully. He writes, "Courage is necessary for remembering because courage allows us to live in an ambiguous world without demanding absolute certainty, security, and perfection" ("Remembering," 89).

memories that "escape conventionalization," describes them in this way: "These are dangerous memories: memories which are threatening because they question the deepest values around which our sense of cohesiveness is organized. They appear to us as an unwelcome presence: an assault on our carefully hewn sense of self."[45] Such memories, filtered through the lens of God's redemption and grace, persist as a shield against sin,[46] complacency, and an exaggerated conception of the self.

Humility razes walls that separate groups, making reconciliation possible. The practice of confessional remembering forms a community that can tell the truth about itself, and in turn frees and equips that community for graceful association with other groups. As they become capable of acknowledging their past without justification and rationalization, their community becomes winsome and inviting to those who hear their story. Kyle Pasewark writes of the way confession of a shameful past, even one that is distant by some generations, can remind us of our common nature with the perpetrators of wrong. He writes, "There is a difference between remembering, on the one hand, that 'We, the likes of us do these things, and when we remember them, we are to remember the agency that belongs to us and our kind,' and recalling, on the other, that, 'You did this to me.' If the latter persists, we cannot escape the past. The former, however, allows the offense to pass into general social memory, to be a warning to all without hatred and retribution against any."[47]

3. Memory Fuels Gratitude

Remembering well enlarges one's capacity for gratitude. Moses commanded the Israelites to perform physical acts of sacrifice, such as abstention from leavened bread, to provide the occasion to testify to their children about the good work of God on their behalf in the exodus, so that the next generation could give thanks along with them. Similarly the half-shekel tax was intended to remind Jews of the ransom God made for their lives (Exod 30:16). The rhythm of life in Israel was punctuated by inconvenient pauses whose sole purpose was to give thanks. Not only time but also place and

45. Lyon, "The Unwelcome Presence," 144. In calling memories "dangerous," Lyon draws on the work of Johann Baptiste Metz, *Faith in History and Society*, 109–10.

46. Volf develops the theme of memory as protective shield against sin, though one that can all too easily "morph into a sword of violence," in Volf, *End of Memory*, 33.

47. Pasewark, "Remembering to Forget," 685.

physical objects called to mind the deeds of Yahweh and incited them to give thanks. Joshua commanded twelve men to gather stones from the Jordan so that in time to come their children would inquire about the meaning of the stones, and they could testify to the deliverance of Yahweh (Josh 4:1–7). The stones stand as a "memorial forever," a catalyst to thanksgiving. Numerous psalms call the people to "remember and give thanks."[48] Stones, altars, and eventually the temple, chiseled upon the land a landscape that, though silent, would speak, directing and shaping hearts toward gratitude.

Jesus gave thanks as he broke bread, both in the miraculous feedings of crowds, and in celebrating the Passover meal with his disciples (Mark 6:41; Luke 22:17). The early church saw the centrality of thanksgiving even as they named the meal, drawing on the verb, *eucharistéo*, to give or return thanks. The words instituting the Eucharist tightly link the memory of Christ with thankfulness, as they call those who partake to, "Take them in remembrance that Christ died for you, and feed on him in your hearts by faith, with thanksgiving."[49] As they remember through the lens of exodus and Eucharist, in the presence of God, believers are enabled to read all of the past, wrongs suffered and inflicted, with thanksgiving.[50] This is in fact the same project Augustine is engaged in throughout the *Confessions*. His goal was, as Albert Outler writes, ". . . in the permissive atmosphere of God's felt presence, to recall those crucial episodes and events in which he can now see and celebrate the mysterious actions of God's prevenient and provident grace."[51]

4. Memory Nurtures Faith

God calls his people to the work of remembering because a well-nourished memory feeds faith in their hearts. Faith, nurtured by memory, has several dimensions in Scripture. At times faith is directly contrasted with fear (Mark 5:36). The ample storehouse of memories of God's previous acts of deliverance is intended to spark confident trust for God's followers in the midst of present crises. Moses, in exhorting the people to "devour" other

48. Pss 105:1–5; 106:21; 107:8.

49. Holy Eucharist: Rite Two, *The Book of Common Prayer of the Episcopal Church*, 365.

50. This is not undisputed, as we will see in aspects of the argument of Volf, examined below.

51. Outler, in introduction to Augustine, *Augustine: Confessions and Enchiridion*, 17.

nations, says, "Do not be afraid of them. Just remember what the Lord your God did to Pharaoh and to all Egypt" (Deut 7:18). Whether or not we like the violence afoot, it is striking that as the Israelites call to mind the salvation God has worked in their past, courage and confident hope are strengthened within them (Isa 40:27–30).

Another dimension of faith that is nurtured by memory is faith in contrast to idolatry. Such faith is marked by single-hearted loyalty to God. With the idolatry that led to exile in mind, Baal Shem Tov, the founder of Hasidism, observed, "Forgetfulness leads to exile; remembrance is the secret of redemption."[52] Various tangible and visual aids called the people back to faithfulness, and there was a fairly high degree of confidence in their efficacy. As the Lord gave Moses instruction for the people about making fringes on their garments, the Lord said, "You have the fringe so that, when you see it, you will remember all the commandments of the Lord and do them, and not follow the lust of your own heart and your own eyes" (Num 15:39, cf. Num 10:10).

Forgetfulness was a primary precursor to idolatry in Israel's history. The psalmist interprets the history of idolatry at Horeb as a failure of memory, writing that it happened because, "They forgot God, their Savior, who had done great things in Egypt . . ." (Ps 106:21). In Judges, we see the Israelites lapse into worship of Baal because, "they did not remember the Lord their God" (8:34). Those who were able to remember God and his covenant, even in the distant land of exile, were described as faithful and loyal. Jonah, after he "remembered the Lord," stated with renewed clarity that "those who worship idols forsake their true loyalty" (Jonah 2:7–8).

Faith fueled by memory makes one strong and capable of action. A lively and well-formed memory is a rich wellspring of courageous and faithful behavior. J. Pederson writes, "When the soul [in Ancient Israelite understanding] remembers something . . . this image is called forth in the soul and assists in determining its direction, its action. . . To remember the works of Yahweh and to seek him, i.e., to let one's acts be determined by his will, is in reality the same."[53] One crucial action that faith-memory promotes is the doing of the commandments (Num 15:40; Ps 103:18). The memory of Yahweh also incites the Israelites to fight for their land and kin (Neh 4:14). Memory makes bold action in the present possible in part because it allows one to imagine an attractive future, on the confident basis

52. Baal Shem Tov, cited in Fleischner, "The Memory of Goodness," 3:159.

53. Pedersen, *Israel*, 1:106–7.

of God's work in the past. It nurtures in the Israelites the ability to conceive alternate possibilities to the obvious doom that appears before them in times of crisis. As they read or hear Scripture, a people who actually have not experienced that past deliverance are called on to widen their horizons of memory through imagination, so that they can forge a path toward a different future. Preachers who can catalyze faithful imagination through memory give their congregations a great gift.

5. Memory Leads to Wisdom

The Hebrew Bible resounds with the recurring theme that a well-developed memory results in wisdom. Wisdom is the capacity to discern a good and faithful path forward, based in part on the failure or success of analogous actions in the past; this is part of the reason wisdom tends to increase with years. The wise person learns not only from his or her own life but also from thoughtful study of the narrative of Israel's ancestors. At a time when Israel needed to choose well the course for the future, Jeremiah counseled them to, "Consider well the highway, the road by which you went" (Jer 31:21). Wisdom consists in the ability to interpret, explain, and put to use in the present the varied events of the past. It involved the ability to make of those fragments a coherent, useful, and compelling narrative. In Joseph's life, after years of gaining perspective, he was able to look back on all that has happened to him and say to his brothers, "Even though you intended to do harm to me, God intended it for good" (Gen 50:20).

Sadly, remembering our past does not inevitably make us wise. Wisdom consists in making good interpretive choices about the meaning of the past, informed by the narrative of Scripture and the renewing work of the Holy Spirit (Rom 12:2). Here, Halbwach's concept of the frameworks through which we remember can illuminate such processes as the psalmist's transformative choice to enter the sanctuary as he recounted his woes, in Psalm 73. What had been oppressive and wearisome became clear and hopeful when he remembered through the framework or lens of the sanctuary of God, joining a community of memory that shaped and informed his own perceptions (Ps 73:17).

The book of Isaiah displays some ambivalence about the desirability of remembering the past. Isaiah 43:18 calls Israel not to remember the former things, and Isa 54:4 promises that they will forget the shame of earlier days. Yet Isa 46:9 calls them to remember the former things, though the former things in this case hearken back to a deeper past even than their history of sin, to the story of the God who is from all eternity. Walter Brueggemann notes the synthesis of appeals to memory and to imagination in Isaiah's poetry. He writes,

> Up until this point [Isa 43:18–19] in the faith and history of Israel, the poets and prophets had continually turned back to the old traditions and articulated their enduring relevance. [Here] they enunciate new actions of God that are discontinuous with the old traditions . . . [The] matter of the end of the old tradition and the presentation of new actions is a dialectical matter. The actions of God are new, but they are cast largely in the molds and images of the old memories so that the discernment and presentation of the new depend profoundly on knowledge about the old.[54]

Remembering the past through the miniscule framework they had been using has proven debilitating and has not lead to wisdom or transformation. It is only in the context of this larger memory that the rest of their story becomes bearable and instructive. As Stanley Hauerwas writes, "Our lives are constituted by discovering we are part of a history we have not created, a history without which we cannot make sense of what we think we have done as well as what we think has happened to us."[55] Isaiah's poetic vision of the beauty of God's eschatological salvation is crafting for Israel a new framework of memory, placing them within a broader history, which sharpens some details and causes others to recede into the background. This process is a crucial dimension of growing in wisdom and wholeness.

The Scriptures portray humanity as growing wise and becoming whole through holding, sifting, and sorting memories in a process of meditation and rumination in the presence of the Lord. This process may be brought on by events that leave us in a state of grief. Shocked at the sight of the devastated city, "Jerusalem remembers, in the days of her affliction and wandering, all the precious things that were hers in days of old" (Lam 1:7). Or it may be occasioned by more joyous events, such as Mary's treasuring of the shepherds' words, pondering them in her heart (Luke 2:19).

Remembering provokes connections that allow us to correctly perceive the significance of events taking place in the present, and the meaning of words we are hearing or reading. In a negative example, the disciples were unable to understand the meaning of Jesus' teaching about the yeast

54. Brueggemann, *Hopeful Imagination*, 2.
55. Hauerwas, "Why Time Cannot Heal," 44.

of the Pharisees, and Jesus attributes this to their lack of remembering the miraculous feedings with five and then seven loaves (Matt 16:9–11). After his resurrection, the disciples remembered various elements of his teaching (John 2:22; 12:16; and 16:4) and his foretelling of the resurrection, in ways that connected the story and validated the resurrection. Their memory increased their understanding, and their growing understanding helped them to recognize the significance of recollected events.

6. Memory Compels Ethical Behavior

Finally, memory compels us to ethical behavior. The Scriptures assume that memory is essential to righteous behavior between human beings. It goads us to generosity, justice, and compassion. Many manifestations of sin toward others are characterized as a failure of memory. One of the most striking examples is found in Jesus' parable of the man who was forgiven a great debt and then refused to have mercy on one who owed him a small sum (Matt 18:30). Conversely, Nathan used a parable to bring about remembrance of David's sin in a way that propelled him to return to ethical behavior (2 Sam 12:7). This is an example of the "dangerous" nature of memory, as it disrupts cherished conceptions of self and other, criticizes present practices, and reshapes future action. Lyon, noting the call to social justice throughout Deuteronomy, writes, "The theology of the Deuteronomist, then, expresses clear practical-moral intent . . . Since this requires a transforming of those values that currently function in Israel's life, its memory calls Israel to take account of the 'unwelcome presence' and, thus, renew its community life."[56]

Memory provokes identification with the needy and inconvenient stranger in one's midst. The writer of Deuteronomy appealed to the Israelite's humble and oppressed past numerous times in his call for them to identify with and therefore show mercy toward sojourners and slaves (Deut 15:12–15; 24:17–18). Memories of receiving the hospitality and provision of God were intended to lead to generous acts toward others. Miroslav Volf observes that it was the memory of God's work, not the Egyptians' cruelty, which was to shape behavior. He writes, "Emulating the Egyptians was to return to Egypt even while dwelling in the Land of Promise. Emulating God was to enact the deliverance God had accomplished for them."[57] One

56. Lyon, "The Unwelcome Presence," 147.
57. Volf, *End of Memory*, 105.

of the chief sins of the "wicked man" in the psalms is his failure to remember the poor (Ps 109:16). Memory of this kind is not spontaneous but must be cultivated and renewed because the poor are so easily marginalized and forgotten. In particular, prisoners easily fade from remembrance because they are physically out of view, as we see with Joseph's fellow prisoners forgetting him for many years. The writer of Hebrews exhorts his audience to remember those in prison (Heb 13:3), imagining themselves as in prison with them. This kind of empathetic identification takes effort; it involves the cultivation of a *habitus* that will issue forth in changed behavior. Through the proclamation of Scripture the church seeks to form a people who remember together the needy in their midst, a people whose love draws their memories back to the poor and forgotten, and whose will to act is shaped by that recollection.

MEANS OF MEMORY IN ISRAEL

We have considered how place, ritual, and narrative practices shape memory for groups. We'll revisit that theme with a focus on Israel and the early church, noting the unique flavor and significance of spatial markers such as land and altars, time markers such as festivals, and the specific ritual of the practice of the Eucharist.

Place

The physical world of the Hebrews was so constructed to spur memory that it is almost more fitting to ask what was *not* called into the service of memory. Land itself, as it was named and then dotted with altars, commemorative stones, and burial sites, all testified to the story of God's involvement with them. The food the land produced was to be eaten with thanksgiving, a reminder of the goodness of the giver of life. Doorposts and the gates of homes bore the words of God, so that every entrance and exit became a moment of remembrance (Deut 6:9). Later the temple and the landscape of the city of Zion made the memory of God precious to worshippers; even the way the mountains surrounded Jerusalem suggested the tender care of God (Ps 125: 2). The body and the garments and items worn on it, from fringes to phylacteries (Deut 11:18) to breastplates bearing the names of the Israelites (Exod 28:29), served as a walking, breathing memorial, a living testimony. Daniel Ben-Amos writes,

[Memory] turns a territory of Earth into a motherland and a homeland, a valley into a setting of a battle, and a mountaintop into a location of revelation. Place names engrave on the land the people's memory of their past. Somewhat paradoxically, burial is an elementary form of transforming the Earth into a vessel that contains collective memory. The tombs of ancestors, saints, martyrs, prophets that are strewn over a land turn a country into holy ground and into a book of memories . . . Memory also transforms objects into symbols, infusing them with meanings they did not have on their own, before memory possessed them . . . Memory, collective and individual, transforms our social and material surroundings into a language that tells us about the past. It intrudes into our daily activities, at times upsetting and at other times rejuvenating our spirit.[58]

Time

Like place, time was marked by a rhythm of pausing to remember the history of salvation and the holiness of God. Whether in the weekly keeping of Sabbath or the more elaborate festivals of Weeks and of Booths (Deut 17:9–17), Israel was called to remember the bitterness of slavery and the miracle of God's deliverance. And of course, all of those times served as occasions to recite and proclaim the story, opportunities for forming a people through the telling of the lively, compelling narrative of Israel's dealings with Yahweh.

Anamnesis in the Eucharist

While Israel was called to remember through the interpretive lens of the exodus, a lens that was focused on justice for a particular people, Volf argues that the paramount locus of God's grace and mercy extended to all is found, for the Christian, in the remembrance of the death and resurrection of Jesus.[59] Debate over the essence of the meaning and proper practice of the Last Supper has polarized the church for centuries, and we will not enter that fray. While not diminishing the Eucharist's meaning to solely that of a memorial, it is striking how powerfully it serves as a transformative locus of memory, identity formation, and healing for those who remember

58. Ben-Amos, "Afterword," 298.
59. Volf, *End of Memory*, 110–11.

as members of Christ's body. D. Stephen Long and Tripp York write, "In an effort to guard against amnesia the Church performs particular liturgical rituals that function as story-telling devices reminding us as to who we are. The Eucharist is the reminder *par excellence*."[60] The remembrance of Christ's death and resurrection forms us as people who can humbly and freely tell the truth about ourselves, interpret the past with gratitude, and extend grace and forgiveness to others. As Rowan Williams reflects, "[In the Eucharist] we are made 'present to ourselves' as people complicit in the betrayal and death of Jesus and yet still called and accepted, still 'companions' of Christ in the strict sense—those who break bread with him."[61]

As the church celebrates Eucharist it forms a holding space, at once safe and transformative, for sifting memories of great pain, whether endured or inflicted. The altar or table provides a sacred space and marks out a holy time within which participants may encounter and integrate their memories in the presence of Christ. Volf writes of the profound impact of Christ's presence in Eucharist: "Even more, to victims Christ offers his own saving presence . . . He shields the sufferer's self so that the wrongdoing can neither penetrate to the core of her identity nor determine her possibilities."[62] In connecting the deeply embodied nature of Eucharist and its power in contexts of physical oppression such as Chile and South Africa, Robert Vosloo writes, "Hereby God has created a space where people can mourn over the injustice to bodies, and keep the memory of those bodies alive. Through the Eucharist Christians remember Christ's broken body. It is the 'dangerous memory' of this broken body that serves as model and source for the body of Christ to embody reconciliation."[63]

The practice of Eucharist also shapes our hope and enlarges our vision for the future. It is not only a reproduction of the past, but an anticipation of the future.[64] Around the table we may imagine an eschatological community of reconciled participants that extends far beyond those who are physically present. We can celebrate that our own sins have been forgiven and will one day be fully redeemed. And we long for the day when Christ,

60. Long and York, "Remembering: Offering Our Gifts," 342.

61. Williams, *Resurrection*, 40.

62. Volf, *End of Memory*, 118.

63. Vosloo, "Reconciliation," 40.

64. Ghislain Ndondji-Tshiwisa-Adidem compares African conceptions of memory, where the goal is reproduction of the ancestral past in the present, with Christian *anamnesis*, which turns by faith toward eschatology, in Ndondji-Tshiwisa-Adidem "An African Reconsideration of Christian *Anamnesis*," 37–40.

whose absence is recognized in the meal, will again be physically present to celebrate it with us fully.[65]

Having considered many of the ways that "happy memory," to use Ricoeur's phrase, serves to shape and enliven individuals and communities toward faithful discipleship, I want to turn now to two less happy, indeed problematic aspects of memory in Scripture, both of which have implications for congregations as they seek to overcome racist pasts and live as reconciled bodies. The first is the fear of being forgotten and the second is the question of whether a kind of forgetting of evil and suffering is salutary and endorsed in Scripture.

THE FEAR OF BEING FORGOTTEN

For the Israelites, being remembered by others and by God was crucial to ongoing existence and honor. Thus, the threat of one's name and good deeds being forgotten surfaced often in Scripture, as threat, curse or fear. Marjorie Sykes notes, "For the Hebrews the name contained the whole of a man's personality and power; the 'memory' of him seems also to have had very much the same content."[66] Absalom was so worried that he had, "no son to keep my name in remembrance," that he built a pillar and with utmost subtlety named it, "Absalom" (2 Sam 18:18). We hear echoes of this fear in God's promise to the faithful eunuchs that God would give them a lasting name (Isa 56:3–5). Numerous cursing passages include some form of the line, "May his name not be remembered," or "May his memory be blotted out" (Job 18:17; Ps 9:5–6, 83:4; Prov 10:7; Jer 11:19). The failure to be remembered was regarded as the ultimate punishment from God, synonymous with obliteration (Exod 17: 14; Deut 32:26; Isa 26:14; Eccl 9:5). Being forgotten meant that one's needs were going unattended to, as we see in exhortations to remember the poor and imprisoned (Gal 2:10; Heb 13:3).

In the realm of ethnic or communal identity, the fragility of memory often becomes a threat to rights and to belonging. Those in the minority and those who have experienced oppression or the repression of their narrative

---

65. Ndondji-Tshiwisa-Adidem writes, "It is by celebrating this absence by means of remembering that the real presence of Jesus is realized to the full. It is in the *anamnesis* of the historical Jesus that the real and true presence of the Risen One is realized" ("An African Reconsideration," 47).

66. Sykes, "Eucharist as 'Anamnesis,'" 115.

by the wider society of course feel this need more acutely. They fear the lack of testimony to their good deeds, their suffering, and to such matters as their land rights and status as members of the community. William James Booth writes of the connection between ongoing memory and justice for those who have suffered within a society. He argues for, "an understanding of justice as the effort to secure persistence, as a community's struggle via memory against the effects of the erosion caused by the passage of the years and by the effort of human hands . . ."[67]

Joshua 22

A striking biblical example of a subgroup striving to preserve its heritage is that of the Transjordanian tribes at the end of the conquest of the Promised Land, as narrated in Joshua 22. After serving valiantly and loyally alongside the other tribes, the tribes of Reuben, Gad and the half-tribe of Manasseh moved to their allotted land across the Jordan. They proceeded to build a large altar, naming it, "Witness."[68] Upon hearing this, the rest of the Israelites immediately prepared for war. They had the foresight to send Phinehas and a small delegation of chiefs ahead of them. Phinehas' speech was no model of cross-cultural dialogue, beginning as it did with accusations and foregone conclusions, rather than open-ended questions. The response of the tribes, on the other hand, modeled the combination of vulnerability and tenacity that makes reconciliation and ongoing relationship possible. They first affirmed their common commitment to the Lord, God of all nations and peoples. Then they made a remarkable confession: "*We did it out of fear.*" Their fear had to do with the potential for collective memory loss or distortion on the part of the majority group, and it was not unfounded.[69] They continue, "We did it from fear that in time to come your children might say to our children, 'What have you to do with the Lord, the God

---

67 Booth, *Communities of Memory*, 117.

68. T. C. Butler writes, "The East Jordan tribes interpret their altar as a perpetual witness that they do belong to Yahweh, a witness which, if accepted, would avoid future confrontations on the subject. The Jordan is a symbol of separation. The altar is a symbol of unity . . . [it] shows that the unifying factor is Yahweh" (*Joshua*, 249).

69. M. H. Woudstra writes, "It was . . . no imaginary danger to suppose that those on the west bank somehow would begin to think they could lay a stronger claim to . . . God than their brothers [sic] in the east. Was not the Jordan an ever-present barrier? Would it not also be a terrible thing if one part of the covenant nation were to tell the other that they had no portion in the Lord?" (*The Book of Joshua*, 327).

of Israel? For the Lord has made the Jordan a boundary between us and you, you Reubenites and Gadites; you have no portion in the Lord'" (Josh 22:24–25). The Transjordanian tribes had place as a constant reminder of separation. What they needed, right where they lived, was a visible symbol of belonging, membership and unity. They needed to keep alive the narrative that included and honored them. After their entire explanation, Phineas proclaims, "Today we know that the Lord is among us, because you have not committed this treachery against the Lord; now you have saved the Israelites from the hand of the Lord" (Josh 22:31).

In his discussion of collective memory, Michael Schudson makes the point that, "Experiences attended to by powerful social institutions are likely to be better preserved than experiences less favored by rich institutional rememberers . . . Whatever past is remembered or commemorated, it must be drawn from the available past, and availability of the past is socially structured."[70]

Joshua led well in asking the leaders of Israel to gather stones from the river, "as a memorial forever" (Josh 4:7). It would have shown even more striking foresight and insight had he commissioned the three Transjordanian tribes to create a memorial that symbolized their part in the battles and in the corporate identity of Israel, and asked them to host a celebration in which they explained the significance of their memorial. That of course is wishful thinking, and such leadership is rare. This passage portrays the poignant longing on the part of a minority group to be included, and to endure, in the broader community of memory. It conveys the fear that their story will be obscured or effaced with the passage of time and the geographical barrier of the Jordan River. Immigrants, Native Americans, and African Americans who choose to join multiethnic congregations face this same fear. The loss that they fear would mean a loss for members of the dominant culture as well, for in the hearing of those stories comes a deeper connection between members, and a richer hermeneutical community.

Bearing Witness

Latent within the fear of being forgotten is the call to bear witness on behalf of others. Often those at risk of being forgotten are somehow compromised in their ability to speak for themselves. Booth writes, "Memory-justice . . . speaks with the voice of the silenced victims. It is the vehicle of their

70. Schudson, "Dynamics of Distortion," 359.

THEOLOGICAL DIMENSIONS OF MEMORY 157

presence, a second life that witnessing and doing justice breathe into them."[71] Bearing witness is a calling that may bring deep joy, but it is also a discipline and even a burden. The tools of remembrance in Scripture are frequently weighty items, like cumbersome breastplates filled with names (Exod 28:29), which must be worn or carried with effort and even suffering. It is not insignificant that stones often spur God and future generations to remember (Gen 12:8; Josh 4:7). As Thomas Long writes, "It is no coincidence that the New Testament word for witness is *martyr*."[72] Ricoeur notes the connection of bearing witness and suffering when he writes, "Testimony is . . . the engagement of a pure heart and an engagement to the death. It belongs to the tragic destiny of truth."[73]

Those who take up this task do so out of love and faithfulness to those who have suffered. Bearing witness lest the past be forgotten has animated the life of Elie Wiesel since he left Buchenwald in 1945. He writes, "Our future depends on our testimony. This is why some of us often overcame our inhibitions, our fear and trembling, and we choose to speak up. For the sake of victims everywhere we remember those who were our friends and companions. We plunge again into our past so as to save the future."[74] Jewish theologian Alan Berger writes, "All are capable of being transformed into witnesses by hearing the survivors' tales. In the words of Ellen Fine, '. . . to listen to a witness is to become one.'"[75]

It is not only the suffering of the dead that must be recalled, but the multifaceted texture of their lives, the joys that enlivened them, and the heroic and ordinary good deeds they performed. Bearing witness to suffering calls those who hear it to mourning, and at times to repentance. It guards against repetition of the evils of the past. Witnessing that celebrates and honors ancestors will call listeners to value and protect the sufferers' descendants and to regard all those around them in transformed ways.

HEALING AND A KIND OF FORGETTING

Justice demands that we remember strenuously and truthfully, as individuals, as members of groups that have done honorable and terrible deeds,

71. Booth, *Communities of Memory*, 157.

72. Long, *Witness of Preaching*, 47.

73. Ricoeur, "Hermeneutics of Testimony," 130.

74. Wiesel, "Future of Remembering," 3:133.

75. Berger, "Bearing Witness," 3:2,333.

and on behalf of those who have suffered at the hands of others. But what does healing demand and require? Is "moving on" from the past, so highly touted in popular psychology today, really the path to happiness and healthy functioning? The mark of healthy people or communities in much secular and church discourse is that they have, "come to closure" and put the past behind them.[76] Here, along the way to considering how to preach about pain suffered by members of various ethnic groups, particularly when members of multiple groups are listening, we will consider the merits and risks of a kind of forgetting. We will take as our primary interlocutor Miroslav Volf, since he has written extensively about the topic and since he has made a bold assertion that deserves consideration. Volf has modified his argument somewhat since *Exclusion and Embrace*, speaking (at times) more carefully about "not calling to mind" and "non-remembrance" in *The End of Memory*. What does he advocate, and what would be the gains and costs of his proposal?

Volf's Advocacy of Forgetting

Volf writes with passion for justice, truth, hospitality, and reconciliation between enemies (the dominant theme of *Exclusion and Embrace*) and for right remembering in the service of healing, and particularly for restoring the capacity to love, on the part of victims of wrongdoing (the theme of *The End of Memory*). In the latter book, Volf makes the point that, despite calls from politicians and psychologists to remember, in service to their visions of justice and truth, memory is not an unambiguous good. Volf limits his theme to the memory of wrongs suffered, and more particularly those who have suffered at the hands of others, as opposed to through illness or natural disasters. Working with insights from Nietzsche, Freud, Dante, and Kierkegaard, Volf develops a theology of "a kind of forgetting," in the service of healing and reconciliation.

Volf notes that victims can be particularly poor at remembering, and that this makes them dangerous.[77] He argues that we have a significant

76. David Augsburger makes the point about contemporary society's rush to come to "closure" and "get on with life" in processes of reconciliation, in *Hate Work*, 92.

77. Volf writes, "The memory of their own persecution makes them see dangers lurking even where there are none; it leads them to exaggerate dangers that do exist and overreact with excessive violence or inappropriate preventive measures so as to ensure their own safety. Victims will often become perpetrators precisely *on account* of their memories" (*End of Memory*, 33).

measure of freedom in how we respond to and configure our memories of past events.[78] Volf synthesizes the insights of Halbwachs about the communal context of remembering through shared frameworks with insights from Scripture, to arrive at two unparalleled sacred frameworks of memory for members of the church, that of the exodus and the passion. He argues that these events form exemplary and even regulative communal memories, which have the capacity to frame incidents in our own lives within the wider story of God's justice, compassion, and redemption.[79] He urges churches to be communities that support individuals in the challenging work of remembering well.[80]

Volf's goals and broad vision of reconciliation, evident throughout his written work, are consistent with the biblical vision of shared forgiveness. *The End of Memory* presents a more nuanced and carefully considered argument for forgetting than did *Exclusion and Embrace*. He has tried to pull back from such strident statements as his assertion that, "Redemption will be complete only when the creation of 'all things new' is coupled with the passage of 'all things old' into the double *nihil* of non-existence and non-remembrance."[81] He continues that in the new world, humans will be able to forget the horrors of history because, "there will stand a throne, and on the throne there will sit the Lamb who has 'taken away the sin of the world' and erased their memory."[82] This is a chilling and disturbing assertion to some who hear it.

Problems with Volf's Theology

Numerous theologians object to this terminology. Stanley Hauerwas writes, "The problem with Volf's non-remembering is not only the implications it seems to have for our current practices, but rather what it implies about God's life. Consummation comes too close to a false eternity."[83] L. Gregory Jones argues that the biblical vision of the kingdom in the *eschaton* is one of

78. Ibid., 25.

79. Volf prefers the language of lenses and frameworks to that of narratives that guide meaning or construct identity, and this is important for his argument for forgetting, considered below (ibid., 103–28).

80. Ibid., 126.

81. Volf, *Exclusion and Embrace*, 136.

82. Ibid., 140.

83. Hauerwas, "Why Time Cannot Heal," 42.

wounds healed, rather than erased. He writes, "Indeed, erasing memories would seem to be much closer to 'uncrucifying Christ' than would healing those memories fully—eschatologically—through the healing wounds of the crucified and risen Christ."[84]

In *The End of Memory*, Volf seems to be initially chastened by his critics, and thus more cautiously asserts the need for "a kind of forgetting," or the choice not to call to mind, at least during this lifetime. He borrows at one point Aleida Assmann's distinction between functional memory, which is identity shaping, and recorded memory,[85] the mass of memories that surround the functional memory. He makes the pragmatic allowance that, "For the sake of flexibility of functional memory, it is essential to keep recorded memory from erasure."[86] He also writes, "I do not mean that certain memories will be erased from each person's cerebral 'hard-drive' so as to make retrieval impossible . . . I propose instead that memories of wrongs, rather than being deleted, will simply fail to surface in one's consciousness—they will not come to mind."[87] This is a softening and a needed clarification of some statements in his earlier work.

Yet Volf makes a number of statements in *End of Memory* that still seem to contradict his stated desire to guard a place for even recorded memory, at least into eternity. Volf values newness and transformation in the *eschaton* much more highly than continuity and duration, and this comes at a cost. As it is for all of us, Volf's eschatological vision is inevitably determinative of his vision for ethics, psychology, and theology in the interim. His eschatological vision reveals the relative value he actually places on remembering and forgetting. He remains convinced, despite some mitigating statements, that a complete forgetting of wrongs suffered will characterize the mental and emotional state of the saints in heaven. He argues that if heaven's inhabitants did remember evils eternally, this would imply the triumph of those evils and evildoers.[88] He also posits that choices to hold

84. Jones, "Healing the Wounds of Memory," 43.

85. Assmann, *Erinnerungsraeume: Formen un Wandlungen des kulterellen Gedaechnises*, cited in Volf, *End of Memory*, 195. He summarizes Assmann, saying, "New configurations of functional memory make selected use of materials from recorded memory. For the sake of the flexibility of functional memory, it is essential to keep recorded memory from erasure."

86. Volf, *End of Memory*, 195 n. 2.

87. Ibid., 145.

88. Volf asks, "If wrongs suffered are permanently inscribed in the minds and identities of the citizens of the world to come, would this not represent a peculiar triumph of

onto painful memories of wrongs suffered, in eternity, would probably indicate a refusal to fully forgive self or others.[89] Rather, when the citizens of
heaven are fully absorbed in the goodness of God, he argues, "the memory
of wrongs will wither away like plants without water."[90]

In defending eschatological forgetting, Volf looks to Augustine for
backing and either mistakes or misrepresents Augustine's position. He
cites Augustine's distinction, in the final pages of *The City of God*, between
mentally remembering evil in eternity and remembering the *feelings* of evil.
Augustine argues that only the former will occur eternally. But Volf goes on
to write of an even more complete forgetting of wrongs personally suffered
than the memory of evil in general, whether one's own or evil that one
observed. He asserts that, "In his [Augustine's] view, the blessed will not
remember having suffered wrongs at all."[91] For this he cites, book 22, chapter 30. However, in this section, after distinguishing between the mental
and emotional remembering of evil, Augustine goes on to state, "Yet such
is the power of knowledge—and it will be very great in the saints—that it
will prevent not only their own past misery but also the eternal misery of
the damned from disappearing from memory. Otherwise, if they were to
lose the knowledge of their past misery how will they, as the psalm says,
'sing the mercies of the Lord for all eternity?'"[92] For Augustine, it is precisely
through remembering sorrows and pain suffered that they will be drawn
to worship the God who mercifully and creatively redeemed them. This
recollection will not be the cause for feelings of tears and sorrow, but for joy
and wonder at the power of God to heal.

In Volf's vision, memory is a vast, thorny, and potent problem, particularly in eternity, and one that might even undo heaven itself. He can
from numerous angles imagine it destroying our experience of heaven,
but he cannot imagine a solution other than memory erasure, whether by
divine or by human agency. Unable to imagine how God could redeem
Auschwitz, he writes, "For if heaven cannot rectify Auschwitz, then the
memory of Auschwitz must undo the experience of heaven."[93] In the face

---

evil rather than its complete defeat?"(ibid., 213).

89. Ibid., 207.

90. Ibid., 214.

91. Volf continues in his footnote, "According to Augustine, the saints in the world to
come will have no memory of offenses that *others* have perpetrated on them" (ibid., 22).

92. Augustine *City of God*, book 22, chapter 30.

93. Volf, *Exclusion and Embrace*, 136.

of this conundrum, erasure of memory appears to be the best God can do. But others have proposed that, as horrific as Auschwitz was, its power to destroy pales in comparison to the power of the resurrected Christ to redeem and heal. Rowan Williams notes the difficulty but looks to the power of the resurrection when he writes, "Simply to be given back the past of wrong and hurt is not of itself a transaction of grace: we have already seen how the bare, context-less recovery of memory can be something regarded only with terror and despair. What happens in the resurrection is that this memory is given back in a particular kind of context—in the presence of Jesus."[94]

Hauerwas finds a similar basis for hope in a capacious vision of the time that will be available for healing in eternity. He draws on Jenson's work with God's duration through and in time, noted above, applying it to the problem of healing and forgiveness: "God makes possible all the time in the world to make our time, our memories, redeemed. Our time can be redeemed because time has been redeemed by Christ."[95] John's vision of the river running through the city of God included a tree whose leaves were for "the healing of the nations" (Rev 22:2). It may be that the leaves are nothing more than amnesiac drugs, inducing mental and emotional obliteration of all wrongs suffered. But the witness of Scripture would suggest that God is capable of a more creative process than the obliteration of memory.

What will *God* remember, in eternity? Only the good deeds and the happy moments, it seems, in Volf's understanding. The cross itself, while a good deed, is deemed too "horrific" to be remembered. In the midst of an argument that the events of the past and the narratives persons tell about them are not as constitutive of identity as is often assumed, Volf extends that argument to the crucifixion. He posits that Christ himself need not remember the cross after it has accomplished its full work and nor will Christ's worshippers. He writes against the idea that Christ was crucified from eternity, and asks, "Why would he have to continue to be 'the Crucified One' after redemption has been completed and unassailably secured in the world to come?"[96] He continues, "Once we have been unalterably redeemed, his death along with our sin can be swallowed in his own divine life . . ."[97] Those "wounds yet visible above, in beauty glorified," of hymn

94. Williams, *Resurrection*, 35.
95. Hauerwas, "Why Time Cannot Heal," 42.
96. Volf, *End of Memory*, 190.
97. Ibid., 191.

writer Matthew Bridges' vision,[98] would disappear in Volf's vision. In fact he argues that eternal remembrance of the cross involves taking ourselves and the effects of our sin on God too seriously and loving God for what God has done, rather than for who God is.[99] How one separates out the being of God from the acts of God is a task that Volf, understandably, does not attempt.

A thorough dialogue with the theological assumptions at work in Volf's Christology here is beyond the scope of the topic of human memory, though the implications of his line of reasoning for trinitarian doctrine here are troubling. Volf asserts that, "The cross of Christ is . . . a stage on the road to resurrection and exaltation . . . a stage that can be left in the past even if its effects last eternally."[100] But if the memory of the cross is forgotten, "swallowed into divine life," to use Volf's term, what will distinguish members of the Trinity from each other? The economic Trinity is inseparable from the immanent Trinity; it is not merely a temporal necessity that will be lifted and done away with in the *eschaton*. If in eternity the cross is forgotten, then incarnation itself must be forgotten, since it implied death in some form. Without incarnation, the Sonship of Christ, the one willingly sent to earth from the Father, would be obliterated, and the Godhead would become an undifferentiated monad. As Pannenberg notes, the understanding of God's "real relationship to time" is tightly tied to an understanding of God as an "intrinsically differentiated unity."[101]

Volf's proposal of divine and human forgetting of the cross in eternity is not incidental or trivial to his project. Rather, it is the inevitable end of an argument for human forgetting of suffering in eternity, since the cross is the emblematic instance of both human and divine suffering. It is fitting that Volf takes his argument to its logical conclusion, but for many readers this end point proves unacceptable and reveals holes in the argument all along the way. In seeking to ground human identity in something more than merely the sum (and narration) of all that a person has experienced, Volf questions the narrative construction of identity that prevails today. Volf is willing to take on cherished assumptions of the field of psychology and theology, and this yields interesting insights. He caricatures late

98. Matthew Bridges, "Crown Him with Many Crowns," 1852, Public Domain. See also Rev 5:11, "Worthy is the Lamb that was slain . . ."

99. Volf, *End of Memory*, 191.

100. Ibid., 191.

101. Pannenberg, *Systematic Theology, Volume I*, 405.

modernity's conception of the individual, which would have one say, "I am what I remember that I have experienced. The more that happens to me and the more of it I remember, the richer my identity."[102] He argues that modernity, in its quest for logical explanations, has focused too much on integrating events into a wider narrative of meaning. This assumes that events in our past are meaningful, and he argues that many horrific events resist the most valiant attempts to cull from them meaning or to integrate them fruitfully into the present.[103] This search for meaning, he argues, also gives too much power to the past as the shaping agent of our identities.

Volf accurately points out the limits of an emphasis on the narrative integration of events for the constitution of identity. Yet his insistence that some events will defy meaning even into eternity grants those events too much power, and grants too little power to God. His solution to great suffering and the pain its memory causes comes at the cost of not only narrative but history itself. The proclamation of the history of God's saving work is crucial to the revelation of God's glory, and God's worship by his followers throughout eternity. The story of the providence, mercy, and salvation God accomplished for his people, a story which reveals his being as loving God, cannot be told apart from the sin, suffering, and death that made it necessary. Pannenberg writes, "History will thus be a demonstration of God, though only at its end."[104]

Volf's elevation of forgetting also entails a devaluation of the good of enduring continuity, of duration over time, for identity. Jaroslav Pelikan, reflecting on the way Augustine narrated the confession of his sins in the presence of a forgiving God, writes, "In that presence it [his narration] could become a way of coming to terms with the continuity of the self by including divine forgiveness within the continuity, and thus of putting the subjectivity of memory into the subjective-objective context of time."[105] For Volf, the narration of woes, even in the context of divine grace and redemption, is still a source of too much potential for harm if it extends into eternity. Williams rightly cautions that, though remembering can be

102. Volf, *End of Memory*, 200.

103. Ibid., 194. Richard Lischer makes a similar point. He cautions about, "the ways in which storytelling falsifies those vast and deep non-narrative domains of human life . . . [The typical shape of a plot] does not always reflect the way things are but mercifully—or arrogantly—imposes a pattern on the disorder and anarchy of life as it is" ("Limits of Story," 30).

104. Pannenberg, *Systematic Theology, Volume I*, 245.

105. Pelikan, *Mystery of Continuity*, 26.

painful because we recall moments of diminishing self and others, the alternative is worse. He writes, "And yet the refusal or denial of memory is likewise diminution, perhaps the deepest diminution of all. If the whole self is the concern and the theatre of God's saving work, then the past of the self must be included in the scope of this work."[106] Williams concludes that, "To know the full scope and the full cost of our untruthfulness and not to be crippled, paralysed, by it is what is given by the risen Christ: memory restored in hope."[107]

Along with history and narrative, a further unintended victim of Volf's theory may be a value on testimony. Volf frequently voices the need for bearing witness. Yet his eschatological perspective on forgetting inevitably shapes values and practices in the present. South African theologian Robert Vosloo, commenting on the rush toward forgetting among perpetrators of crimes in South Africa, writes, in critique of Volf, "It may be better to talk about memories healed than about transgressions forgotten, especially in a climate where the rhetoric of a static view of reconciliation reigns. The real challenge and hope lie not in a certain kind of forgetting, but in remembering well."[108] Vosloo concludes, "Amnesia is indeed the great enemy of an ethic of responsibility."[109]

If one's best hope lies in the belief that all that is painful on earth will be forgotten, including the cross, this will tend to suppress or diminish the value of those stories of pain for today. This could have damaging implications for pastoral counseling and for preaching and testifying in church. Church is the place where our memories matter, much as they may need perspective or even outright correction. As Hauerwas puts it, "The possibility of reconciled memory between peoples who have wronged and been wronged by one another is but another name for church. To be such a church takes time and in the taking becomes time in God's very life."[110]

106. Williams, *Resurrection*, 29.

107. Ibid., 42.

108. Vosloo, "Reconciliation," 36.

109. Ibid., 37.

110. Hauerwas, "Why Time Cannot Heal," 46.

CONCLUSION: THEOLOGY OF MEMORY AND THE FORMATION OF ETHNICALLY DIVERSE CONGREGATIONS

I have taken Volf on here and strenuously argued that memories matter, eternally, because stories and selves matter eternally to God. Our memories of God's work matter as well, from creation to exodus, from cross to Pentecost. Of course we worship God for what God did, and we will do so eternally. God's actions are of one piece with God's being, and the proclamation of those actions will not cease simply because some of those stories involve the memory of pain. The kings of the nations will bring their glory into heaven (Rev 21:24), and that glory will be in part their testimony of God's work on their behalf, redeeming terrible acts they perpetrated or suffered. We will eternally sing of how God has redeemed us, and in part that will be how God has worked through our national and ethnic history. National identity will be transcended but not forgotten, since it will form part of the testimony that will propel worship forever.

This chapter has asserted that memory is essential to our nature as humans, and to our capacity to faithfully follow and worship God. Through disciplined individual and corporate practices of remembering well, Israel and the church became and becomes a body of people marked by humility, gratitude, faithfulness, and wisdom. Memory forms the basis for ethical behavior, acts of compassion and justice toward others. The fear of being forgotten runs through the Old Testament, demonstrating how central memory was considered to the ongoing honor and inclusion of individuals and groups. The chapter examined Volf's proposal for a kind of forgetting, appreciating aspects of the intent of that proposal but critiquing eschatological and christological implications of his enthusiasm for divine and human forgetting. Let us turn now to consider some of the implications of this study for churches that are striving to build unity and foster ethnic diversity.

First, congregational leaders who strive to build into their members the disciplines of remembering well together will find that those disciplines transfer well to the development of the cross-cultural communication skills that are essential for building trust and forging partnerships in multiethnic churches. The practice of remembering and recounting one's own past, and the past of one's ethnic group, with truthfulness, humility, gratitude, faith, and wisdom, shapes individuals and communities that can build bridges effectively across boundaries. Churches that encourage testimony and storytelling along these lines create a space for connections to be made and for understanding to grow.

Second, in addition to the benefits reaped as members learn to remember and tell their own stories well, the practice, discipline, and skill involved in learning to remember Israel's and the church's past as their own is a skill that trains listeners in empathetic imagination. The empathetic process involves, "the suspension of one's own frame of reference in order to enter the perceptual and emotional world of the other."[111] Listeners grow in the ability to extend themselves toward the other and are more able to hear stories of suffering and joy, testimonies of immigrant journeys, etc., and if not count them as their own, at least incorporate them into our mental framework of what life can entail. In a sermon given on Remembrance Sunday, Helen Oppenheimer said, "Exercising historical imagination is not itself Christian love, but it could be a way of laying good foundations. Getting into the habit of thinking of other people as real is a kind of basis for Christian love; and it is harder than it sounds."[112]

Norma Rosen, writing on how non-Jews may grow in empathy and solidarity with the suffering of the Jews and others in the Holocaust, urges the use of vivid imagery to strengthen memory. She writes, "But entering into a state of being that for whatever reasons makes porous those membranes through which empathy passes, or deep memory with its particular 'there-ness,' so that we can move, as far as it is given to us to do so, into the pain and hence the meaning of the Holocaust—that too is a kind of memorial."[113] The choice to commemorate the suffering of others is in itself an act of generosity; it involves a choice to learn that history and engage with it. It requires the activation of the will, which, as has been noted above, was for Augustine intimately connected with desire and love.

Third, as a church gains a reputation as a community that values the pasts of all its members, and views learning those pasts as an integral part of its life together, trust will grow among members of minority cultures, both in the church and in the surrounding community. Like the Transjordanian tribes, minority members need confidence that the churches they join will be places where their memories are welcomed and can be reinforced for subsequent generations. George Van Alstine, the white pastor of Altadena

111. Hendry, "Empathy," 354.
112. Oppenheimer, "Remembering," 421.
113. Rosen, "Second Life of Holocaust Imagery," 58; Berger, "Bearing Witness," 2336.

Baptist church, has noted the trust that has been gained in their community as several members of their ethnically mixed congregation started observing Black History Month, covering the sanctuary with large prints of African and African American leaders and hosting a lecture series.[114]

Individual and collective memory limits and accentuates our capacity to hear and interpret information, and this has significant implications for preaching texts. Memories told can unite listeners, sparking recognition that leads to solidarity. Preachers who appreciate the power of memory are better equipped to preach biblical texts, interwoven with experience, in ways that provide new interpretive frameworks for memories. The goal of such proclamation is to shape new communities of memory, deeply connected to the history of Israel and the church, communities that are capable of working toward reconciliation, justice, and love.

114. From interview with George Van Alstine, August 2, 2007.

7

Teach Us to Remember Well: Preaching to Shape a Reconciled People

Ethnic diversity in congregations adds a messy complexity that must be accounted for in pastoral leadership, and particularly in preaching. When that diversity is lived out in a community marked by grace, justice, and reconciliation, its presence provides unparalleled opportunities for individual and communal healing and transformation. Such churches offer their members and surrounding communities startling and hopeful visions of the shared life the gospel makes possible. They equip their members to serve and lead well in their neighborhoods, schools and work settings, where race continues to divide our nation. No arbitrary measure of diversity is biblically mandated for every congregation, but every congregation is called to reach out across cultures and to welcome others in cross-culturally, and churches reap huge rewards when they do. Here we'll fill out the picture as we draw from interviews with pastors and churches that are intentionally striving to live into ethnic diversity.[1]

1. Those interviewed include: Rev. Kerwin Manning of Pasadena Church of God, Rev. George Van Alstine of Altadena Baptist Church, Rev. Ken Fong of Evergreen Baptist Church, Rev. Danny Martinez of Church of the Redeemer, and Jack Hakimian of Unshakable Ministries. Rev. Curtis Chang, former pastor of The River Church Community of San Jose, was consulted informally. Hope Christian Fellowship of San Gabriel, CA, Pasadena Church of God, Evergreen Baptist Church of Los Angeles, and Church of the Redeemer in Los Angeles, were visited.

The lens of collective memory has provided a conceptual framework as we've looked at the challenges that arise when individuals from different backgrounds gather together in churches. While this lens does not equally highlight all of the dynamics of ethnicity, it has proven a helpful magnifier of both the problems and opportunities in multiethnic community, and the preaching that shapes and animates it. By examining how groups construct and transmit their memories, and then considering key theological and ethical dimensions of memory, we have sought to demonstrate that the remembering practices individuals and groups engage in not only reveal but in turn shape their character. That character will in turn limit, prohibit, or foster their capacity to hear Scripture proclaimed, as well as their ability to forge connections with those outside their ethnic group.

This chapter focuses on the task of preaching, considering the homiletical goals and strategies that can foster the growth of ethnic diversity in congregational life. We will first look at preaching a word that comes *out of* the heart of one's community, considering some of the ways preachers can pay greater attention to the context of our congregations, allowing memory to more deeply indwell and shape their proclamation. Then we'll look at how the Word of God speaks *into* that community, engaging and shaping the practices of memory that take place there. Preaching can foster transformed practices of remembering that lead to healing, repentance, and greater faith. The spoken word can make the past (our own, our nation's, and that of Israel and the church) available to the congregation as a potent resource for reconciliation, hospitality, and love in the present. The proclamation of the gospel can shape a congregational culture that is capable of breaking down barriers between ethnic groups within it that may have long histories of hostility and prejudice, or at least misunderstanding and mutual avoidance.

Globally, history has shown the potential for violence and other harm where there is a tight overlap and mutual reinforcement of ethnic and religious passions. Yet, history also shows that membership in ethnic-specific religious communities has functioned positively to preserve an ethnic group's values and identity for countless immigrants (whether they came freely or as slaves). Given the history of racism and the effacement of ethnic identity that many minority groups have endured throughout this nation's history, the choice of Christian minority people to affiliate along ethnic lines has served several good purposes. For Native Americans, forced assimilation and denial of their culture was linked with indoctrination into

Christianity. The sparseness of Christian faith among the indigenous people of America today is in large part a legacy of that severing of ethnic identity from its creative expression in faith, and highly indigenized expressions of faith such as Eagles Wings Ministries[2] are some of the most promising signs of a way forward for authentic gospel engagement for these groups. Among African Americans, examples can be found of Christianity bringing both cultural loss and preservation, but in general the mono-ethnic black church has been a powerful contributor to ethnic heritage and healthy identity formation, as well as an advocate and resource for social justice.

This may well be a critical time in United States history, with unprecedented opportunities for ethnic reconciliation. Our nation has gained a certain level of distance from the Civil Rights struggles. Ethnically mixed marriages continue to increase, causing greater permeability in ethnic groups. Racial harmony, integration, and justice are particularly strong desires articulated by many youth today. The church has an opportunity to seize, and yet many continue to argue that it is too costly. We still hear arguments such as this one from Gary McIntosh and Alan McMahan: ". . . that heterogeneity is to be the norm in the universal church . . . while homogeneity is to be the norm in the local church . . . is this not the more biblical model?"[3] These authors argue from a pragmatic perspective that rapid church growth is more likely in homogeneous settings.

Arguments for ethnic specificity may also carry the subtle implication that those who affiliate with multiethnic congregations are denying their ethnic identity or are refusing to stand in solidarity with others of their ethnic background. *Ethnic identity* can become the card that trumps all other concerns. Especially when conceived of in terms of in terms of individual preference and image, a strong focus on this can reflect a modern, Western preoccupation with the individual and his or her sense of self. This conception often has little to do with a biblical understanding of identity formation, in which identity is viewed as a gift we receive and an image with which we are marked by our Creator. In Scripture we see that image nurtured through membership in family and in faith communities, and through risky journeys that involve encounters with others who may be radically different.[4]

---

2. See http://www.eagleswingsministry.com/people/index.htm.

3. McIntosh and McMahan, *Being the Church in a Multi-Ethnic Community*, 120.

4. Examples include the strengthening of values that resulted from the journeys and encounters with strangers that occurred for Abraham and Sarah, the Exiles (most

PREACHING THAT COMES FROM THE COMMUNITY

To use McClure's phrase, churches growing toward greater diversity seek a homiletic that "persuades text to meet experience" in ways that name the struggles, joys and unique flavor of ethnic groups represented, while also speaking a universally applicable word that persuades experience(s) to meet text, allowing the Word to interpret, celebrate, and at times judge or mourn those experiences, in the context of a congregation that seeks truth and grace together.

Preachers speak a word that comes *from* the heart of the community, a word that is shaped and indwelt by the memories shared there. This book has been an extended argument for preachers to pay greater attention to context, to what has happened and is happening in the communities and congregations in which they do their work. Preachers will be aided in several ways if they preach out of a greater awareness of the shaping power of memory, and particularly narratives of the past as they have been constructed within the ethnic groups to which individual members belong. They must listen well to how their members have already been formed as they come to the sermon event, since their capacity to hear, retain, and interpret the Word is both stunted and sharpened by that formation. Heightened consciousness of the dynamics of memory will enable preachers to navigate conflicting interpretations and will extend the range of experiences to which they appeal as they preach.

Barth rightly condensed the purpose of preaching to one simple challenge when he wrote, "The task of the sermon is to make space for the Word of God."[5] How can preachers make that space, and what can the Word of God do when given the space in which to do its work? Much of the work of making a safe and fecund space for our listeners to encounter God through preaching takes place outside the pulpit, as preachers engage in the priestly and pastoral work of attending to their members' encounters with Scripture in informal settings, learning the narratives of their wounds, sins and joys, engaging the wider community so as to be able to broaden the diversity of voices that address the congregation and empowering softer voices to preach and testify. Here we will consider five practices that preachers can

---

emblematically Daniel and his friends), Peter with Cornelius, Philip with the Ethiopian eunuch, and more implicitly in the disciples' encounters with the Gerasene demoniac and other Gentiles.

5. Barth, *Homiletics*, 122.

pursue as they seek to let their faith community's context inform and shape their preaching.

1. Reading the Bible Together

It sounds obvious, but one of the primary tasks of every congregation is simply to learn to read the Bible together. That endeavor is complicated by the multiple hidden histories and hermeneutical vantage points of a diverse body of readers. But church only moves forward with the belief that it is *possible*. A robust confidence in God's power to bring about shared understanding is a crucial dimension of pastoral leadership. We read together not only to understand but to be transformed by Scripture together. We bring to our reading the belief that the Word of God carries the capacity to unite and reconcile us as we come together in humility before it.[6] Shared understanding and unity come both as the fruit of earnest effort, and as gifts of the Holy Spirit. In the pulpit, preachers aid in that communal endeavor as they educate regarding the background of Scripture, rein in error, raise questions, spark conversations, and testify to their passion and love for the Word. However, to do this well in the sermon, preachers need to be on the ground, participating with ears wide open in the ongoing discussions of the Bible that are ideally taking place in their congregation in various less formal settings than the sermon. This too often falls off the schedule of pastors, but it is an invaluable source for connecting with and knowing members.

Sometimes this Bible study may be specifically designed as a feed-forward instrument, which both prepares the congregation for the proclaimed word and helps the pastor to prepare, following the model of John McClure's *Roundtable Pulpit*.[7] But it need not be focused toward the sermon to be enlightening for preachers. For example, a white pastor of a multiethnic

---

6. See Col 3:16; Eph 4:15. Michael G. Cartwright writes, "We know now in part (1 Co 13:10), even with respect to Scripture, but we will read the text better when we read it in communion with one another as a witness to the capacity of the gospel to reconcile us" ("Wrestling with Scripture," 113).

7. McClure writes, "Collaborative preaching embodies a participatory form of persuasion. While the sermon remains a non-interactive, single-party communication event, it is embedded within, and represents an actual interactive, multiple party communication event, the sermon roundtable. The sermon avoids being coercive or manipulative inasmuch as it is faithful to the collaboration and feedback that actually took place at the sermon roundtable prior to preaching" (*Roundtable Pulpit*, 56).

church in Georgia recently led a Bible study on the healing of the centurion's slave (Luke 7:1-10), intending to focus on the faith of the centurion. He
was caught off-guard when the African Americans raised the question of
why Jesus did not order the centurion to free his slave. He reflects, "Those
of us who were white had accepted slavery as part of the social landscape
of this passage, part of the background to the real meaning and power of
this story."[8] This is the kind of learning that needs to go on for pastors, and
the unidirectional nature of the sermon limits its capacity to instruct them.

2. Gathering Feedback: Hearing What They Heard

Powell's study of the widely varying details that North American and Russian listeners remembered of the Prodigal Son story, cited in chapter 4,
demonstrates well that culture and lived history affect our capacity to hear
and remember. Multiethnic churches are settings where the possibilities for
"missing" due to cultural differences are unusually high. Preachers in such
congregations need to be especially eager to seek out feedback and to con-
vey an approachable demeanor that welcomes constructive criticism. Some
pastors are highly intentional about feedback, organizing weekly gather-
ings with rotating groups of people who evaluate the sermon's effectiveness.
For most pastors that is not likely to become a permanent feature of their
schedule, but it could be something done occasionally, and should at least
occur informally throughout the year.

Miscommunication is inevitable in cross-cultural communication,
and it need not be viewed as a failure, but as an opportunity for laughter,
growth, and deepened relationship. For example, at one of the churches
I visited a white preacher engaged in some gentle ribbing of Jesus at the
opening of a sermon, as a way to provoke curiosity about Jesus' unorthodox
behavior at a party. A Honduran woman called him that week and shared
that it had offended her to hear Jesus "ridiculed." In her cultural context,
such humor was perceived as irreverent. As the preacher humbly expressed
appreciation for her perspective, their conversation became a redemptive
moment of grace, resulting in greater affection for each other. Their efforts
to understand each other call to mind the comments of John Peters. After a
survey of the history of the idea of communication he concludes,

---

8. Stroupe, "Looking on the Other Side," 22.

> Communication sometimes masquerades as the great solution to human ills, yet most troubles in human relationships do not come from a failure to match signs and meaning . . . [I]n relations among friends . . . what might be called a failure to communicate is more often a divergence of commitment or a deficit of patience. Communication . . . is more basically a political and ethical problem than a semantic or psychological one . . . We ought to be less worried about how signs arouse divergent meanings than the conditions that keep us from attending to our neighbors and other beings different from us.[9]

Peters' words echo the wisdom of the apostle Peter, who wrote that love covers a multitude of sins (1 Pet 4:8). Multiethnic churches have myriad opportunities to learn that truth.

3. Letting Many Voices Proclaim the Word

Jack Hakimian, a pastor of African and Armenian descent, reflected on his difficult choice to leave the church that had been instrumental in his conversion, a mostly white church with an all-white preaching staff. He said, "If I could just *once* have heard the Word from someone who looked and sounded like me, or like the friends [Latino and black young people] I was bringing to church, I would have stayed."[10] Hakimian's words are haunting, not only for white pastors, but for all pastors who hope their church's preaching ministry will find resonance with a diverse group of listeners.

HCF is a church with a great deal of ethnic diversity, and has had an ethnic mix at every level of its leadership. Yet it has proven difficult to find and equip a diverse preaching team. A Hispanic leader has preached occasionally, but the rest of the preaching team has been white. This year, for the first time, two Asian Americans and one black lay leader preached, and the excitement in the air after those services was striking. Broadening the base of preachers may involve more forethought and leadership training than writing a sermon does, so it is easily postponed. But the benefits are clear. Most churches have a few lay people who are gifted to preach occasionally, especially with some investment in their development.

Short of preaching, moments of testimony can broaden the base of speakers up front and can give another setting in which diverse stories are

9. Peters, *Speaking Into the Air*, 269.

10. From interview with Jack Hakimian, spring 2006, at Fuller Theological Seminary.

told. At HCF, a Cambodian woman named Sarah recently approached the microphone, with a map of Africa on the screen behind her. She shyly said, "I have been asked to lead the congregation in prayer for the Sudan today because I too have lived through genocide." Many who had shared a pew with her had never known that, though they knew that she was Cambodian. This woman would never be willing to preach a sermon, but her offering of her story and herself as an intercessor on behalf of Sudan was a gift to the congregation. Rowan Williams's words interpret well the gift Sarah gave as she shared her painful memory.

> We might say that the community lives in the exchange, not sim-
> ply of *charisms* in Paul's sense, but of *stories*, of memories. My par-
> ticular past is there, in the Church, as a resource for my relations
> with my brothers and sisters—not to be poured out repeatedly and
> promiscuously, but as a hinterland of vision and truth and accep-
> tance, out of which I can begin to love in honesty. My *charism*,
> the gift given me to give to the community, is my *self*, ultimately;
> my story given back, to give me a place in the net of exchange, the
> web of gifts, which is Christ's church. My self is to be given away
> in love, not because it is worthless, but because it is supremely pre-
> cious, given to me by the hand of God as he returns my memory.
> Out of my story, the Spirit of the risen Jesus constitutes my present
> possibilities of understanding, compassion and self-sharing.[11]

It is the great privilege and calling of pastors to draw forth that gift-giving from their members, by learning what those stories are, believing in their worth for the whole congregation, and making space for those stories to be told.

4. Knowing the Ethnic Memories in Our Midst

For that self-sharing to happen, someone with real interest in Sarah needed to have sat with her and earned her trust, drawn her out and heard her story. Barth speaks with the heart of a pastor when he exhorts, "Preachers must love their congregations. They must not want to be without them . . . If preaching is to be congregational, there must also be openness to the real situation of the congregation and reflection upon it so as to be able to take it up into the sermon. Living with their congregations, preachers live out a

---

11. Williams, *Resurrection*, 43–44.

story with them, and they are constantly agitated by the question, 'How is it with them?'"[12]

As we know the experiences that have shaped the interpretive and hearing capacities of our listeners, our love for them grows, and our desire grows to connect the stories of Scripture with their stories. We become more attuned to the cultural complexity and richness within Scripture itself, and better able to bring its themes to bear on the experiences of our listeners. James Nieman and Thomas Rogers write, "Knowing more about an ethnic group obviously gives substantive materials that permit an immediate connection with the lives of our hearers both before and during the sermon. Mentioning these insights is also an important way of validating ethnic groups that have often been ignored or undervalued . . . Biblical texts begin to speak in vibrant new ways when the preacher is committed to a particular ethnic group."[13] Preachers who have invested in this kind of pastoral care find within themselves a deep desire to speak a word of freedom, healing, and grace, and a deep confidence that the gospel Christ proclaims can offer it.

Pastors of multiethnic churches have pursued several creative strategies to deepen not only their knowledge of their members, but to increase the knowledge of each other's backgrounds within the whole congregation. The Rev. Mark Lau Branson's former church[14] initiated movie nights that were hosted by members of different ethnic groups. Their task was to choose a movie that would help others get to know the dynamics of their ethnic group better. They hosted lively discussions after the movies. The Rev. Ken Fong has worked hard to help his Asian American members get to know the Latino culture that predominates near their building. Through after-school programs, they have developed relationships with youth, and from there have entered into the festivals and commemorations that are significant to them, such as *quinceañera* celebrations (marking a girl's fifteenth birthday).

Pastors can develop their knowledge of another culture in various ways. They can invest time to read and in other ways educate themselves about the ethnic histories and current realities in their community. This investment earns trust, since minority people tire of being the educators of ignorant outsiders. When possible, travel and language learning can be

---

12. Barth, *Homiletics*, 84.

13. Nieman and Rogers, *Preaching to Every Pew*, 31.

14. Rockridge United Methodist Church of Oakland, CA.

powerful tools for building trust and gaining insight. Pastors also broaden their cultural reach as they read and listen to sermons by preachers of other ethnicities than their own.

5. Knowing and Embracing Our Own Ethnic Story

In my interviews, as with the much more extensive ones Nieman and Rogers conducted, a consistent theme that arose was the need to know and love one's own culture and ethnicity. The path to that love will almost always involve a process of anger and mourning over the pain that has been inflicted on others by members of one's own culture. But self-loathing cannot be where leaders land. Nieman and Rogers write, "Enough self-awareness is needed to claim one's own personal identity without apology. We are bid to show a curious blend of humility and strength."[15] As Rowan Williams's words above show, we offer our *selves* to the body of Christ, but we are only able to make that offering if we know and love ourselves. This is true in preaching as well; preachers are more effective as they recognize and appreciate the particular vantage point their cultural context has given them for hearing Scripture and understanding life. The Rev. Curtis Chang recalled that one of the most effective sermons he preached, in a congregation where Asian Americans are a minority, was a sermon on hospitality that included an extended story of a lavish Chinese banquet. He exhibited love for and a delight in his own ethnic heritage and was able to offer it as a gift to his congregation.

PREACHING SHAPES THE COMMUNITY OF MEMORY

If preaching is making space for the Word of God, what can that Word do when given room to move? Preachers can proclaim words that foster practices of faithful remembering, both of the biblical Word and of the stories represented by each member. Such preaching cultivates the ability to laugh together, to confess painful truth to one another, and to imagine a new future together. It trains members to serve well in their communities, and it enables them as a congregation to persevere. It is grounded in a high view of the agency of God to act within the sermon event. Preachers both humbly depend on the Holy Spirit's capacity to transform lives through

---

15. Nieman and Rogers, *Preaching to Every Pew*, 29.

the preached word, and they confidently trust in it. Here, David Lose's critique of Campbell's postliberal homiletic is apt: "In a postliberal homiletic, preaching is not about proclaiming the gospel by which the Holy Spirit creates faith, but rather it is the means by which to inculturate participants more deeply in their tradition while training them in the habitual practices of their community."[16] Preachers can benefit from the deep concern that postliberals and virtue ethics thinkers show for the formation of character, their attention to habits, and their attunement to the shaping power of narrative and the centrality of the community of faith. Yet we lean away from the flattening of the agency of the Holy Spirit and the reduction of the miraculous and eventful nature of the sermon that can ensue from their line of reasoning. As Ray Anderson has written, "It can be said that Jesus is not only the subject of proclamation (the one about whom we preach), but he is himself the proclaimer in every act of proclamation (the one who proclaims himself through every event of preaching)."[17] Such an understanding leads us to expect the preaching event to be a moment in which God is really present, mysteriously yet powerfully at work.

That is good, because racial reconciliation in the context of the deep divisions that have plagued North American (and world) history calls for nothing less than a miracle of new hearing and understanding. As Willimon notes, "All gospel induced speaking and hearing tends to be miraculous . . . There is no other way to bring the event of Jesus Christ to comprehension through speech other than as miracle, that is, as an instance of the self-giving, the self-revelation of God." He concludes, "I think Acts would also tell us that, whenever by the grace of God our preaching overcomes some cultural boundary, we are right to rejoice that God continues to work wonders through the word."[18]

With specific regard to memory, the proclaimed word engages listeners on a number of levels. We see the prophets, Jesus, and the apostles striving to expose amnesia and other faulty memory practices (toward nostalgia, melancholy, bitterness, or pride). The writers of Scripture also sought to make narratives of the past (from the Exodus to the cross and resurrection) accessible to those who were not eye-witnesses to those events, so that they could foster wisdom and faith, enabling hearers who had become alienated from their history (such as the readers of Hebrews)

16. Lose, *Confessing Jesus Christ*, 123.
17. Anderson, *Shape of Practical Theology*, 56.
18. Willimon, "Everyone Whom the Lord Calls," 6, 9.

to receive and own it as their story. They prophesied and proclaimed as a means of shaping the capacity to remember well. Memory is an aspect or function of the imagination, and lively preaching allows the Word of God to engage the imagination.[19] Garrett Green writes, "Proclamation . . . can be described as an appeal to the imagination of the hearers through the images of Scripture. The preacher's task is to mediate and facilitate that encounter by engaging his or her own imagination, which becomes [a] link between scripture and congregation."[20]

The ability to learn from the past is a skill that is not cultivated well in society today. Massive quantities of fragmented bits of information assault us from multiple forms of media, and assimilating it trains us well today to *process* information but not to understand it, reflect upon it, or remember it. Web news-watchers may be captivated by a story for a moment, and even forward it to their "community" or post it in their blog, but their attention is quickly drawn to the next scintillating story. However, church is formed by a people who are, and who *remain*, captivated by the same story.

Thus, a large part of the preaching task is *reminding*. Reminding unfortunately has connotations that are negative or neutral at best. One who becomes highly talented at reminding will not be likely to make the news in the same way as one who becomes highly talented at innovating. Reminding is a close cousin to nagging, and can feel like a wearisome task that fosters only resentment in those who receive it. It is difficult to gauge when someone needs reminding, and can be perceived as patronizing when it is given and not needed. Reminders can be difficult to welcome even when they are needed. We tend to need reminding to do difficult or laborious things, whereas our natural ability to remember to do pleasurable things is obviously stronger. Reminding tends to imply greater maturity on the part of the one doing the reminding, as seen in its centrality to the task of parenting. In a society that highly values egalitarianism, it is feared that acknowledgement of greater maturity on the part of a teacher implies inferiority on the part of the learner. So the role of the "remind-er" (or

---

19. Charles H. Cosgrove and W. Dow Edgerton state, "Reflection has access to experience only by means of the imagination. Lived experience is available to us insofar as it is transformed into the symbolic forms of the imagination, especially language. These first-order transformations both preserve experience and construct it according to the imaginative world, forms, and dynamics available to us. If I want to reflect on my experience, I must reflect on it as it resides (preserved and constructed) in my imagination" (Cosgrove and Edgerton, *In Other Words*, 10).

20. Green, *Imagining God*, 149.

remembrancer, as it was called in English courts) is resented and diminished in many areas of late modern society. Yet it is crucial to the church's discipleship. The writer of Hebrews notes our tendency to "drift away" from the things we have heard (Heb 2:1). While drifting is an evocative image, Lancelot Andrewes (1555–1626) highlighted the verb's even more striking classical Greek meaning, "to leak and run out." He did so in a sermon on Jesus' exhortation to remember Lot's wife. The antidote to the natural human tendency to leak, according to Andrewes, was the preaching of Scripture. He observed, "In [the] office of preaching we are employed as much about *recognosce* [know again/remember] as about *cognosce* [perceive]; as much in calling to their minds the things they know and have forgot, as in teaching them the things they know not, or never learnt."[21] He urged preachers to labor particularly hard to bolster remembrance of the narrative of history found in Scripture. He preached, "But the storehouse, and the very life of memory, is the history of time: and a special charge have we, all along the Scriptures, to call upon men to look to that."[22]

Preaching interacts with memory in multiple ways, from unearthing and naming memories that have been left unspoken in church, to interpreting and reframing painful or debilitating ones. But core to the task of preaching is the basic, unglamorous task of reminding, strengthening and shaping the memory skills of hearers, toward the end that they would live lives of bold faith as they endeavor to reach out within their congregations and engage their communities fruitfully. It is hoped that preachers can view reminding not as a chore, akin to reminding children to brush their teeth, but as a sacred, urgent, and joyful calling. Here we'll explore six ways that preaching engages and shapes memory and consider how the preached Word may further various goals and purposes of multiethnic churches.

1. The Preached Word Makes the Past Useful for Discipleship

Various speakers and writers of words in Scripture have sought to use memory for growth, healing, and greater fidelity to God. It begins with the narration of the life of Joseph in the book of Genesis, which in many ways forms a template for remembering well, as it displays poignantly the integration and healing of a painful past. Exiles narrated his story even as

21. Andrewes, "Remember Lot's Wife," sermon preached before Queen Elizabeth at Hampton Court, 1594, in Davis, *Imagination Shaped*, 30.

22. Ibid., 31.

they sought ways to articulate their recent past. Joseph endures the pain of being forgotten, a fact that the narrator emphasizes by stating it both positively and negatively: "Yet the chief cupbearer did not remember Joseph, but forgot him" (Gen 39:23). The hinge of the narrative occurs when the cupbearer does remember him, stating, "I remember my faults today" (Gen 41:9). Later, in an ambivalent attempt at forgetfulness, Joseph names his son Manasseh, or *Making to Forget*, though of course his very name would call to mind his past in its every utterance. After a long journey through grief, Joseph shows remarkable insight at the end of his life, saying to his brothers, "Even though you intended it [their betrayal of him] to do harm to me, God intended it for good, in order to preserve a numerous people" (Gen 50:20). Joseph is able to place his story within the larger narrative of God's purposes for redemption. The writer of the Joseph cycle in Genesis is teaching the Israelites how to open up their narration of difficult recent events, to consider if they may fit into a larger narrative of God's purposes. Preachers share in this calling as they seek to do the same for their congregations, so that they too can find the fingerprint and work of God as they look back upon their lives, so that the past can be a source of faith rather than of bitterness. They do this in part through highlighting exemplary memory in Scripture, and the Joseph narrative is a rich resource for this.

In Scripture, we see numerous instances of speakers using words to recall the past to listeners in ways that will inform godly behavior in the present. Nathan's vivid image and stark narrative of the heartless sheep thief (2 Sam 12:1–6) provoked David to recall his recent past and integrate it with his newly heightened sense of outrage at injustice. After connecting the parable with David, the Lord through Nathan proceeds to review for David God's history of working on his behalf (2 Sam 12:7–8). "I anointed you . . . I rescued you . . . I gave you . . ." Then the Lord asks David to recall his own actions: "You despised . . . You struck down . . . You killed . . ." Nathan's proclamation of God's word was a powerful antidote to the amnesia that royal privilege can permit; it enabled David to look his past squarely in the face and to confess it truthfully. The recollection of his past gave meaning to David's present and contained the seed of a redeemed future.

In a similar strategy, Jesus provokes the curiosity of the woman at the well by using the vivid imagery of living water, and then, in an *Ecce homo*-like shift, he suddenly tells her the truth about her past (John 4:17–18). While her immediate response to this invitation to confession is evasion, Jesus' knowledge of her past later forms the very center of her testimony.

Her essential proclamation of the identity of Jesus is, "He told me everything I have ever done" (John 4:39). Her encounter with Jesus has made it safe and fruitful to tell the story of her past. Preachers share in Jesus' ongoing ministry as they speak the truth to their congregations in ways that lead to repentance.

Jesus teaches about people who do not have access to their past in usable ways, as cautionary tales for his listeners. One such person was the unforgiving servant (Matt 18:23–34), who was forgiven an enormous sum of money, only to turn to one who owed him a small amount and demand payment. His recent past failed to form a memory in his consciousness or his character that could function as a source of wisdom or kindness. Jesus is clearly teaching that our memory of God's grace toward us should lodge lastingly and deeply within us and should serve as a transformative wellspring for our behavior toward others. One implication of this parable is simply that we are all too prone to forgetfulness, and so preachers should not apologize for sermons that remind people of the basic truths regarding the grace of God and the need to extend forgiveness to our neighbor.

The rich man who refused to care for Lazarus is an example of a man who failed to remember and learn from the wisdom of the more distant past (that of Moses and the prophets), and who came from a household marked by impaired memory (Luke 16:19–31). In heaven he begs Abraham to send Lazarus to warn his five brothers, but Abraham replies that they can listen to Moses and the prophets. That heritage of memory is available as a source of ethical guidance for them, but they have not engaged with it in ways that would shape their practices toward the poor. Jesus appeals to his listeners to follow a better path, by remembering their ancestors and learning from their righteousness and their failures. Elsewhere he calls them to remember the faithfulness of Noah (Luke 17:26), the ambivalence of Lot's wife (Luke 17:32), and the freedom and pragmatism of David (Matt 12:3-4). Here, as a preacher he models the role of the sage, who calls the community to wisdom through disciplined reflection on the past.

The epistles abound with calls to put the past to work. The hearers of Hebrews are warned to learn from the disobedience of Israel so that they can enter into God's Sabbath rest (Heb 3:7–19). Paul and Peter engage in the work of reminding as part of their pastoral zeal for the people in their care. Peter describes that process when he writes, "Therefore I intend to keep on reminding you of these things, though you know them already and are established in the truth that has come to you. I think it right, as long as

I am in this body, to refresh your memory . . . I will make every effort so that after my departure you may be able at any time to recall these things . . . . I am trying to arouse your sincere intention by reminding you that you should remember the words spoken in the past by the holy prophets, and the commandments of the Lord and Savior spoken through your apostles" (2 Pet 1:12–15; 3:1–2).

As a pastoral leader who reminds his listeners, Peter does not usurp from them the task of remembering; rather he *reminds them to remember*. His goal is to strengthen within them the capacity to draw upon the wisdom of the past, and also the *tendency* to turn to it as their first response, their first source of guidance. Preachers today are engaged in that same task, of proclaiming the stories and the prophetic teachings of Scripture in ways that cause them to land deep within memory. Memory then becomes a storehouse of treasures old and new that evoke godly responses to the issues and questions listeners face each day.

2. The Preached Word Forms a Humble People

While the preached word forms many character qualities within its hearers, perhaps none is as essential to the pursuit of racial reconciliation as humility. Humility enables people to hear Scripture speak words of judgment and of grace upon their ethnic heritage. It springs from the memory of God's gracious, saving work on our behalf. A humble heart frees people from the fear of failure and from the need for certainty in communication events. It lends tolerance for ambiguity, and cultivates an eagerness to gain the perspective of others. As Hauerwas writes, "The Christian story teaches us to regard truthfulness more as a gift than a possession and thus requires that we be willing to face both the possibilities and threats a stranger represents."[23]

Humility bears the fruit of laughter and freedom in our relationships. Humor is closely linked to humility because laughter brings us back to our human finitude, not as something against which we must chafe, but as a source of joy and gratitude, and of dependence on God and one another. The uncertainty inherent in cross-cultural communication attempts causes errors that can either lead to shame and offense, or to good-natured laughter. Philip Keane, who has developed a moral theology of imagination, sees humor as a key component of the development of imaginative capacities.

---

23. Hauerwas, *Community of Character*, 10.

He writes, "Humor is one of the best ways to help us get past the human tendency to absolutize the relative, to help us remember that only God is God. Humor confronts us with the incongruous in our lives. Through dealing with incongruity, humor reminds us that, as finite beings, we do not have logical answers to all the problems we face."[24] The ability to laugh, at oneself and at the situation, is a sign that grace is present and growing in the congregational culture.

In a similar vein, Penny Becker notes the role of laughter in her study of congregations that moved toward greater ethnic inclusivity in the Chicago area. She observed of City Baptist Church that, "Through sermons, as well as in other forums, the pastor provides an interpretive rationale for multicultural ministry and an opportunity for members to laugh good-naturedly at their own discomfort and find ways of moving beyond it before it becomes the basis for prolonged and painful conflict."[25] The ability to laugh at our own blunders and those of others is a sign that our memories are being healed and redeemed. During a recent sermon on reconciliation, pastor Kerwin Manning, an African American, grinned as he moved among his ethnically mixed congregation rubbing black members' forearms, demonstrating the way he was greeted by strangers at his almost entirely white Christian college. What had been a source of pain remains now only as a source of affection and laughter.

Preaching can foster a gracious humility in a few ways. It can tell the stories of cross-cultural mishaps and blunders that abound in Scripture, from Abraham and Sarah's awkward negotiations with different customs in new lands (Gen 12:10-20) to Naaman's blustering about his superior rivers (2 Kgs 5:12), to the struggles of the early church to incorporate the Gentiles in Acts, Galatians, and 1 Corinthians. The book of Acts in particular abounds with awkward moments and misperceptions of meaning. Peter's interaction with Cornelius portrays both men bumbling their way toward understanding the new words and works of God (Acts 10). Neither could come to understanding without the other, and their awkward exchanges reflect that uncertainty and incompleteness.

In addition, preachers can model humility and dependence on God through their sermons. One source for that humility is the very improbability and even impossibility of multiethnic congregations thriving apart from God's frequent work to rescue and redeem and the inadequacy most

24. Keane, *Christian Ethics and Imagination*, 67.
25. Becker, "Making Inclusive Communities," 459.

pastors feel for the task of leading them. Though this could lead to paralysis or anxiety, for many pastors this becomes a source of delight and of gratitude to God for giving them this ministry. Often their leadership is strengthened by the narratives of the improbable servants God chose in Scripture. Rev. Jeff Bassette demonstrates this well in a sermon entitled *One New People*:

> I can imagine God talking to one of the angels in the time of Jesus, saying, "I've got just the guy to build my church: Peter." The angels object, "But he's so parochial, so provincial, he's never had a close friendship with a single Gentile." God responds, "Yes, that's right, but that's just his starting point. I have a whole life journey for him to walk. At the right time, I will tell him to broaden out his soul to include non-Jews freely as my people, and when I tell him he will do it with a whole heart, and lead others to do the same. Yes, Peter is my man." And there might have been a similar conversation about unlikely Paul.
>
> I can see God doing the same when he dreamt of this multiethnic church in Los Angeles, Hope Christian Fellowship. Leaning over to one of his angels and saying, "I've chosen just the guy to get this started. God points to the most mono-ethnic of the fifty states, Vermont, to a town of five hundred people, to a young man who'd never had one friend from another culture than his own, and says, with a twinkle in his eye, "If I can create a multi-ethnic church through him, he'll know full well it was my work and not his, and so will everyone else." If God brought you here to this church, then you are part of that work of God, too.[26]

Willimon reflects with humility on his own preaching as he writes,

> One of the great joys of the preaching ministry is to be able to witness the rather miraculous ability of the Holy Spirit to grant, in our listeners, a hearing, a response that is not of our devising, a response that is better than our preaching . . . Even with preaching as poor as mine . . . Someone from a race my race has abused and degraded for centuries came up to me after Sundays' sermon and said, "God really spoke to me through you." I have no other satisfactory explanations for such events than that they are miracles, gifts of the still active Holy Spirit.[27]

---

26. Rev. Jeffrey Bassette, sermon preached at Hope Christian Fellowship of San Gabriel, July 15, 2007.

27. Willimon, "Everyone Whom the Lord Calls," 9.

A different aspect of humility that comes into play particularly for multiethnic congregations is the task of recounting the histories of our own ethnic groups as truthfully as possible. Though not directly related to preaching, it is something that preaching can model and can make safe as it shapes a culture of grace and truth. It is costly to be known. It is easier to maintain a rose-colored lens on one's own complicity or that of one's ancestors when one is not in regular contact with those who have borne the brunt of that history. Remembering well in the presence of others involves a humble confession of need and a risky expression of willingness to be changed. As we choose to remember in church, we are implicitly acknowledging that our own memory-constructing capacities are faulty. Too often we have remembered our personal and national past through the distorting lenses of self-justification, self-condemnation, nostalgia, diminishment, and exaggeration.

Nietzsche insightfully named the role of pride in the repression of memories of which we are ashamed. He wrote, "'I have done that,' says my memory. 'I cannot have done that,' says my pride, and remains inexorable. Eventually memory yields."[28] Nietzsche is right about the human tendency, but he did not tell the whole story. Membership in a community of faith can be a powerful antidote to pride, which may even undo its effects on memory. When acts of confession are made safe by a culture of grace, a more clear-eyed look at the past becomes possible. We enter the community of faith confessing that we need others, and we need the Word of God, to re-collect us, to give context, shape, and clarity to our memories. The preached word, in particular, allows the metaphors, images, stories, and promises of Scripture to speak into painful pasts with a healing word of redemption, grace, and love. It names ways the Spirit of God may have been at work in events that are difficult to interpret and integrate into the present. In turn it names the presence of God in the joyful experiences in our pasts, so that they become sources of gratitude and hope for the future.

3. The Preached Word Heals Wounded Memories

Whether issues of ethnicity are directly involved or not, listeners come to church in need of restoration, integration, and interpretation of painful

---

28. Nietzsche, *Jenseits von Gut und Böse*, cited in Miroslav Volf, *Exclusion and Embrace*, 247.

past events.[29] Through proclamation of God's mercy, forgiveness, and redemption, through stories that connect with and interpret listeners' own struggles, and through testimony, sermons can open spaces in which listeners may grieve over sins committed and wounds suffered and where they may mourn losses together.[30]

Jesus proclaimed words that restored dignity to those who had suffered shame, such his declaration to the woman with the flow of blood that she was a daughter with strong faith (Mark 5:34). One of the most dramatic instances of Jesus speaking restoration into a past riddled with failure and shame took place by the Sea of Tiberius, in the reinstatement of Peter. Jesus graciously refocused Peter's life around Peter's pastoral calling, his love for Christ, and the invitation to follow him. He spoke words that redeemed his past, recasting it within the larger narrative of Jesus' life and mission.

Rowan Williams suggests that simply exercising the capacity to remember the past is a part of healing, as it lifts us above or beyond that past; we are more than the sum of our past experiences and we are not determined solely by them. He writes, "The self's transcendence is in its memory, precisely in its recollection *now* of another reality, a past reality, both distinct from and part of the present situation. Memory affirms that the present situation has a context; it, like the self, is part of a continuity, it is 'made' and so it is not immutable. By learning that situations have wider contexts, we learn a measure of freedom and detachment from (or transcendence of) the limits of the present. Things may be otherwise; change occurs."[31]

The work a preacher does in this area is much like that of a patient and skillful quiltmaker, who can gather scraps and fragments and see a pattern emerging. Scripture provides the template that gives meaning and even

29. I have avoided the term, "healing of memories," to avoid some of the excesses and distortions of the inner healing movement that flourished in the 1970s and 1980s within charismatic and evangelical circles. Specifically, some strains of it encouraged people to go back and imaginatively change their memories, in ways that do not reflect sound psychological practice. Yet, it is an apt term for the way the Holy Spirit through the Word interacts with memories.

30. Wilkes addresses the connection between remembering and mourning personal failures when he writes, "Remembering involves mourning because we constantly have to put to death the illusions that we have erected for ourselves. In remembering there is a constant re-evaluation of the past as we see it through our present vision, and we are given the opportunity to put to death our past cruelty and insensitivity" ("Remembering," 89).

31. Williams, *Resurrection*, 30.

beauty to the pieces, as they are placed and given perspective by the surrounding pieces. John Hendrix, in an address to seminary faculty, praised the capacity of gifted teachers to connect the scattered pieces of students' lives in healing ways. He said,

> Life for most of us is made up of small pieces and fragments, much like an old fashioned piecework quilt . . . Each of us is made up of scraps that did not quite fit the garment at the time. We leave the leftovers everywhere—in the attic, the closet, under the bed, tucked away on a shelf. It often takes another person to discover them. They are puzzled as to why such a beautiful piece was discarded. They begin to show us how it all fits together—mismatched colors, ragged edges, and scraps. These patterns make no sense at all at first sight, but some people come along who show us how they blend together. We call these people teachers.[32]

We could also call such people preachers. The comfort that a quilt provides makes it an especially apt metaphor for the healing ministry that preaching can perform. Preachers go about their work of listening with compassion throughout the week, finding the fragments in the stories they hear from their members and in the wider community context, and searching for interpretive keys in the Scriptures that can lend a pattern to those fragments, one that might enable listeners to see and embrace the work of God in their lives.

4. The Preached Word Re-Members the Body of Believers

The above section primarily addressed how the preached word can augment personal integration of painful pasts; here the focus is on how preaching can foster unity and healing between people. Chapter 6 noted the ways that the writer(s) of Deuteronomy sought to help the Israelites draw upon their past enslavement as a source of compassion toward the aliens in their midst. That past is exponentially more distant from hearers today, but the task of preachers continues to be to present the Scriptures as the family photo album, as *our* story. Hauerwas writes, "Our lives are constituted by discovering we are part of a history we have not created, a history without which we cannot make sense of what we think we have done as well as what we think has happened to us."[33]

32. Hendrix, "Making the Trip," 419.
33. Hauerwas, "Why Time Cannot Heal," 44.

Not only do preachers display the characters of Scriptures as scenes from our family photo album, but they invite listeners to place our images of ourselves in the album and thus to see them anew.[34] When placed side by side in the album, our uncanny resemblance to conniving Jacob emerges; our likeness with the image of Christ does as well. When images are framed within the biblical narrative, new vistas and vantage points appear that transform our gaze upon ourselves and upon others. The album is so arranged that it functions as a primer in the art of seeing the beauty and delighting in it, which in turn transforms relationships.[35] David Hart reflects on this process, in a consideration of the delight members of the Trinity have in each other. He writes,

> The Christian thought of God's creative agape . . . belongs to the thought of the Trinity: it is a love always of recognition and delight . . . generous in truly wanting the other. Thus the "ethical" must belong, for theology, to an aesthetics of desire . . . A Christian ethics cannot help but concern itself with the cultivation of desire, with learning to desire the other because the other is truly desirable, because every other is truly beautiful; the moral task is to love because one truly sees and to see because one truly loves: to educate the vision to see the glory of *this particular one.*[36]

Preachers must cultivate their own vision of the beauty of all who are in their care. Their preaching will then exude the love that ensues from that vision, and that preaching can also function as instruction in the art of seeing and celebrating beauty. So it is part of the vocation of the preacher to cultivate within himself a deep sense of the created goodness of humanity, and particularly the beauty in ethnic diversity.

Fondness and affection also grows as members of a diverse community tell and hear each other's stories, and as we help each other to place

34. Lischer reflects, "When we make a family photo album we do not do so to prove the existence of our ancestor or to provide a record of their appearance. We do it for our children and grandchildren in order to make a meeting possible, to enlarge their sense of identity and place in a family of love. Which is precisely our purpose in narrative preaching . . . not to prove points about Jesus but to evoke the one who is always among us, but hidden" (*End of Words*, 125).

35. Dykstra observes, "What people see is an indication of what they care about and can care about. It is an indication of the depth and breadth of their compassion, of the scope and quality of their loves and desires and of the intensity of which they feel . . . The quality of our lives is, in turn, shaped by what we see. Acts of attention do not leave us unchanged" (*Vision and Character*, 51).

36. Hart, *Beauty of the Infinite*, 265.

those scenes next to scenes within the biblical narrative. In that process, we come to *resonate* with one another, and empathy grows for each other.[37] Hearing testimonies of God's redemption of a painful past may provoke identification or recognition on the part of listeners with God's work in their histories, and they may recognize anew that that they are profoundly loved, held, and valued by God as well.

Remembering well together is also an act of hospitality and inclusion. The desire to hear the painful and joyful pasts of others is a harbinger of growing capacity within a congregation to honor and include the other. In the very act of hearing, dignity may be restored. This act is costly, requiring time, patience, and generosity. Kathy Black notes the time-consuming nature of shared remembrance and its potential to unite congregations.[38] It often takes the form of reminiscence, which is a leisurely form of narration,[39] and thus runs counter to the "drive-through" culture of many churches today. Preachers can model and nurture a high capacity and desire to hear the reminiscences that matter to congregants. This conveys value and care and fosters intimacy. Roger Schank and Robert Abelson note, "The listener performs a very important role for a storyteller. He or she reveals, usually implicitly, which stories he or she wants to hear."[40]

Remembering well together requires hospitality for another reason. Stories that highlight memories of a minority will simply not immediately appeal to everyone. Preachers tend to prefer the ease of familiarity, so predominantly white, suburban churches hear stories of soccer dads on the sidelines in sermons on righteous anger, instead of Fannie Lou Hamer's speeches surrounding the Democratic Convention in 1963.[41] But, that story will resonate deeply with the collective memory of many African Americans who may be present, and it will expand the memory stores of everyone

37. Clayton Schmit, drawing on the work of Walter Ong, gives insight into resonance in art and preaching. He writes, "Resonance is the capacity that allows for that which is interior to one person to reciprocate with that which is interior to another person. Just as a piano sounding the tone low 'E' causes the low 'E' string on a nearby bass violin to sound in sympathy (or perhaps, more accurately, in symphony), the sound of one person speaking communicates a sympathetic understanding in his or her listeners" (*Too Deep for Words*, 12).

38. Black, *Culturally Conscious Worship*, 87.

39. Casey notes, "When we reminisce, a certain laxity of direction or purpose abounds that disallows, or at least discourages, the kind of intensified build-up so characteristic of story-telling . . ." (*Remembering*, 106).

40. Schank and Abelson, "Knowledge and Memory," 41.

41. Charles Marsh tells this story well in *God's Long Summer*, 33-44.

who hears it. So, preachers must extend themselves to learn and draw upon a broader base of illustrative material. Then, they must be willing to risk offering that material to their congregations, even when it will not yield the desired fruit of immediate resonance that a more readily accessible illustration will. This will develop the congregation's capacity for empathy, both within their walls and as they go out into the world.

5. The Preached Word Envisions a New Community

Not only does society today not train us well to remember, but it does not articulate a compelling vision of a future that is worth hoping for. Multiethnic churches that are vibrant, joyful centers of reconciliation and healing proclaim, by their life and their words, the kingdom that is coming. Interviews and observation show that preachers in multiethnic churches tend to refer often to the eschatological visions of the reconciled nations found in Revelation 7 and 21. Pastors who strive for ethnic diversity tend to be visionaries, and they draw inspiration from the images of unity and healing found in Scripture. Long writes, "An eschatological perspective allows us to preach the prophetic call for justice not on the basis of guilt, moralism, or some misguided obedience to a principal of political correctness, but on the basis that the prophets themselves did: a joyful, even festive response to God's in-breaking future."[42]

That vision is not only tied to the future, but is anchored by the past, by glimpses of God's work that have already been seen. Preachers draw upon a congregation's cherished memories, of bold risks taken and of moments when reconciliation became possible, to inspire future faithfulness. Walter Brueggemann describes this aspect of the preaching task.

> What a commission it is to express a future that none think imaginable! Of course this cannot be done by inventing new symbols, for that is wishful thinking. Rather, it means to move back into the deepest memories of this community and activate those very symbols that have always been the basis for contradicting the regnant consciousness. Therefore the symbols of hope cannot be general and universal but must be those that have been known concretely in this particular history. And when the prophet returns, with the community, to those deep symbols, they will discern that hope is

42. Long, "Preaching God's Future," 201.

not a late, tacked-on hypothesis but rather the primal dimension
of every memory of this community.[43]

So, the preacher paints vivid pictures of the shape the kingdom of God
might take in their community. She lays bare the emptiness of the vision of
the good life put forth by marketing experts, and seeks to whet the appetite
of her listeners for the abundant life Christ promised. She testifies invitingly
to the joy that is the fruit of that pursuit. She tells compellingly the stories
of saints throughout history who have staked their lives on a vision of God's
beloved community.

6. The Preached Word Sends Members Out in Mission

Ideally, one of the fruits born of the multiethnic church is that it prepares its
members to serve and lead effectively in a multicultural society. Preaching
does this in part when it celebrates the many examples of people throughout Scripture who crossed borders and negotiated cultural marginality to
fulfill God's mission, from Joseph to Ruth to Daniel, and from Ananias to
Paul. Because the church has a basis for reconciliation in the cross of Jesus
Christ, it can be a safe place to practice, and to fail at, communication with
those from very different backgrounds, equipping them with tools that
will enable them to bring the practices of Jesus into their workplaces and
neighborhoods.

Also, the church can play a key role in nurturing youth that are secure in their ethnic identities and confident and motivated to interact with
strangers. Most children raised in public schools today know the rhetoric of
tolerance, but tolerance alone is not adequate to the task of genuine shared
life. Youth who can articulate a biblical vision for unity, forgiveness, and
love of the most unlikely of neighbors will be able to lead their peers in
that endeavor. Hauerwas notes, "The church's first task is to help us gain a
critical perspective on those narratives that have captivated our vision and
lives. By doing so, the church may well help provide a paradigm of social
relations otherwise thought impossible . . . The church [witnesses] to the
kind of social life possible for those that have been formed by the story of
Christ."[44]

43. Brueggemann, *Hopeful Imagination*, 66.
44. Hauerwas, *Community of Character*, 12.

One way churches foster that, for youth and adults, is by addressing racist incidents and tendencies from the pulpit and calling listeners to a higher standard. This takes prophetic courage and pastoral sensitivity. Shortly after the terrorist attacks of September 11, 2001, the Rev. Ken Fong hosted an evening for their church and the community. He invited the Middle Eastern members of his church to participate in a panel discussion to broaden and deepen understanding for the congregation. This began a series of conversations that have continued to build the cultural intelligence of his congregation over the last several years.

As the church seeks to equip its members to be effective in a society that is not oriented toward reconciliation, another virtue that preaching can cultivate is the ability to learn from and emulate each other. Preachers do that in part by sharing what they are learning from wise contemporary leaders and from the resources of the past. Imitation is not highly prized in our independent culture, but it has been an esteemed value in the church throughout history. Disciples by their nature are followers, who look to another for direction and a model or pattern of life. For Christians that is inextricable from the ability to learn from the past with humility, heeding the call in Job 8:8 to "ask the former age, and consider what their ancestors have found" (cf. Deut 32:7; Isa 46:9; Jer 6:16; Heb 10:32). As Lancelot Andrewes considered the church's calling to learn humbly from the past, he noted two types of stories in Scripture: *memento et fac* (remember and do likewise) and *memento et fuge* (remember and flee). He cites as examples Jesus' prophetic word that every generation will remember the beautiful deed of the woman who anointed him at Bethany (Mark 14:9), and Jesus' exhortation to remember and flee from the behavior of Lot's wife (Luke 17:32).

As we learn to learn from biblical history, we cultivate a posture of teachability and humility that hopefully can transfer to the ability to learn from each other in church. Hauerwas writes, "For internal to the story itself is the claim that we cannot know the story simply by hearing it, but only by learning to imitate those who now are the continuation of the story."[45] In an interview, Kerwin Manning posited that there is a double challenge for black pastors who seek to broaden their congregational base, because, "Black people have always had to sit at the feet of white people and learn from them. It's a new skill for white people, and it doesn't come naturally." As workplaces diversify at every level, workers of every ethnic background

45. Ibid., 152.

are learning how to learn from and be led by people from other ethnic groups than their own. Ideally the church of coming decades will not lag in this skill but will in fact prove a cutting edge training ground for it.

7. The Preached Word Inspires Hearers to Persevere

Multiethnic church life is challenging, and it calls for pastoral leadership that is both visionary and patient. Preaching must name that cost honestly, and call its members to gladly (or at least willingly) pay it. In a sermon calling his congregation to pursue deeper relationships with those outside their own ethnic group, Pastor Bassette offered the analogy of how adding color adds cost, along with value, at a print shop. It adds beauty but also complexity, and thus it takes more time and involves more opportunity for error.

Emerson and Smith describe the difficulty of multiethnic congregational life as follows: "[The costs are much higher for members] because of the increased complexity of demands, needs, and backgrounds, the increased effort necessary to create social solidarity and group identity, and the greater potential for internal conflict."[46]

This exploration of the dynamics of social remembering has highlighted the sources of difficulty in understanding and trusting one another beyond one's own ethnic group. It has hopefully also underscored the mutual correction, healing, and hope that can come as we interpret our past in a context of diversity, and specifically the opportunities that arise when we remember in church, allowing our memories and memory construction practices to be shaped, corrected and renewed by the proclamation of the gospel. As Dykstra observes, "Moral communities . . . show me what I am not yet able to see on my own. Such communities may involve me in activities that I would fear on my own. They may bring me up short against what I refuse to admit, and jar me back into reality."[47] But such choices involve effort: efforts to hear Scripture from disturbing new angles, efforts to hear the pain and anger of others, and efforts to look honestly at parts of our histories of which we are not at all proud. Along the way, those who embark on such a journey inevitably become weary; the warts of one's fellow travelers become all too apparent, and churches that ask much less of their members begin to look attractive.

46. Emerson and Smith, *Divided by Faith*, 145.
47. Dykstra, *Vision and Character*, 57.

At such times, preachers must act as bold visionaries who believe in the possibility and who proclaim the goodness, beauty, and joy of re-deemed and reconciled fellowship. They do this in part by tying the stories of the church's journey to similarly sweaty journeys and arduous processes of sanctification and redemption in Scripture. Such biblical images can interpret current struggles in ways that lead to hope and faith. Preachers also help their congregants to embrace the goodness of the biblical dis-ciplines of waiting and persevering, letting God's future emerge as a gift, rather than scrambling to fashion their own futures. While perseverance is by its nature never easy, it is made more possible when those doing so are helped to remember the past, to discern the work of God in the pres-ent, and to imagine the future that God is bringing. When preachers of the Word heighten these perceptual capacities within their congregants, those listeners are emboldened to walk forward into that future together. Their multiple messy pasts do not impede that walk, but rather are healed in the course of walking as they are retrieved, redeemed, and reclaimed by God for new purposes and are then offered freely to one another.

CONCLUSION

My engagement with this topic arose out of participation in Protestant congregations in North America and observation of that landscape with a mixture of affection, pride, and discouragement. I have rejoiced on numer-ous occasions as I have seen the church live out its biblical calling to be a center of reconciliation, healing, and advocacy for the needy, and I have mourned my own and others' inability to sustain efforts to embody those and other virtues well. Particularly troubling and puzzling to me has been the persistence of ethnic segregation in churches, even in communities that are highly diverse and rather well integrated in other institutions. Adding to the puzzlement have been suggestions that churches that are ethnically diverse grow more rapidly and encounter less "turbulence" if they downplay ethnicity as a source of identity, avoiding references to it in the pulpit and other areas of congregational life. This strategy seemed to miss a precious opportunity to celebrate the beauty and goodness of God, who created people and cultures with rich diversity. It also seemed to skirt crucial atten-tion to issues of justice and reconciliation. Awareness of this tension led to a desire to explore ethnic identity and affiliation choices as they interact with religious identity and affiliation, and to examine congregational practices and homiletical choices in relation to ethnic diversity.

As one who believes strongly in the transformative power of the preached word, I wanted to explore the role preaching could play in furthering unity and connection across ethnic lines. I have sought to provide some cognitive tools that might enhance the awareness and competence of preachers who desired to broaden the diversity of their current churches, as well as those who may already lead diverse churches and yet fear their preaching is landing on some ears with more helpful effect than on others. I placed memory at the nexus of this exploration of ethnicity, church, culture, and preaching as a way to focus the questions and issues. While memory has been predominantly conceived in Western culture as individual, inward, and private, its corporate and communal dimensions have been brought to light through certain pioneers in sociology, anthropology, political history, and philosophy in recent decades, and some theologians have begun to benefit from that. But homileticians have not yet given sustained attention to its implications for preaching.

If, as has been argued, the significant thrust of the New Homiletic may be summarized as a *turn toward the listener*, then becoming attuned to the shaping memories of one's congregation, and to those of the ethnic groups represented there and in one's broader community, may simply be one more way of completing that turn. Yet, as sensitive as the Spirit of God seeks to be toward listeners, the Word of God is not content to stop at turning toward them. It seeks to turn *us*, to shape and transform hearers. It does so in part through calling into question distorting and isolating habits of remembering, and urging listeners toward commemorative practices that foster humility, faith, and love. I hope you will continue the conversation about how your own communities narrate their pasts and how that construction of meaning may enhance, distort, or even completely hinder their capacity to hear Scripture. Greater cognizance of this would not only change how a pastor preached a text but would also deepen every member's longing to live close to, indeed in hearing distance of, the voices of others.

Bibliography

Alderfer, Clayton. "Embedded Intergroup Relations and Racial Identity Development Theory." In *Racial Identity Theory: Applications to Individual, Group, and Organizational Interventions*, edited by Chalmer E. Thompson and Robert T. Carter, 237–63. Mahwah, NJ: Lawrence Erlbaum, 1997.

Allen, O. Wesley. *The Homiletic of All Believers: A Conversational Approach to Proclamation and Preaching*. Louisville: Westminster John Knox, 2005.

Allen, Ronald J. "The Turn to the Listener: A Selective Review of a Recent Trend in Preaching." *Encounter* 64/2 (2003) 166–96.

———. "Two Approaches to Theology and Their Implications for Preaching." *Journal for Preachers* 19/3 (1996) 38–48.

Allen, Ronald J., Barbara Shires Blaisdell, and Scott Black Johnston. *Theology for Preaching: Authority, Truth and Knowledge of God in a Postmodern Ethos*. Nashville: Abingdon, 1997.

Allport, Gordon W., and Leo Postman. *The Psychology of Rumor*. New York: Henry Holt, 1947.

Amaladoss, Michael. *Beyond Inculturation: Can the Many Be One?* Delhi: Vidyajyoti Education and Welfare Soc., 1998.

Ammerman, Nancy, Jackson W. Carroll, Carl S. Dudley, and William McKinney. *Studying Congregations: A New Handbook*. Nashville: Abingdon, 1998.

Anderson, Ray. *The Shape of Practical Theology: Empowering Ministry with Theological Praxis*. Downers Grove, IL: InterVarsity, 2001.

Andrews, Dale P. "New to Whom?" *Homiletix e-Forum*, American Academy of Homiletics (September 2006) 1–3.

Antze, Paul, and Michael Lambek. *Tense Past: Cultural Essays in Trauma and Memory*. New York: Routledge, 1996.

Appiah, Kenneth. "Identity, Authenticity, Survival: Multicultural Societies and Social Reproduction." In *Multiculturalism: Examining the Politics of Recognition*, edited by Amy Gutmann, 149–64. Princeton, NJ: Princeton University Press, 1994.

Assmann, Jan. "Collective Memory and Cultural Identity." *New German Critique* 65 (1995) 125–33.

Auerbach, Erich. *Mimesis: The Representation of Reality in Western Literature*. Translated by Willard R. Trask. New York: Doubleday, 1957.

Augsburger, David. *Hate-Work: Working Through the Pain and Pleasures of Hate.* Louisville: Westminster John Knox, 2004.

Augustine. *Augustine: Confessions and Enchiridion.* Library of Christian Classics 7. Translated by Albert C. Outler. Philadelphia: Westminster, 1955.

———. *The City of God Against the Pagans.* Translated by Henry Bettenson. London: Penguin, 1972.

———. *Confessions.* Translated by Henry Chadwick. Oxford: Oxford University Press, 1991.

———. *The Trinity.* Translated by Stephen McKenna. Washington DC: The Catholic University of America Press. 1962.

Austin, John Langshaw. *How to Do Things with Words.* Cambridge, MA: Harvard University Press, 1955.

Avis, Paul D. L. *God and the Creative Imagination: Metaphor, Symbol and Myth in Religion and Theology.* New York: Routledge, 1999.

Bacon, Francis. *The Advancement of Learning, Novum Organum, New Atlantis.* Great Books of the Western World 30. Chicago: Encyclopedia Britannica, 1990.

Baddeley, Alan. "Psychology of Remembering and Forgetting." In *Memory: History, Culture and the Mind,* edited by Thomas Butler, 33–60. Cambridge: Blackwell, 1989.

Bakhurst, David. "Social Memory in Soviet Thought." In *Collective Remembering,* edited by David Middleton and Derek Edwards, 203–26. London: Sage, 1990.

Barth, Karl. *Church Dogmatics.* Vol. I/1. Translated by G. T. Thomson. Edinburgh: T. & T. Clark, 1936.

———. *Church Dogmatics.* Vol. I/2. Translated by G. T. Thomson and Harold Knight. Edinburgh: T. & T. Clark, 1956.

———. *Homiletics.* Translated by Geoffrey W. Bromiley and Donald E. Daniels. Louisville: Westminster John Knox, 1991.

———. *The Preaching of the Gospel.* Translated by B. E. Hooke. Philadelphia: Westminster, 1963.

———. *The Word of God and the Word of Man.* London: Hodder & Stoughton, 1928.

Becker, Penny Edgell. "Making Inclusive Communities: Congregations and the 'Problem' of Race." *Social Problems* 45/4 (November 1998) 451–72.

Bellah, Robert, and Richard Madsen, William M. Sullivan, Ann Swidler, and Stephen M. Tipton. *Habits of the Heart: Individualism and Commitment in American Life.* Berkeley: University of California Press, 1985.

Ben-Amos, Dan. "Afterword." In *Cultural Memory and the Construction of Identity,* edited by Daniel Ben-Amos and Liliane Weisberg, 297–300. Detroit: Wayne State University Press, 1999.

Berger, Alan. "Bearing Witness: Second Generation Literature of the *Shoah.*" In *Remembering for the Future: Working Papers and Addenda,* edited by Yehuda Bauer et al. Oxford: Pergamon, 1989.

Black, Kathy. *Culturally Conscious Worship.* St. Louis: Chalice, 2000.

———. "Promises and Problems of a Multiethnic Church." In *The Conviction of Things Not Seen: Worship and Ministry in the 21st Century,* edited by Todd Johnson, 141–52. Grand Rapids: Brazos, 2002.

Blair, Edward P. "An Appeal to Remembrance: The Memory Motif in Deuteronomy." *Interpretation* 15/1 (January 1961) 41–46.

Bonhoeffer, Dietrich. *Christology.* Edited by Edwin Robertson and translated by John Bowden. London: Collins, 1966.

Booth, W. James. *Communities of Memory: On Witness, Identity, and Justice.* Ithaca, NY: Cornell University Press, 2006.

Branson, Mark Lau. "Ecclesiology and Leadership for the Missional Church." In *The Missional Church in Context: Helping Congregations Develop Contextual Ministry*, edited by Craig Van Gelder, 94–126. Grand Rapids: Eerdmans, 2006.

———. "Intercultural Life and Adult Formation: Community, Narrative, and Transformation." EdD dissertation, University of San Francisco, 1998.

———. *Memories, Hopes, and Conversations: Appreciative Inquiry and Congregational Change.* Herndon, VA: Alban, 2004.

Broadus, John. *On the Preparation and Delivery of Sermons.* New York: Hodder and Stoughton, 1898.

Brockman, John. *The Third Culture: Beyond the Scientific Revolution.* New York: Simon & Shuster, 1995.

Brown, Delwin, Sheila Greeve Davaney, and Kathryn Tanner, eds. *Converging on Culture: Theologians in Dialogue with Cultural Analysis and Criticism.* Reflection and Theory in the Study of Religion. Oxford: Oxford University Press, 2001.

Browning, Don. *A Fundamental Practical Theology: Descriptive and Strategic Proposals.* Minneapolis: Fortress, 1996.

Brueggemann, Walter. *Finally Comes the Poet: Daring Speech for Proclamation.* Minneapolis: Fortress, 1989.

———. *Hopeful Imagination: Prophetic Voices in Exile.* Philadelphia: Fortress, 1986.

———. "The Social Nature of the Biblical Text for Preaching." In *Preaching as a Social Act: Theology and Practice*, edited by Arthur Van Seters, 127–65. Nashville: Abingdon, 1988.

Budde, Michael. *The (Magic) Kingdom of God: Christianity and Global Culture Industries.* Boulder, CO: Westview, 1997.

Burke, Peter. "History as Social Memory." In *Memory: History, Culture and the Mind*, edited by Thomas Butler. Oxford: Blackwell, 1989.

Butkus, Russell A. "Dangerous Memory and Social Justice." *Religious Education* 82 (1987) 426–46.

Butler, T. C. *Joshua.* Waco, TX: Word, 1983.

Buttrick, David. *Homiletic: Moves and Structures.* Philadelphia: Fortress, 1987.

Campbell, Charles. *Preaching Jesus: New Directions for Homiletics in Hans Frei's Postliberal Theology.* Grand Rapids: Eerdmans, 1997.

Cartwright, Michael G. "Wrestling with Scripture: Can Euro-Americans and African-Americans Learn to Read Scripture Together?" In *The Gospel in Black and White*, edited by Dennis L. Ockholm, 71–116. Downers Grove, IL: InterVarsity, 1997.

Casey, Edward. *Remembering: A Phenomenological Study.* Bloomington: Indiana University Press, 1987.

Castells, Manuel. *The Information Age: Economy, Society and Culture.* Vol. 2, *The Power of Identity.* Oxford: Blackwell, 1997.

Childers, Jana. *Preaching as Theatre: Performing the Word.* Nashville: Abingdon, 1998.

Childs, Brevard. *Memory and Tradition in Israel.* Naperville, IL: Allenson, 1962.

Clancy, Robert A. D. "The Old Testament Roots of Remembrance in the Lord's Supper." *Concordia Journal* 19/1 (January 1993) 35–50.

Clapp, Rodney. "How Firm a Foundation: Can Evangelicals Be Nonfoundationalists?" In *The Nature of Confession: Evangelicals and Postliberals in Conversation*, edited by Timothy R. Philips and Dennis L. Ockholm, 81–92. Downers Grove, IL: InterVarsity, 1996.

Clark, David K. "Relativism, Fideism and the Promise of Postliberalism." In *The Nature of Confession: Evangelicals and Postliberals in Conversation*, edited by Timothy R. Philips and Dennis L. Ockholm, 107–20. Downers Grove, IL: InterVarsity, 1996.

Cokley, Kevin. "Critical Issues in the Measurement of Ethnic and Racial Identity: A Referendum on the State of the Field." *Journal of Counseling Psychology* 54/3 (2007) 224–34.

Conde-Frazier, Elizabeth, S. Steve Kang, and Gary Parrett. *A Many Colored Kingdom: Multicultural Dynamics for Spiritual Formation*. Grand Rapids: Baker Academic, 2004.

Connerton, Paul. *How Societies Remember*. Cambridge: Cambridge University Press, 1989.

Cornell, Stephen. "That's the Story of Our Life." In *We Are a People: Narrative and Multiplicity in Constructing Ethnic Identity*, edited by Paul Spickard and W. Jeffrey Burroughs. Philadelphia: Temple University Press, 2000.

Cosgrove, Charles H., and W. Dow Edgerton. *In Other Words: Incarnational Translation for Preaching*. Grand Rapids: Eerdmans, 2007.

Cousar, Charles B. "Paul and Multiculturalism." In *Many Voices, One God: Being Faithful in a Pluralistic World*, edited by Walter Brueggemann and George W. Stroup. Louisville: Westminster John Knox, 1998.

Craddock, Fred B. *As One Without Authority*. St. Louis: Chalice, 2001.

Crites, Stephen. "The Narrative Quality of Experience." In *Why Narrative? Readings in Narrative Theology*, edited by Stanley Hauerwas and L. Gregory Jones. Grand Rapids: Eerdmans, 1989.

Crowley, Paul. *In Ten Thousand Places: Dogma in a Pluralistic Church*. New York: Crossroad, 1997.

Daniel, Reginald G. "Multiracial Identity in Brazil and the United States." In *We Are a People: Narrative and Multiplicity in Constructing Ethnic Identity*, edited by Paul Spickard and W. Jeffrey Burroughs. Philadelphia: Temple University Press, 2000.

Davis, Ellen F. *Imagination Shaped: Old Testament Preaching in the Anglican Tradition*. Valley Forge, PA: Trinity, 1995.

Davis, H. Grady. *Design for Preaching*. Philadelphia: Fortress, 1958.

Deddo, Gary. "Persons in Racial Reconciliation: The Contributions of a Trinitarian Theological Anthropology." In *The Gospel in Black and White: Theological Resources for Racial Reconciliation*, edited by Dennis L. Okholm, 58–70. Downers Grove, IL: InterVarsity, 1997.

Descartes, Rene. *Discourse on Method and Meditations*. Translated by Laurence J. Lafleur. Indianapolis: Bobbs-Merrill, 1960.

DeYoung, Curtiss Paul, Michael O. Emerson, George Yancey, and Karen Chai Kim. *United by Faith: The Multiracial Congregation as an Answer to the Problem of Race*. Oxford: Oxford University Press, 2003.

Dykstra, Craig. *Vision and Character: A Christian Educator's Alternative to Kohlberg*. New York: Paulist, 1981.

Dyrness, William. *The Earth is God's: A Theology of American Culture*. Maryknoll, NY: Orbis, 1997.

Ebeling, Gerhard. *Word and Faith*. London: SCM, 1963.

———. "Word of God and Hermeneutic." In *The New Hermeneutic*, edited by James Robinson and John B. Cobb, 78–110. New York: Harper & Row, 1964.

Eliot, T. S. *Notes Toward the Definition of Culture*. New York: Harcourt, Brace & World, 1940.

Elizondo, Virgilio. *The Future is Mestizo: Life Where Cultures Meet.* Bloomington, IN: Meyer-Stone, 1988.

Emerson, Michael O., and Christian Smith. *Divided by Faith: Evangelical Religion and the Problem of Race in America.* Oxford: Oxford University Press, 2000.

Erikson, Erik. *Identity, Youth and Crisis.* New York: Norton, 1968.

Esler, Philip F. "Collective Memory and Hebrews 11: Outlining a New Investigative Framework." In *Memory, Tradition, and Text: Uses of the Past in Early Christianity,* edited by Alan Kirk and Tom Thatcher, 151–72. Atlanta: SBL, 2005.

Eslinger, Richard. *Narrative Imagination: Preaching the Worlds That Shape Us.* Minneapolis: Fortress, 1995.

———. *The Web of Preaching: New Options in Homiletic Method.* Nashville: Abingdon, 2002.

Fentress, James, and Chris Wickham. *Social Memory.* Oxford: Blackwell, 1988.

Fleischner, Eva. "The Memory of Goodness." In *Remembering for the Future: Working Papers and Addenda,* vol. 3: *The Impact of the Holocaust and Genocide on Jews and Christians,* edited by Yehuda Bauer. Oxford: Pergamon, 1989.

Flory, Richard W. "Conclusion: Toward a Theory of Generation X Religion." In *GenX Religions,* edited by Richard Flory and Donald E. Miller. New York: Routledge, 2000.

Foster, Charles R., and Theodore Brelsford. *We are the Church Together: Cultural Diversity in Congregational Life.* Valley Forge, PA: Trinity, 1996.

Foucault, Michel. *Language, Counter-Memory, Practice: Selected Essays and Interviews.* Edited by Donald F. Bouchard. Ithaca, NY: Cornell University Press, 1977.

Frederickson, Scott. "The Missional Church in Context." In *The Missional Church in Context: Helping Congregations Develop Contextual Ministry,* edited by Craig Van Gelder, 44–64. Grand Rapids: Eerdmans, 2007.

Frei, Hans W. *The Eclipse of Biblical Narrative: A Study in Eighteenth and Nineteenth Century Hermeneutics.* New Haven, CT: Yale University Press, 1974.

———. *The Identity of Jesus: The Hermeneutical Bases of Dogmatic Theology.* Philadelphia: Fortress, 1975.

———. "Response to 'Narrative Theology: An Evangelical Appraisal.'" *Trinity Journal* 8 (1987) 22–23.

Friesen, Duane K. "An Anabaptist Theology of Culture for a New Century." *Conrad Grebel Review* 13 (1995) 33–51.

Fulkerson, Mary McClintock. "We Don't See Color Here." In *Converging on Culture: Theologians in Dialogue with Cultural Analysis and Criticism,* edited by Delwin Brown et al., 140–47. Oxford: Oxford University Press, 2001.

Gadamer, Hans-Georg. *Truth and Method.* New York: Crossroad, 1988.

Garro, Linda. "The Remembered Past in a Culturally Meaningful Life: Remembering as Cultural, Social and Cognitive Process." In *The Psychology of Cultural Experience,* edited by Carmella C. Moore and Holly F. Mathews, 105–50. Cambridge: Cambridge University Press, 2001.

Gedi, Noa, and Yigal Elam. "Collective Memory: What Is It?" *History and Memory* 8 (1996) 30–50.

Geertz, Clifford. *Interpretation of Cultures.* New York: Basic, 1973.

Geffre, Claude. "Christianity and Culture." *International Review of Mission* 84 (1995) 17–35.

Gillis, John R. "Memory and Identity: The History of a Relationship." In *Commemorations: The Politics of National Identity,* edited by John R. Gillis, 3–26. Princeton, NJ: Princeton University Press, 1994.

Ginn, Richard J. *The Present and the Past: A Study of Anamnesis.* Allison Park, PA: Pickwick, 1989.

Goh, Jeffrey C. K. *A Postliberal Vision of Church and World.* Louvain Theological and Pastoral Monographs. Louvain, Belg.: Peeters, 2000.

González, Justo, and Catherine G. González. "The Larger Context." In *Preaching as a Social Act: Theology and Practice*, edited by Arthur Van Seters, 29–54. Nashville: Abingdon, 1988.

Green, Garrett. *Imagining God: Theology and the Religious Imagination.* Grand Rapids: Eerdmans, 1989.

Gregg, David. *Anamnesis in the Eucharist.* Bramcote, UK: Grove, 1976.

Gross, David. *Lost Time: On Remembering and Forgetting in Late Modern Culture.* Amherst: University of Massachusetts Press, 2000.

Guder, Darrell, ed. *Missional Church: A Vision for the Sending of the Church in North America.* Grand Rapids: Eerdmans, 1998.

Gudykunst, William B. "Uncertainty and Anxiety." In *Theories in Intercultural Communication*, edited by Young Yun Kim and William Gudykunst, 123–56. Newbury Park, CA: Sage, 1988.

Habermas, Jürgen. *The Theory of Communicative Action.* Vol. 1, *Reason and the Rationalization of Society.* Translated by Thomas McCarthy. Boston: Beacon, 1981.

Halbwachs, Maurice. *The Collective Memory.* Translated by Francis J. Ditter Jr. and Vida Yazdi Ditter. New York: Harper Colophon, 1950.

———. *On Collective Memory.* Edited and translated by Lewis A. Coser. Chicago: The University of Chicago Press, 1992.

Harrison, Nonna Verna. "Human Community as an Image of the Holy Trinity." *St. Vladimir's Theological Quarterly* 46 (2001) 347–64.

Hart, David Bentley. *The Beauty of the Infinite: The Aesthetics of Christian Truth.* Grand Rapids: Eerdmans, 2003.

Hauerwas, Stanley. *A Community of Character: Toward a Constructive Christian Social Ethic.* Notre Dame: University of Notre Dame Press, 1981.

———. *Truthfulness and Tragedy: Further Investigations in Christian Ethics.* Notre Dame: University of Notre Dame Press, 1977.

———."Why Time Cannot and Should Not Heal the Wounds of History But Time Has Been and Can Be Redeemed." *Scottish Journal of Theology* 53/1 (2000) 33–49.

Hawn, C. Michael. *One Bread, One Body: Exploring Cultural Diversity in Worship* Herndon, VA: Alban, 2003.

Hendrix, John. "Making the Trip in Imagination and Memory." *Review and Expositor* 86 (1989) 417–29.

Hendry, H. C. "Empathy." In *Dictionary of Christian Ethics and Pastoral Theology*, edited by David J. Atkinson and David H. Field, 343–44. Downers Grove, IL: InterVarsity, 1995.

Herrmann, Douglas J., and Roger Chaffin, eds. *Memory in Historical Perspective: The Literature Before Ebbinghaus.* New York: Springer, 1988.

Hervieu-Léger, Danièle. *Religion as a Chain of Memory.* Translated by Simon Lee. New Brunswick, NJ: Rutgers University Press, 2000.

Higham, John. "The Amplitude of Ethnic History: An American Story." In *Not Just Black and White: Historical and Contemporary Perspectives on Immigration, Race and Ethnicity in the United States*, edited by Nancy Foner and George M. Fredrickson, 61–81. New York: Russell Sage, 2004.

———. "Multiculturalism and Universalism: A History and Critique." In *New Tribalisms: The Resurgence of Race and* Ethnicity, edited by Michael Hughey, 212–36. New York: New York University Press, 1998.

Hilkert, Mary Catherine. *Naming Grace: Preaching and the Sacramental Imagination.* New York: Continuum, 2005.

Hingia, Teresia. "Inculturation and the Otherness of Africans: Some Reflections." In *Inculturation: Abide by the Otherness of Africa and Africans,* edited by Peter Turkson and Frans Wijsen. Kampen: Kok Pharos, 1994.

Hollinger, David. *Postethnic America: Beyond Multiculturalism.* New York: HarperCollins, 1995.

Hopewell, James. *Congregation, Stories and Structures.* Philadelphia: Fortress, 1987.

Hutton, Patrick H. *History as an Art of Memory.* Hanover, VT: University Press of New England, 1993.

Jenson, Robert W. *Systematic Theology.* Vol 1. Oxford: Oxford University Press, 1997.

Jeter, Joseph, and Ronald Allen. *One Gospel, Many Ears: Preaching for Different Listeners in the Congregation.* St. Louis: Chalice, 2002.

John Paul II. *Fides et Ratio.* Encyclical Letter. 1998. Online: http://www.vatican.va/holy_father/john_paul_ii/encyclicals/documents/hf_jp-ii_enc_14091998_fides-et-ratio_en.html.

———. *Redemptoris Missio.* Encyclical Letter. 1990. Online: http://www.vatican.va/holy_father/john_paul_ii/encyclicals/documents/hf_jp-ii_enc_07121990_redemptoris-missio_en.html.

Jones, L. Gregory. "Healing the Wounds of Memory: The Dynamics of Remembering and Forgetting." *Journal of Theology* 103 (1999) 35–51.

Jones, Serene. "Cultural Labor and Theological Critique." In *Converging on Culture: Theologians in Dialogue with Cultural Analysis and Criticism,* edited by Delwin Brown et al., 158–75. Oxford: Oxford University Press, 2001.

Kammen, Michael. "Some Patterns of Memory Distortion in American History." In *Memory Distortion: How Minds, Brains, and Societies Reconstruct the Past,* edited by Daniel Schacter, 329–45. Cambridge, MA: Harvard University Press, 1995.

Kansteiner, Wulf. "Finding Meaning in Memory: A Methodological Critique of Collective Memory Studies." *History and Theory* 41 (2002) 179–97.

Kay, James F. Review of *Preaching Jesus: New Directions for Homiletics in Hans Frei's Postliberal Theology,* by Charles Campbell. *Theology Today* 56/3 (1999) 403–5.

Keane, Philip S. *Christian Ethics and Imagination: A Theological Inquiry.* New York: Paulist, 1984.

Kelley, Shawn. *Racializing Jesus: Race, Ideology and the Formation of Modern Biblical Scholarship.* New York: Routledge, 2002.

Kim, Jaegwon. "Culture." In *The Oxford Companion to Philosophy,* edited by Ted Honderich, 185. Oxford: Oxford University Press, 2005.

Kirk, Alan. "Social and Cultural Memory." In *Memory, Tradition and Text: Uses of the Past in Early Christianity,* edited by Alan Kirk and Tom Thatcher, 1–24. Atlanta: SBL, 2005.

Kittel, Gerhard, ed. *Theological Dictionary of New Testament.* Vol. 1. Grand Rapids: Eerdmans, 1985.

Kroeber, A. L., and Clyde Kluckhohn. *Culture: A Critical Review of Concepts and Definitions.* New York: Vintage, 1952.

Lash, Nicholas. *Easter in Ordinary: Reflections on Human Experience and the Knowledge of God.* Charlottesville, VA: University Press of Virginia, 1988.

Lausanne Committee on World Evangelization. *The Willowbank Report on Gospel and Culture*. 1978. Online: http://www.lausanne.org/willowbank-1978/lop-2.html

Le Goff, Jacques. *History and Memory*. New York: Columbia University Press, 1992.

Lindbeck, George A. *The Nature of Doctrine: Religion and Theology in a Postliberal Age*. Philadelphia: Westminster, 1984.

Lischer, Richard. *The End of Words: The Language of Reconciliation in a Culture of Violence*. Grand Rapids: Eerdmans, 2005.

———. "The Limits of Story." *Interpretation* 38/1 (1984) 26–38.

Long, D. Stephen, and Tripp York. "Remembering: Offering Our Gifts." In *The Blackwell Companion to Christian Ethics*, edited by Stanley Hauerwas and Samuel Wells, 332–45. Malden, MA: Blackwell, 2004.

Long, Thomas G. "And How Shall They Hear? The Listener in Contemporary Preaching." In *Listening to the Word: Studies in Honor of Fred B. Craddock*, edited by Thomas G. Long and Gail R. O'Day, 167–88. Nashville: Abingdon, 1993.

———. "Preaching God's Future: The Eschatological Context of Christian Proclamation." In *Sharing Heaven's Music: The Heart of Christian Preaching*, edited by Barry L. Callen, 191–202. Nashville: Abingdon, 1995.

———. *The Witness of Preaching*. Louisville: Westminster John Knox, 2005.

Long, Thomas G., and Gail R. O'Day, eds. *Listening to the Word: Studies in Honor of Fred B. Craddock*. Nashville: Abingdon, 1993.

Lose, David J. *Confessing Jesus Christ: Preaching in a Postmodern World*. Grand Rapids: Eerdmans, 2003.

———. "Narrative and Proclamation in a Postliberal Homiletic." *Homiletic* 23/1 (1998) 1–14.

Lowry, Eugene L. *Doing Time in the Pulpit: The Relationship Between Narrative and Preaching*. Nashville: Abingdon, 1985.

———. *The Homiletical Plot: The Sermon as Narrative Art Form*. Atlanta: Westminster John Knox, 1980.

———. *The Sermon: Dancing the Edge of Mystery*. Nashville: Abingdon, 1997.

Lyon, K. Brynolf. "The Unwelcome Presence: The Practical Moral Intention of Remembering." *Encounter* 48/1 (1987) 139–49.

Lyotard, Jean-Francois. *The Postmodern Condition: A Report on Knowledge*. Translated by Geoff Bennington and Brian Massumi. Minneapolis: University of Minnesota Press, 1984.

MacIntyre, Alasdair. *After Virtue: A Study in Moral Theory*. Notre Dame: University of Notre Dame Press, 1984.

Mankowski, Eric, and Julian Rappaport. "Stories, Identity, and the Psychological Sense of Community." In *Knowledge and Memory: The Real Story*, edited by Robert S. Wyer Jr., 211–26. Advances in Social Cognition 8. Hillsdale, NJ: Lawrence Erlbaum, 1995.

Marti, Gerardo. *A Mosaic of Believers: Diversity and Innovation in a Multiethnic Church*. Bloomington: Indiana University Press, 2005.

Marsh, Charles. *God's Long Summer: Stories of Faith and Civil Rights*. Princeton, NJ: Princeton University Press, 1997.

McClure, John S. *Other-Wise Preaching: A Postmodern Ethic for Homiletics*. St. Louis: Chalice, 2001.

———. Review of *Preaching Jesus: New Directions for Homiletics in Hans Frei's Postliberal Theology*, by Charles Campbell. *Journal for Preachers* 21/2 (1998) 35–37.

———. *The Roundtable Pulpit: Where Leadership and Preaching Meet*. Nashville: Abingdon, 1995.

McGrath, Alister. "An Evangelical Evaluation of Postliberalism." In *The Nature of Confession: Evangelicals and Liberals in Conversation*, edited by Timothy R. Philips and Dennis L. Ockholm, 23–44. Downers Grove, IL: InterVarsity, 1996.

McIntosh, Gary, and Alan McMahan. *Being the Church in a Multi-Ethnic Community: Why it Matters and How It Works*. Indianapolis: Wesleyan, 2012.

McKenzie, Steven L. *All God's Children: A Biblical Critique of Racism*. Louisville: Westminster John Knox, 1997.

McMickle, Marvin A. *Preaching to the Black Middle Class: Words of Challenge, Words of Hope*. Valley Forge, PA: Judson, 2000.

Meacham, John A. "Reminiscing as a Process of Social Construction." In *The Art and Science of Reminiscing: Theory, Research, Methods and Applications*, edited by Jeffrey D. Webster and Barbara K. Haight, 37–48. Washington DC: Taylor & Francis, 1995.

Metz, Johann Baptist. *Faith in History and Society: Toward a Fundamental Practical Theology*. Translated by David Smith. New York: Seabury, 1980.

Middleton, David, and Stephen D. Brown. *The Social Psychology of Experience: Studies in Remembering and Forgetting*. London: Sage, 2005.

Miles, Margaret. *Image as Insight*. Boston: Beacon, 1985.

Min, Anselm Kyongsuk. *The Solidarity of Others in a Divided World: A Postmodern Theology After Postmodernism*. New York: T. & T. Clark, 2004.

Misztal, Barbara. *Theories of Social Remembering*. Maidenhead, UK: Open University Press, 2003.

Moltmann, Jürgen. *The Trinity and the Kingdom*. Translated by Margaret Kohl. Minneapolis: Fortress, 1993.

Moore, Carmella C., and Holly F. Mathews. *The Psychology of Cultural Experience*. Cambridge: Cambridge University Press, 2001.

Nagel, Joane. "Constructing Ethnicity: Creating and Recreating Ethnic Identity and Culture." In *New Tribalisms: The Resurgence of Race and Ethnicity*, edited by Michael W. Hughey, 237–72. New York: New York University Press, 1998.

Ndondji-Tshiwisa-Adidem, Ghislain. "An African Reconsideration of Christian Anamnesis." *Exchange* 27/1 (1998) 35–51.

Newbigin, Lesslie. *The Gospel in a Pluralist Society*. Grand Rapids: Eerdmans, 1989.

———. *Trinitarian Faith and Today's Mission*. Richmond, VA: John Knox, 1963.

Nieman, James R., and Thomas G. Rogers. *Preaching to Every Pew: Cross-Cultural Strategies*. Minneapolis: Fortress, 2001.

Nora, Pierre. "Between Memory and History: *Les Lieux de Mémoire*." In *History and Memory in African-American* Culture, edited by Genevieve Fabre and Robert O'Meally, 284–300. New York: Oxford University Press, 1994.

Olick, Jeffrey K., and Joyce Robbins. "Social Memory Studies: From 'Collective Memory' to the Historical Sociology of Mnemonic Practices." *Annual Review of Sociology* 24 (1998) 105–40.

Omi, Michael, and Howard Winant. *Racial Formation in the United States from the 1960s to the 1990s*. New York: Routledge, 1994.

Oppenheimer, Helen. "Remembering." *Theology* 98 (1995) 419–23.

Ortiz, Manuel. *One New People: Models for Developing a Multi-Ethnic Church*. Downers Grove, IL: InterVarsity, 1996.

Otto, Randall E. "The Use and Abuse of *Perichoresis* in Recent Theology." *Scottish Journal of Theology* 54 (November 2001) 366–84.

Padilla, C. Rene. "The Unity of the Church and the Homogeneous Unit Principle." In *Exploring Church Growth*, edited by Wilbert R. Shenk, 117–31. Grand Rapids: Eerdmans, 1983.

Pannenberg, Wolfhart. *Systematic Theology, Volume I*. Grand Rapids: Eerdmans, 1991.

Pasewark, Kyle. "Remembering to Forget: A Politics of Forgiveness." *Christian Century* 112 (1995) 683–85.

Pederson, J. *Israel: Its Life and Culture*. 2 vols. Oxford: Oxford University Press, 1926.

Pelikan, Jaroslav. *The Mystery of Continuity: Time, History, Memory, and Eternity in the Thought of Saint Augustine*. Charlottesville: University Press of Virginia, 1986.

Peters, John Durham. *Speaking into the Air: A History of the Idea of Communication*. Chicago: The University of Chicago Press, 1999.

Phan, Peter C. *In Our Own Tongues: Perspectives from Asia on Mission and Inculturation*. Maryknoll, NY: Orbis, 2003.

Placher, William C. "Paul Ricoeur and Postliberal Theology: A Conflict of Interpretations?" *Modern Theology* 4/1 (1987) 35–52.

———. *Unapologetic Theology: A Christian Voice in a Pluralistic Conversation*. Louisville: Westminster John Knox, 1989.

Plato. *Phaedo*. Translated by H. N. Fowler. In *Euthyphro. Apology. Crito. Phaedo. Phaedrus*. Loeb Classical Library 36. Cambridge, MA: Harvard University Press, 1914.

———. *Theaetetus*. Translated by H. N. Fowler. In *Theaetetus. Sophist*. Loeb Classical Library 123. London: W. Heinemann, 1921.

Pohl, Christine D. *Making Room: Recovering Hospitality as a Christian Tradition*. Grand Rapids: Eerdmans, 1999.

Pollock, David C., and Ruth E. Van Reken. *Third Culture Kids: The Experience of Growing Up Among Worlds*. Yarmouth, MA: Intercultural, 1999.

Powell, Mark Allan. *What Do They Hear? Bridging the Gap between Pulpit and Pew*. Nashville: Abingdon, 2007.

Rahner, Karl. "Theology in the New Testament." *Theological Investigations* 5. Translated by Karl H. Kruger. Baltimore: Helicon, 1966.

Ramsey, G. Lee, Jr. *Care-full Preaching: From Sermon to Caring Community*. St. Louis: Chalice, 2000.

Resner, Andre. *Preacher and Cross: Person and Message in Theology and Rhetoric*. Grand Rapids: Eerdmans, 1999.

Rice, Charles. *Interpretation and Imagination: The Preacher and Contemporary Literature*. Philadelphia: Fortress, 1970.

Ricoeur, Paul. "The Hermeneutics of Testimony." In *Essays on Biblical Interpretation*, edited by Lewis Mudge, 119–54. Philadelphia: Fortress, 1980.

———. *Memory, History, Forgetting*. Translated by Kathleen Blamey and David Pellauer. Chicago: The University of Chicago Press, 2004.

Rodriguez, Rafael. "What is 'Historical' about the Historical Jesus?" Paper presented at the Society of Biblical Literature, December 2007.

Rose, Lucy Atkins. *Sharing the Word: Preaching in the Roundtable Church*. Louisville: Westminster John Knox, 1997.

Roxburgh, Alan J. "Missional Leadership: Equipping God's People for Mission." In *Missional Church: A Vision for the Sending of the Church in North America*, edited by Darrell Guder, 183–220. Grand Rapids: Eerdmans, 1998.

Schank, Roger C., and Robert P. Abelson. "Knowledge and Memory: The Real Story." In *Knowledge and Memory: The Real Story*, edited by Robert S. Wyer Jr., 1–86. Advances in Social Cognition 8. Hillsdale, NJ: Lawrence Erlbaum.

Schlesinger, Arthur, Jr. *The Disuniting of America: Reflections on a Multicultural Society.* New York: Norton, 1992.

Schmit, Clayton. *Too Deep for Words: A Theology of Liturgical Expression.* Louisville: Westminster John Knox, 2002.

Schudson, Michael. "The Dynamics of Distortion in Collective Memory." In *Memory Distortion: How Minds, Brains, and Societies Reconstruct the Past*, edited by Daniel Schacter, 346–64. Cambridge, MA: Harvard University Press, 1995.

Schuman, Howard, Hiroko Akiyama, and Barbel Knauper. "Collective Memories of Germans and Japanese About the Past Half-Century." In *Surveying Memory Processes*, edited by Daniel B. Wright and George D. Gaskell, 427–54. East Sussex, UK: Psychology, 1998.

Schwartz, Barry. "The Social Context of Commemoration: A Study in Collective Memory." *Social Forces* 61 (1982) 374–401.

Sharp, Douglas R. *No Partiality: The Idolatry of Race and the New Humanity.* Downers Grove, IL: InterVarsity, 2002.

Sitze, Bob. *Your Brain Goes to Church: Neuroscience and Congregational Life.* Herndon, VA: Alban, 2005.

Smith, James K. A. *The Fall of Interpretation: Philosophical Foundations for a Creational Hermeneutic.* Downers Grove, IL: InterVarsity Press, 2000.

———. *Who's Afraid of Postmodernism? Taking Derrida, Lyotard, and Foucault to Church.* Grand Rapids: Baker Academic, 2006.

Spero, Moshe Halevi. "Remembering and Historical Awareness—Part II: Psychological Aspects of a Halakhic State of Mind." *Tradition* 19/1 (1981) 59–75.

Stanczak, Gregory. "Strategic Ethnicity: The Construction of Multi-Racial/Multi-Ethnic Religious Community." *Ethnic and Racial Studies* 29/5 (2006) 856–81.

Steimle, Edmund A., Morris J. Niedenthal, and Charles L. Rice. *Preaching the Story.* Philadelphia: Fortress, 1980.

Stott, John R. W., and Robert Coote, eds. *Down to Earth: Studies in Christianity and Culture.* Grand Rapids: Eerdmans, 1980.

Stroupe, Nibs. "Looking on the Other Side: Preaching in a Multicultural Society." *Journal for Preachers* 29/4, (2006) 21–25.

Sykes, Marjorie H. "The Eucharist as 'Anamnesis.'" *Expository Times* 71/4 (1960) 115–18.

Tanner, Kathryn. *Theories of Culture: A New Agenda for Theology.* Minneapolis: Augsburg Fortress, 1997.

Tanouye, Ellen. "Festivals: Celebrating Community, Story and Identity." In *People on the Way: Asian North Americans Discovering Christ, Culture, and Community*, edited by David Ng, 177–88. Valley Forge, PA: Judson, 1996.

Taylor, Charles. "The Politics of Recognition." In *Multiculturalism: Examining the Politics of Recognition*, edited by Amy Gutman, , . Princeton, NJ: Princeton University Press, 1994.

Terdiman, Richard. *Present Past: Modernity and the Memory Crisis.* Ithaca, NY: Cornell University Press, 1993.

Teske, Roland. "Augustine's Philosophy of Memory." In *The Cambridge Companion to Augustine*, edited by Eleonore Stump and Norman Kretzmann, 148–58. Cambridge: Cambridge University Press, 2001.

Thompson, Chalmer E., and Robert T. Carter. "Race, Socialization, and Contemporary Racism Manifestations." In *Racial Identity Theory: Applications to Individual, Group, and Organizational Interventions*, 1–14. Mahwah, NJ: Lawrence Erlbaum, 1997.

Thompson, James. *Preaching Like Paul: Homiletical Wisdom for Today*. Louisville: Westminster John Knox, 2001.

Thompson, John Arthur. *Deuteronomy: An Introduction and Commentary*. Downers Grove, IL: InterVarsity, 1974.

Ting-Toomey, Stella. "Communicative Resourcefulness: An Identity Negotiation Perspective." In *Intercultural Communication Competence*, edited by Richard L. Wiseman and Jolene Koester, 72–111. Newbury Park, CA: Sage, 1993.

Tisdale, Leonora Tubbs. *Preaching as Local Theology and Folk Art*. Minneapolis: Fortress, 1997.

Tracy, David. *Blessed Rage for Order: The New Pluralism in Theology*. New York: Seabury, 1975.

Troeger, Thomas. *Imagining a Sermon*. Nashville: Abingdon, 1990.

———. *Preaching and Worship*. St. Louis: Chalice, 2003.

Vanhoozer, Kevin. "Pilgrim's Digress: Christian Thinking on and about the Post/Modern Way." In *Christianity and the Postmodern Turn*, edited by Myron Penner, 71–104. Grand Rapids: Brazos, 2005.

———. "The World Well Staged? Theology, Culture, and Hermeneutics." In *God and Culture: Essays in Honor of Carl F. Henry*, edited by D. A. Carson and John D. Woodbridge, 1–30. Grand Rapids: Eerdmans, 1993.

Veldsman, D. P. "Remembering as Socio-Historic Dynamic of Religious Experience." *Scriptura* 42 (1992) 1–11.

Vidu, Adonis. *Postliberal Theological Method: A Critical Study*. Paternoster Theological Monographs. Cambria, CA: Paternoster, 2005.

Volf, Miroslav. *The End of Memory: Remembering Rightly in a Violent World*. Grand Rapids: Eerdmans, 2006.

———. *Exclusion and Embrace: A Theological Exploration of Identity and Otherness*. Nashville: Abingdon, 1996.

———. "Theology, Meaning, and Power." In *The Nature of Confession: Evangelicals and Liberals in Conversation*, edited by Timothy R. Philips and Dennis L. Ockholm, 45–66. Downers Grove, IL: InterVarsity, 1996.

———. "The Trinity is Our Social Program: The Shape of Social Engagement." *Modern Theology* 14 (July 1998) 403–23.

Vosloo, Robert. "Reconciliation as the Embodiment of Memory and Hope." *Journal of Theology for Southern Africa* 109 (2001) 25–40.

Warren, Rick. *The Purpose Driven Church: Growth Without Compromising your Message and Mission*. Grand Rapids: Zondervan, 1995.

Waters, Mary. "The Costs of a Costless Community." In *New Tribalisms: The Resurgence of Race and Ethnicity*, edited by Michael W. Hughey, 273–97. New York: New York University Press, 1998.

Webb, Stephen H. *The Divine Voice: Christian Proclamation and the Theology of Sound*. Grand Rapids: Brazos, 2004.

Webster, Jeffrey D., and Barbara K. Haight. "Memory Lane Milestones: Progress in Reminiscence Definition and Classification." In *The Art and Science of Reminiscing: Theory, Research, Methods and Applications*, 273–86. Washington DC: Taylor & Francis, 1995.

Weldon, Mary Susan. "Remembering as a Social Process." In *The Psychology of Learning and Motivation: Advances in Research and Theory*, vol. 40, edited by Douglas L. Medin, 67–120. San Diego: Academic Press, 2001.

Wertsch, James. *Voices of Collective Remembering*. New York: Cambridge University Press, 2002.

Westbury, Chris, and Daniel C. Dennett. "Mining the Past to Construct the Future: Memory and Belief as Forms of Knowledge." In *Memory, Brain, and Belief*, edited by Daniel L. Schacter and Elaine Scarry, 11–34. Cambridge, MA: Harvard University Press, 2000.

Whitney, Diana, Amanda Trosten-Bloom, and David Cooperridger. *The Power of Appreciative Inquiry: A Practical Guide to Positive Change*. San Francisco: Berrett-Koehler, 2003.

Wiesel, Elie. "The Future of Remembering." In *Remembering for the Future: Working Papers and Addenda*, edited by Yehuda Bauer et al., 3:3128–33. Oxford: Pergamon, 1989.

Wilder, Amos. *The Language of the Gospel: Early Christian Rhetoric*. New York: Harper & Row, 1964.

Wilkes, James R. "Remembering." *Theology* 84 (March 1981) 87–95.

Williams, Rowan. *Resurrection: Interpreting the Easter Gospel*. London: Darton, Longman & Todd, 1982.

Willimon, William H. *Conversations with Barth on Preaching*. Nashville: Abingdon, 2006.

———. "'Everyone Whom the Lord Our God Calls': Acts 2 and the Miracle of Pentecost: Preaching in a Multicultural Context." *Journal for Preachers* 25 (2006) 3–9.

Wilson, Paul Scott. "Beyond Narrative: Imagination in the Sermon." In *Listening to the Word: Studies in Honor of Fred B. Craddock*, edited by Thomas G. Long and Gail R. O'Day, 131–46. Nashville: Abingdon, 1993.

Wilson-Kastner, Patricia. *Imagery for Preaching*. Minneapolis: Fortress, 1989.

Wolterstorff, Nicholas. *Art in Action: Toward a Christian Aesthetic*. Grand Rapids: Eerdmans, 1980.

Wood, Laurence W. *Theology as History and Hermeneutics: A Post-Critical Conversation with Contemporary Theology*. Lexington, KY: Emeth, 2005.

Woudstra, M. H. *The Book of Joshua*. Grand Rapids: Eerdmans, 1981.

Wuthnow, Robert. *Christianity in the Twenty-First Century: Reflections on the Challenge Ahead*. Oxford: Oxford University Press, 1993.

Yoder, John Howard. "How H. Richard Niebuhr Reasoned: A Critique of *Christ and Culture*." In *Authentic Transformation: A New Vision of Christ and Culture*, edited by Glen H. Stassen, D. M. Yeager, and John Howard Yoder, 31–90. Nashville: Abingdon, 1996.

Zizioulas, John. *Being as Communion: Studies in Personhood and the Church*. Crestwood, NY: St. Vladimir's Seminary Press, 2002.

www.ingramcontent.com/pod-product-compliance
Lightning Source LLC
Chambersburg PA
CBHW030820270326
41928CB00007B/821